JOHN TERRY

JOHN TERRY
My Winning Season

HarperSport

An Imprint of HarperCollins*Publishers*

First published in UK in 2005 by
HarperSport
an imprint of HarperCollins*Publishers*
London

© JGT Promotions Limited 2005

1

A CIP catalogue record for this book is
available from the British Library

ISBN 0 00 721450 2

Set in 11.25/16 pt Linotype Sabon by
Rowland Phototypesetting Ltd, Bury St Edmunds, Suffolk

Printed and bound in Great Britain by
Clays Ltd, St Ives plc

The HarperCollins website address is
www.harpercollins.co.uk

Contents

PICTURE CREDITS

Plate section page, from top to bottom

Acknowledgments

I'd like to thank Ollie Holt, who had the huge task of helping me put my thoughts down on paper in such a short space of time. It was worth the effort, Ollie!

To Aaron Lincoln, my agent and my friend and confidante, thanks for all your support, mate.

To my publishers HarperCollins, and especially Michael Doggart and Tom Whiting, for having faith in me and opening my eyes to the world of book publishing.

To everyone at Chelsea FC, especially José, Roman, the current squad, and all those who stood by me as a YTS coming through the ranks. I couldn't have done it without you guys.

Last, but not least, thanks to my family – my mum Sue, dad Ted and brother Paul – who were there for me from the beginning, and my fiancée Toni.

1 Mourinho – 'The Special One' Arrives

I missed the first five days of the Jose Mourinho era. I was still licking my wounds from England's quarter-final exit from Euro 2004 at the hands of Portugal. Still thinking about Wayne Rooney limping off in the first half. Still thinking about that header from Sol Campbell that the Swiss referee Urs Meier disallowed. Still thinking about the penalty shoot-out and the painful journey home.

The new Chelsea manager said that those of us who had been involved in the tournament could report late for pre-season training. But I was still burning with curiosity about what the new guy was like, so Frank Lampard and I made it our business to ring the other lads every day to find out how the new regime was treating them. We called them so often we were driving them mad.

The news wasn't good. The boys said it was running, running and more running, every footballer's worst nightmare. They made it sound like some sort of boot camp. Scott Parker said he was so shattered when he got home at the end of each day that he just collapsed into bed and went straight to sleep.

I thought it was going to be cold showers and army assault courses. 'Make sure you bring an extra set of lungs with you,' Scottie said.

Lamps and I were on the phone to each other a fair amount over those five days. We didn't like the sound of it at all. We were quaking. Lamps is a good runner. He'll often go on long laps of the training ground off his own bat at our new head-quarters in Cobham anyway. He astounds the rest of us with his stamina and his appetite for running. He's a one-off like that. But even he seemed a bit daunted by the reports that were coming back to us of the new manager's attitude.

It's not that we're lazy. The previous manager, Claudio Ranieri, had run the nuts off us. It's just that every player loves working with a football. I can run as many sprints as you want as long as I've got a ball at my feet. It's just the mindless slog around and around a training pitch that I can't stand. That saps my enthusiasm. It sounded to me like we were in for a long haul with the new guy. And I felt surprised. It wasn't what I had expected.

So when I arrived at Harlington for my first day, it was with a feeling of apprehension. Not quite dread, perhaps, but not far off. Perhaps Scottie could see it in my face when I arrived. As soon as I saw him he started laughing. Lamps and I had fallen for it hook, line and sinker. It was the lads' idea of a joke. Something to get us back for having an extra five days of holiday. It was a wind-up.

I still couldn't quite bring myself to believe it, though. I still wanted to see the proof. Then I did my first session under Mourinho and it was great. It was all ball work. There was a bit of running but it was all with the ball at your feet. 'We don't do running here,' the manager said when he spoke to me afterwards. 'Don't worry, I'm not going to have you doing lap after lap of the field.' I think he'd been in on the joke. There was a glint in his eye.

The fitness coach, Rui Faria, said something to me that day that made a big impression on me, too. 'If you have a pianist,' he said, 'he doesn't run around the piano, does he? He plays the piano and he practises on it. He gets to know it inside out. He gets to know everything about it and how it responds when you touch it. That's what we do with the football.'

I felt a great sense of relief. Partly because the manager's approach already seemed like a breath of fresh air and the kind of training regime that would get the most out of the players. My first impressions were very good. I knew instantly this was a guy I was going to enjoy working for. The training routine was particularly important to me because I had been bothered for some years by a persistent problem in the little toe on my left foot that had really begun to wear me down under Claudio.

In previous years, the pain had got so bad midway through the season that I had had to miss training now and again. Because we did so much running in training, I started to get worn out by the middle of the season. I started to feel like I needed a rest. And that was made worse by the toe problem. Under the new manager that never happened. The pain from the toe resurfaced. But I never felt tired. I was always raring to go. I was always desperate to play.

Footballers are paid to play football, not to run, and Mourinho got that spot on. We loved that right from day one.

We are players, not long-distance runners. The other thing with the manager was that tactically he was spot on, too. Certain things he drilled us in during the pre-season, certain situations, actually occurred during league games at the start of the Premiership season. That made him look pretty good in our eyes. He just pays attention to small details and they make a big difference.

I had first become aware of Mourinho when he took his FC Porto team to the UEFA Cup Final against Celtic in Seville in 2003. There was quite a lot of publicity about the game in England because Celtic were involved and Martin O'Neill was the manager. Celtic fans streamed over there in their tens of thousands and colonized Seville, so the atmosphere at the game looked fantastic.

But it was also notable because Porto were there. I knew Porto had won the European Cup when they beat Bayern Munich in the final back in 1987 but I wasn't aware of them doing much since. And yet here they were winning a fantastic final 3–2, with some terrific players like Deco. They looked like a great side. It was obvious their manager knew what he was doing.

I found out more about him when Porto beat Manchester United in the first leg of their Champions League second-round tie at the Estadio do Dragao the following spring. Mourinho had predicted Porto would get United in the draw, just like he was to predict we would meet Barcelona in the second round of the Champions League the year after. I remember Mourinho making fun of Sir Alex Ferguson in the press conference afterwards. One of the press boys told him Ferguson was upset about something. And Mourinho said he would be upset, too, if his side had just been beaten by a team that cost a pittance to put together!

Then, of course, there was the famous image of Mourinho running down the touchline at Old Trafford with his arms above his head after Costinha had scored the last-minute equalizer in the second leg that put United out of the competition. In a way, that was the result that really rocketed him into the big time, although I think he had already been approached by English clubs by then.

Soon, the rumours started circulating that he was coming to Chelsea. I didn't pay them too much attention. Partly, I suppose, because despite all his eccentricities, I liked Ranieri. He had been very good to me and he had established me as a first-team regular. I owed him a lot and I certainly wasn't about to start agitating for him to be replaced.

But by the time the end of the season came around, it was obvious that Ranieri was on his way out. He came to me and thanked me for the nice things the players had been saying about him but told me that the fight was over and that he knew the club wanted him out. It's the way football is. At least Claudio got a wonderful send-off after his last match in charge against Leeds at the Bridge on the final day of the season. After the fans had cheered him round the pitch, the players came on to form a guard of honour for him before he walked down the tunnel.

About the same time, the new manager was winning the Champions League with Porto. They beat Monaco, who had beaten us in the semi-final, fairly comfortably. By then,

Mourinho was being linked very strongly with us. He seemed like a brilliant manager. It was impossible to argue with his achievements. And practically speaking, it was hard to escape the conclusion that we should have beaten Monaco but he actually did it.

Ranieri got us close to winning the Champions League but not quite close enough. And it's all about very fine lines at that level. We should have closed out the game against Monaco and we didn't. And the club took the view that we needed somebody who could take us that extra step and break the domination of Arsenal and Manchester United in the Premiership.

Footballers are practical people. We are used to our teammates being bought and sold and we are used to managers coming and going, too. We are used to people we have worked with for several years having to leave without even getting the chance to say goodbye. So even though I was probably Ranieri's biggest fan at the club, we were all still looking forward to the fresh start and the kick up the arse under the new manager that could take us to the next step. Looking at it now, it's obvious Mourinho has taken us to a new level. It's been a privilege to work with him.

The fact is that the club was improving but he has quickened that process. He has speeded everything up. And he has made everything feel more solid. He is in total control and he makes sure all of us are brimming with confidence. He is an excellent man-manager, a clever tactician and he prepares for the opposition more thoroughly then any manager I have ever known.

I know that when he was at Porto, he gave Paolo Ferreira, the right-back he brought with him to Chelsea, a DVD of action involving Jerome Rothen, the Monaco left-winger, before the Champions League Final in Gelsenkirchen. He does not give us DVDs but he does give each of us a dossier before every game with detailed information about our opponents.

It's always lying on top of our clothes in the changing room when we walk back in after training a couple of days before the game. The manager says it's up to us whether we take it home and read it or whether we choose not to. It's not like he's giving us homework and he's going to test us on it. But you know the test's going to come. The test is going to come in the match. So I always take mine away and read it thoroughly when I get home.

I read what's pertinent to me, the work he's done on my opponent and the stuff that might affect me as part of the defensive unit. It's usually about three or four pages long. Always devoted to the opposition. It will have sections about formations, set-plays, their key players. How many times they score from set-plays. What kind of runs their players make.

If we're playing United, there might be a section pointing out that if I'm marking van Nistelrooy at a corner, out of the last ten games he has made ten runs at corners to the near post. So I know that's probably where he's heading. If it's Liverpool, there might be a diagram of the pattern of the runs made by Milan Baros. And there might be a reminder about Steven Gerrard's ability to spray the ball from deep and have us back-pedalling.

I find it useful. It helps to cut out surprises. Of course you can't prepare for everything. Football would be boring if you could. But you might as well prepare for as much as you can. Otherwise, you're just being negligent. You're being lazy. I want to do everything I can to win and if reading the manager's dossier is going to help me, I'll read it every time. If he's done the graft, it must be for a reason. He thinks it's useful and he's the boss so I think it's the least I can do to study it for a while.

I liked Mourinho from day one. I had met him once before a couple of days before we flew out to Portugal for Euro 2004. He came to the England team hotel in Manchester to talk to me and Joe Cole, Wayne Bridge and Lamps. I think Rafael Benitez did the same with the Liverpool boys. He said very complimentary things to all of us.

Basically, he sat us down and told us we were going to win things. He turned to Lamps and said he believed he had just taken charge of the best midfielder in the world. He said to Coley that he wanted him to demonstrate the commitment and the maturity and the consistency to cement a regular place. He said he believed I was one of the best defenders in the world. And he told Bridgey he felt he was the best left-back in Europe.

He told us how he was going to come in and make things happen. We were all playing for our country, he said, but none of us had won anything and he was going to change that. I was worried about what he would be like because he always came across as a very strict character in his television interviews, but nothing could have been further from the truth. He's a very friendly guy. He sat all of us down and told us about his ambitions. Right from the start, I was impressed because he didn't have to bother with any of that. He could have waited until pre-season to meet us but he made the effort to come and seek us out in Manchester. That's what he's like: always going the extra mile.

And when Lamps and I reported back for training at Cobham, he soon made a point of taking us aside again. He said a couple of things to us about how we were the best at what we did. Even in training, he would say things like 'you are the best I've worked with'. I don't know if he meant it deep down but it did the trick with me. I came away from those early training sessions feeling as if I was ten-feet tall.

I was on tenterhooks about whether he was going to make me captain or not. Marcel Desailly had been the captain most of the time I had been at the club and before that it was Dennis Wise. I had learned a lot from both of them and I was vice-captain to Marcel. Marcel had your respect instantly because of everything he had achieved in the world game. He had authority without needing to say anything.

Marcel was a terrific bloke as well. Maybe from the outside, he looked as though he might have been a bit aloof but he was the absolute opposite of that. At that time when he joined the club, a lot of the first-team players wouldn't speak to the youth-team lads like me because they considered themselves too important. That was just the way it was in those days. But Marcel wasn't like that at all.

He was brilliant to me. He would always make ten minutes to speak to me after training if there was something I wanted to ask him or some advice I needed. He was an absolute hero of mine anyway. Just talking to Marcel Desailly was a big thrill for me back then. And he was great with the other young lads, too. He'd give out pairs of boots to the lad who cleaned his boots and sometimes he'd give away tracksuits and that kind of thing to the YT lads. It doesn't seem like much now but it meant a lot then. He had won everything there was to win in the game but he was so generous spirited. He was a real class act.

He wasn't particularly vocal on the pitch, whereas Wisey was vocal. He was very vocal. Everybody knew what they should be doing and if they weren't doing it, he let them know about it. He was an inspirational kind of guy, too, a player who would set the tone with a fierce tackle or a bit of argy-bargy, a player that opponents were often wary of. Sometimes, you could see that they were nervous of him just by looking in their eyes.

As Marcel's vice-captain, I was desperate to succeed him when he retired. He had left the club at the end of the previous season and when Mourinho arrived, the manager had given an interview on Sky where he had made it plain that either me or Lamps would be the new skipper. I felt I was ready for the role. I would have been delighted for Lamps if he had got it but that didn't stop me doing everything I could to sway the manager's thinking towards me.

I was first in to the training ground in the morning. I was at the front of every run we went on, even though there weren't that many. I gave everything in training just like I always do. I thought I might not have had enough time to impress him because we set off on the pre-season tour of America a few days after I reported back. Lamps and I never talked about it and it was clear that whichever of us got it would be happy for the other.

On the flight to Seattle, the manager came to the back of the plane and asked me if he could sit and talk to me for ten minutes. The first thing he asked me was which trophy I was most eager to win. Straight away, I said the Premiership. We had a good chat and he said he felt he had seen enough to show him that the other players respected me. He wanted me to be captain. I was absolutely buzzing.

He told me he wanted me to be there for the lads always. That was the number one priority for the captain in his mind. 'Even if you think they are wrong, you stick with them,' he said. 'Even if you have to tell me something I might not like, always stick with the players.' He wanted me to organize club events like paint-balling and go-karting and he wanted everyone to go. If someone missed it, then he wanted to know the reason why.

I don't know too much about team spirit at other clubs but we all get on very well. It sounds calculating but I think that's because we work at getting on well. It's not just the old style, let's go out and get pissed kind of thing that used to be a football club's idea of team bonding. We still have nights out all together. Very occasionally, we all still go to a nightclub together. But because football has changed, because the media watch us so carefully and because the influx of foreign players has brought a change in club culture, there is no point in thinking that trying to get everyone to go out and get blind drunk together is going to work as a bonding mechanism.

We all look out for each other, on and off the pitch. There was one time before I had the alarm system properly done on my house in Surrey when I woke up and was convinced I could hear noises outside. I've got this arrangement with Scottie and Glen Johnson that, because we all live close to each other, we don't keep our mobiles on silent at night.

So I rang Scottie and he was around at my gate in about one minute flat. I crept down the stairs with a baseball bat in my hand and saw him standing at the gates. He had a baseball bat, too. Then Johnno arrived and soon the three of us were prowling around the outside of the house with our baseball bats at the ready. We must have looked a pretty sight. There was no one there, of course.

Captaincy suits me. If I'm honest, I like being bossy and telling people what to do. It's important to organize the team and make sure they're following instructions. And it means more to be respected than liked by your team-mates. Having said that, I reckon I have both. I'm respected at Chelsea because I know the club well and I've seen the ups and downs here. They know I'm not passing through. I'm here for the long term. I accept that I might annoy team-mates because you need to tell players off if they're doing something wrong, but I hope they take it on the chin and learn.

Likewise, if someone wants to have a go at me, I have to take it, too. I'm there first and foremost for my team-mates. They know that I would do anything for them. It's my job to be Jose's voice on the pitch. I have to be the link between the players and the manager. Jose said at the start of the season that there would be times when the players couldn't hear him because of the crowd or because someone is on the opposite side of the pitch, and that is where he needed me to step in. I hope I've fulfilled that role for him. I certainly haven't got a problem raising my voice on a football pitch. You could never accuse me of not being a talker.

The duties of captaincy aren't just confined to the first team either. We have a players' pool. If anyone gets fined for being late for a team meeting or training, the money goes in there. We use that money to try to help some of the younger lads with things like driving lessons and driving tests. I know how difficult it was paying for that kind of thing when I was earning £46 a week on YTS, so we try to make a contribution. We pay for them to go paint-balling or go-karting now and again, too. They bring me receipts sometimes so I can reimburse them for stuff. There have been plenty of dodgy ones. I'm getting good at spotting them now.

I think being captain has brought the best out of me. I relish it. I love the responsibility and the responsibility has been good for me. On and off the pitch. It's made me even more aware that I have a duty not to let my club down in any way. I'm representing the club and I thrive on that. I'm a very proud captain and I don't want anything to taint the honour I have been given.

I know it's a cliché, but even though I'm the skipper, we've got a lot of leaders in the team. The manager encourages that. Before the first pre-season game, he introduced the idea of having a huddle in the dressing room a few minutes before every game. Steve Clarke, the assistant manager, came to me an hour before the kick-off of the game against Celtic in Seattle and said that the manager wanted us to go through this routine before every match.

He wanted one player to give a team talk in the huddle and

over the course of the season, he wanted every player to take a turn at doing it. When the player who was in charge finished his team talk, he had to yell, 'Who are we?' The lads had to respond by shouting out 'Chelsea'. And we'd repeat that several times and then head out to the pitch.

I was a bit taken aback. I had to talk to a couple of the lads and explain the new routine to them. I'd never come across anything like that before, although I suppose you see a lot of teams going into pre-match huddles now. We do ours in the privacy of the dressing room. A lot of teams conduct theirs on the pitch. I don't know how they can hear each other sometimes. Anyway, in Seattle, I was wracking my brains about what to say. I felt as nervous as if I'd been about to make a best man's speech. I don't think it was particularly Churchillian when the time came. I just did a lot of effing and blinding and out we went.

I did about eight of them over the course of the season. Lamps did about the same. Didier Drogba did a few. We had a couple of dodgy ones. When William Gallas did it, he was staring down at the floor, not looking at anybody and his English, which is usually good, went to pieces. When he got to the end of his speech he went, 'Where are we?' We all cracked up. 'We're at Stamford Bridge!' we all yelled out, and that broke the ice.

A couple of people prefer not to do them but, on the other hand, the player who did it best was Scottie, before the Newcastle game at St James' Park in the Carling Cup. His was so inspirational the hairs on the back of my neck were standing on end. He got me so pumped up for that game. He was so good some of the staff wanted to go out and play. He was staring at everyone, looking them right in the eye, talking about how Newcastle might have great fans but we were going to shut them up and how this was going to be our first shot at silverware and we weren't going to blow it. It was unbelievable.

So we soon got into the swing of how the manager wanted things to be done. Even in that first friendly match in Seattle, he gave me a little wake-up call at half-time. He told me I should have been shouting at Babayaro earlier in the game and giving him a bollocking for failing to make a covering run on his winger. I thought I'd upset him already. But, generally, we did well in that game. We looked good. We looked sharp. Even then, I thought we might have a chance of doing great things in the season ahead.

We did a lot of work on that pre-season tour. People tend to write those trips off as money-making exercises that are more of a hindrance to a team than a help. But we laid a lot of the foundations of what was to come while we were out in America. We learned a lot from Jose in those first few weeks.

He didn't drill the defence in the same way that, say, George Graham used to do at Arsenal when he tied the back four together with a piece of rope to drum it into them that they had to move up as a unit. There was nothing like that. But most of our pre-season work was based around defensive organization and defending as a team and that stayed with us for the whole season.

He wanted us to defend solidly and he wanted that process to start with the forwards. It was made absolutely clear to the midfielders that they always had to track their runners. No excuses. No exceptions. He never wanted to see situations where the defence was overloaded. He never wanted to see us caught one on one with an attacker at the back. He wanted the full-backs tucked in and plenty of cover. Once he drummed that into us, that was it. It stuck.

I'd never worked with Ricardo Carvalho, who'd been signed from Porto and was going to be my central defensive partner for a large chunk of the season. But we didn't do any formal sessions together, just the two of us set apart from the rest. What tended to happen was that if it was clear I would be playing alongside Ricky or William Gallas the next day, then the manager would organize a short-sided game after training on Friday and we would be alongside each other in that. We learned each other's games that way and it worked perfectly.

So even though the transformation the team went through under Mourinho felt pretty seamless, it was obvious that a lot of what we went on to achieve was down to him. His whole approach was a breath of fresh air. His team meetings were sharp and focussed, not the long, drawn-out boring affairs I know some managers seem to lapse into. Jose's meetings, always on the day before a game, last 10 or 12 minutes. The points are made briefly but with emphasis. It's almost as if he's underlining something on a page while he's talking. When he's finished, the priorities are very clear in your mind. You know what's important.

In some meetings with previous managers, I've seen players looking about when the boss has been talking, their concentration wavering and then going totally. People have started to fidget, sometimes even whisper to each other. It's not like that in Mourinho's meetings.

In common with other clubs, we use an information system called Prozone which gives us information about ourselves and how far we have run, how many sprints we have made, where we have made our runs and what direction we have made them in. We get the same information about the other team and that's what we tend to focus on more. After 12 minutes dissecting the information the Prozone has given us and a couple of other things, he calls it a day. That's it. Finished.

Every player stays fully focussed throughout. No exceptions. He shows us a few clips of the opposition, analyses some of their favourite set-plays and talks about their players and what we can do to expose their weaknesses. It's very authoritative. And believe me, it holds our attention.

But it's not just what he says. It's the timing of the meeting and it's the location. I'm in danger of starting to sound pretentious here but it's only since Mourinho has arrived at the club that I've begun to realize the importance of things like that. For instance, the room where we hold the team meeting is detached from the main training ground complex. It's not in the same building where we have our lunch in the canteen and get changed in the changing rooms.

It's in a smaller building on the way to the training pitches. It sounds silly but once we get in that room, we move into game mode. The game might still be more than 24 hours away but suddenly there's a new intensity about everything that doesn't drop until the final whistle blows the following afternoon.

We come out of that team meeting and we head straight into training ready to put into practice everything we have just learned.

You believe you are playing your opponents in that final training session. Everything you are doing is with them in mind. Your whole week has been building up to this point. You've read the dossier the manager has prepared, you've listened to what he has had to say at the team meeting and by Friday afternoon you feel ready. Actually, you feel more than ready. You're chomping at the bit, desperate to get out there and prove you're the best again.

When we got back from the pre-season tour of America, he got us all together again. He said that as he looked around the room he saw a lot of very good players. He saw a lot of players who had represented their country with distinction at major finals. But he said he didn't see anyone who had won a Premiership medal. He pointed out to us that football was a short career and it was about time we started having something to show for it. He said he had won the Champions League and the UEFA Cup and what had we won: nothing. He said he was bringing a winning mentality with him and he was going to turn us into winners, too.

I think those comments were aimed particularly at the English lads. And he was right. Players like me and Lamps and Coley were painfully aware that we were considered top players and yet we had no medals to show for it. Chelsea hadn't won a trophy for five years. When it came to the 'put your medals on the table' test, we would come up empty. There were other players in the team now like Paolo and Claude Makelele who had won the Champions League, too, and we wanted to have what they had.

It was no use earning the money we were earning, living in a nice house, driving a nice car, if we weren't winners. Nobody wants to be known as a loser. We wanted medals. We wanted trophies. We wanted something to show for all the hard work we were putting in. And I suppose most of all we wanted respect from our fellow players. We didn't want to be known as spoilt little rich boys from fashionable Chelsea who had all that money behind them and still couldn't beat Man United and Arsenal. We had come close to titles or cups a few times but that wasn't good enough. And that was why there was a hunger burning in us that we kept stoking every game of the season. We were desperate to win things.

Sometimes that hunger matters more than anything. For a long time, that was Manchester United's gift. That hunger that they had. The hunger that players like Gary Neville and Roy Keane made sure was always there. The hunger that Ferguson created in them. When that group of local lads came through the youth team together, Ferguson had been able to mould them and instil in them great professionalism. Look at what a long and brilliant career Ryan Giggs has had. And the Neville brothers. And Paul Scholes. And David Beckham.

With players like Gary Neville and Keane still at Old Trafford, that hunger is still there. It will always be there. That's why they're such great pros. If United have slipped a little bit in the last couple of years, it has been because Ferguson has struggled to convince players who have come into the club from outside that they need to adopt the same levels of dedication and commitment as Gary and Keane. But if you can harness that hunger as a manager, if you can keep a player hungry, then that's the greatest gift of all.

And Mourinho has that gift. He kept us hungry from that first friendly in Seattle right through to the last game of the season at Newcastle. That's why we only lost one league game. That's why we didn't fall away even when we knew we had it won. That's why I was desperate to play in every game and why I was so upset to miss the last two even though the title was ours by then. That's why Lamps didn't miss a game all season.

Mourinho made us feel we were part of something special. Made us feel that we didn't want to be left out. That we didn't want to miss a single moment of a special season. At a time when players are criticized for not caring about their football enough, he tapped into the fear of being considered a loser that most players must feel at some time in their careers. He made us feel that we could be great players if we wanted it enough. We believed in him and everything he predicted happened like he said it would. Well, everything except Liverpool, and no one could have foretold the bizarre way their story was to unfold.

Sometimes, over the course of the season, he has seemed more like a friend than a manager. He will sit with us in the canteen in the morning, chatting over a piece of toast. About what was on the telly the night before, about the match that was on, or the news of the day, or which restaurant we had been out to. It's like having a mate around the place some of the time.

Sometimes, he might come across as hard and ruthless but

there are other sides to him as well. He treats people with consideration. And he doesn't just look after first-team players or people who he thinks might be useful to him. He does things that no other manager I've ever worked with would have thought of doing. He cares about people at all levels of the club and that's why he's built the best team spirit we have ever had. Towards the end of the season, he found out that one of the guys who had worked at the training ground doing odd jobs for about 20 years and who is Chelsea through and through had a birthday coming up. His name is Frank Steer.

Frank used to do a bit of stewarding at the old training ground at Harlington near Heathrow. He used to do all sorts actually and all the lads love him. He does similar stuff at the new training ground in Cobham, which we moved to around the turn of the year. He organizes the rota for having the players' cars washed and generally busies himself around the building. He's always around the dressing-room area on match days at the Bridge. He's a diamond bloke. So, out of the blue, Jose treated Frank to a weekend with the team that he will remember for the rest of his life.

When we played at Southampton, Frank sat up at the front of the team bus with the manager on the journey down there the day before the game. He ate with us in the evening and he came into the team meeting. He was in the dressing room before the game and then, during the match, he sat with the rest of the staff just behind the dug-out at St Mary's. He had a great couple of days. He absolutely loved it. He's still talking about it now. We can't shut him up.

I thought the whole thing reflected incredibly well on the

manager. It's the kind of thing that has started to set us apart from other clubs, I think. It's the kind of thing that has built our team spirit up very quickly to a point where it's the best I've ever known. The togetherness runs through the club. It's not just in the first team, not just in the squad, but right through the staff and the administration. There's an overwhelming feeling of everyone pulling together in the same direction. There is no suggestion of tensions or people breaking off into cliques.

When Bridgey got injured in the FA Cup tie at Newcastle in February, the manager was the first one down to the hospital to see him. He reassured him about everything. And the rest of us set up a rota for visiting him so that he would have mates coming to see him every day. We all stand up for each other and stick by each other. I think that's why other players look at what we have built here with a degree of envy. That's why it makes me laugh when people talk about us buying the Premiership. Anybody who knows anything about it knows it's about so much more than money and that's where the manager has been so influential.

So it is easy to see him as a friend. It's easy to have a laugh and a joke with him and to confide in him. But as soon as you step on to the training pitch, he goes into a serious mode. He becomes your boss and we respect that. But his man-management is fantastic and he has a knack of knowing exactly how games are going to unfold. Tactically, you would just not believe how good he is. We have these meetings and he is always absolutely spot on. Nothing is left to chance before a game because he covers every single angle. There are no surprises because he's mapped it all out beforehand.

When a substitution happens, you know exactly what shape you're going to play before the sub even steps on to the pitch. We always know exactly what to expect. I have complete trust in him as a man and a manager, and when you have that combination, it makes you a better player. He's definitely the best manager I've worked with and I'm praying he stays at Chelsea for a long, long time.

He's a clever man. He knows exactly what he is doing when he makes his statements. Something that has been lost in all the various controversies he has attracted over the season is that every time he gets criticism, it takes pressure off us. There's been nothing negative about any of the players all season. He's taken all the flak. And that's been worth a few points all on its own.

However much you might try to deny it, it gets to you if you are coming in for criticism every week or if there are controversies playing out around the players. It takes its toll. But every time the heat was on, it was the manager who was under fire. When there were negative headlines, he was the one getting it in the neck. Not us. He was the one who was shouldering everything and letting us get on with the football. And it worked like a dream for the players.

Nothing is left to chance with him. However hot-headed he might sometimes appear, nothing just slips out. Everything is planned. The players realize that and we are all very appreciative of the way he's taken the pressure off us before big games. It's also had the effect of uniting us behind him even more than we would have done before.

When a UEFA official described him as the 'enemy of football' after the first leg of the Champions League tie against

Barcelona, it made us want to rally round and make sure we got past Barcelona for him. It created a siege mentality inside the club. Again, there was probably a degree of planning about that. Ferguson was a genius at doing that when he was at Aberdeen. Managers have done it down the years. The feeling that no one likes us, we don't care, has done wonders for team spirit down the years.

I like the fact that he's passionate about his football anyway. I like the fact he's not afraid to stand up for himself. And when he leaps up off the bench and pumps his fist when we score a goal in a big game, that's great to see, too. It's like he's one of us. He's feeling it as deeply as we are and players like that. It's better than a guy standing there showing no emotion. You want somebody to inspire you. I'd be disappointed if we scored and he was just sitting there on the bench doing nothing. All he's doing is showing how much he wants to win and that makes us even more desperate to give the victory to him.

Even though we consider him a mate, there is still something there that marks out the territory between boss and player. There is a line you know not to cross with Jose. You can have a normal conversation with him about what was on the television last night or where you ate or what match you watched. But there is that line. And when you even think about crossing it, you get nervous. When there was all the publicity about the new contract he had signed towards the end of the season, there was plenty of speculation about how much his new annual salary was. Some time around then, there was one day at training where we were all daring each other to ask him how much he was earning.

It was a warm-down day so it was all pretty relaxed and chilled out and we were doing a few exercises out on the pitch. The rest of the lads were egging me and Lamps on to do it. They were saying that we were the captains so we should take the plunge. My bottle was going, though. I didn't want to get involved. I didn't want to go there. In the end, it was Eidur Gudjohnsen who had the biggest balls. 'I wouldn't mind being your agent,' he piped up, trying to fish for a bit of information. But the manager just laughed it off. 'Don't believe everything you read,' he said. 'It's all rubbish.'

That's his style, really. Quiet authority. When it comes to half-time team talks, he's certainly not a tea-cup smasher. He's not a Neil Warnock or a Barry Fry. He swears plenty and always in English but it's all calm and considered. He's lost it a few times but mostly he's quite self-possessed. He was angry during the interval when we played at Bolton, the game when we sealed the championship. He accused us of not wanting it badly enough. And because we had rarely seen him that riled, it made a big impact. We went out and got it sorted in the second half.

But normally, he's calm and methodical. When we first get back to the dressing room after the half-time whistle has gone, he lets us thrash out what's happened in the opening 45 minutes amongst ourselves for a while. He likes to sit there going through his notes before he says anything. He doesn't panic or rush to judgement. He makes those 15 minutes at half-time seem quite leisurely and considered.

Whatever his wages are, he earned his money in his first season at Chelsea. He kept us together. He kept us calm and focussed. He never even looked like folding under the pressure when it was at its height. And that was reflected in the players. Players from Arsenal and Manchester United kept saying we were bound to have a blip and that our lack of experience of being in the title race would bring us down in the end. But that never happened.

That was down to the manager more than anything else. That was down to the confidence he instilled in us and the organization he brought to us. We felt like a golfer with a rock-solid swing. Even though we were doing the equivalent of heading down the back nine in a Major, we knew we were going to hold it together and stay on our game.

We might have one of the most expensive squads in the Premiership but experience tells you that success doesn't automatically follow. We spent more money the season before and didn't win a thing. You have to work really hard. Those people who say it's all about the money should see us in training every day and all the preparation that goes into winning.

You have to work really hard and you have to have talent. And you have to have a talented manager. We've got that. When Jose Mourinho arrived at Stamford Bridge, we got the best geezer in the business. We're lucky to have him. Long may he reign.

2 Superstitious Minds and Happy Beginnings

My life at Chelsea is ruled by superstition. I started last season with a couple and ended up with about 30. If something works for me, no matter how small or how inconsequential other people might think it is, I have to repeat the same routine and the same rituals again and again and again. I had a few of them going already before the first Premiership game of the season against Manchester United at Stamford Bridge. For instance, I have to sit on the same seat on the team coach. On every trip. Not only that. The people sitting at the table with me have to be the same. And they have to occupy the same places, too. On every trip.

We stayed at a hotel the night before the United game and took the coach the short distance to the ground. I don't sit right at the back. The Portuguese boys occupy one of those two tables and the French lads, usually playing cards, sit at the other. There was a story in the papers in the summer about the French lads betting for huge sums of money but that's never happened while I've been on the bus. It usually seems to be about a fiver as the top stake. But that doesn't stop William yelling and whooping every time he wins a hand. If you heard him, you could be excused for thinking he'd just hit the jackpot at Caesar's Palace.

Anyway, I sit on the table in front of the French lads with Lamps, Eidur and the physio, Billy McCulloch. Billy's a real star. He's one of the lads and he's a great mimic. Everyone loves him. Lamps and Eidur sit in the window seats and I have to have the seat next to Eidur on the aisle. And Billy sits opposite me. If he goes to the stadium early to do a bit of preparatory work, I call him and tell him to get back to the hotel so he can come with us on the coach. He has to be in his seat.

I know it's getting ridiculous. It's got to the point where if Eidur isn't there, I can't have anyone else sitting in his seat. It just wouldn't be right. It would be tempting fate. Oh, and I have to have three sips of water from the bottle on every journey we take on the team coach. Not two sips. Not four sips. Three sips. It's just the way it is.

If you think that's weird, it gets weirder. Don't ask me to explain it. In the toilets next to the home dressing room at the Bridge, we have got two sit-down toilets in the normal stall-type bogs and three urinals. I always have to use the urinal on the right hand side. If we're waiting to go out at half-time and someone's using the one on the right, I still stand there waiting for him to finish even if the other two are vacant. Imagine how that looks. I feel like an idiot doing it sometimes but it has to be done.

On the day we played Charlton away at the end of November, the pre-match food at the hotel where we stayed in south London was really bad. I looked at the chicken and it was all pink and red in the middle. So all I had was a glass of apple juice and three bananas. Not really enough to get me through 90 minutes. Not in the ideal world anyway. But I scored twice that game. So for most of the rest of the season, I had three bananas for my pre-match meal.

I just kept adding new superstitions like that all season. By the spring, it got to mad levels. When we're sitting in the team meeting at the training ground, I always have to have the same seat. I arrived for it once and Eidur was already sitting in my seat. I asked him to move and he looked at me like I was crazy and told me in fairly stark terms to go and sit in one of the seats at the back. I said, 'Eidur, I have got to have that seat', but he wouldn't shift. In the end, the manager was standing there waiting to start the meeting while he and I were still debating about the seat. He gave it to me in the end though.

Oh yeah, and my seat has to be directly in line with the right-hand side of the screen that the manager does his presentations on. I get funny looks sometimes because if the chair's a little bit out of line, I have to shuffle along in it until it's in exactly the right spot.

On home-match days, we almost always arrive under our own steam rather than on the coach, and I always have to park my car in the same spot in the underground car park at Stamford Bridge. No room for error or compromise. So when I drove in at lunchtime on the day of the game against Barcelona in the Champions League and there was another car there, I was a bit unsettled. 'No problem,' I thought, 'I'll come back and move it when they've gone.'

So every hour, I went back to the car park to see if my spot had become free. But every time, the same car was still there. In the end, it got to about two hours before the game and I was still fretting about it. When I sat down for my pre-match meal, I gave my keys to one of the kit men and asked him if he could go and move it for me. He looked at me like I was mad. 'You want me to do it, now?' he asked. I nodded. I just told him he had to do it. I told him he couldn't lie to me, either. He had to get the car into that spot. He came back and said he'd done it. When I went back to it after the game, I was relieved to see it was in its proper place. Given the result we got that night, that car absolutely, definitively, emphatically had to be in that spot every single match after that.

I need all those superstitions to be observed before the match build-up begins properly. I don't know why it is. I think a lot of sportsmen are superstitious. I went to Wimbledon on the middle Saturday this year with my girlfriend and I was lucky enough to be sitting in the Royal Box during Andy Murray's magnificent five-set match with David Nalbandian.

It was a great day and an incredible match, the best drama I've ever witnessed at Wimbledon. It was a real privilege to be there. It was great sporting theatre even though I was gutted for him that he couldn't quite close it out. But I couldn't help noticing that when Murray hit a great shot or served an ace, he always gestured to the ball-boys that he wanted the same ball back immediately. He was absolutely insistent about it. He got quite impatient if they didn't understand what he meant immediately. Even though it's obvious that one particular ball isn't going to have special powers, it was clearly important to him mentally to get the same one back. He was saying to himself that that was his lucky ball.

With some sportsmen, it's just a case of lucky underpants or not shaving. I noticed during the summer that the England cricketer Jon Lewis said he didn't have his hair cut for as long as possible after a good performance. I could relate to that. I know that when we're on England trips, Gary Neville always has to sit in the same seat on the team coach, too. At United, he and Beckham always used to sit next to each other before Becks moved to Madrid.

I wanted everything to be absolutely spot-on before we played United. We knew it was going to be a massive game. We knew it might even define our season. The pressure was already building on the manager because of his high profile and his confident predictions and because he had told the press he was 'the special one'. They were lying in wait for him and waiting for him to fail. If we didn't get a result against United, then the pressure on him and on us would build and build. But if we won, we knew it would give us a launch pad for the rest of the campaign.

We expected United to be serious challengers for the title but we thought Arsenal would be our main rivals. They had gone through the whole of the previous season unbeaten which hadn't been done since the 19th century, and they seemed to start the new season the same way. I remember going into the dressing room on a couple of occasions after matches we had won and putting the Arsenal game straight on and they were tearing teams apart.

They played some terrific football in those early stages of the season. They set the pace just like they had the season before. They still looked as if they were in a class of their own. We won five or six games on the spin and I thought that no matter how well we played, they seemed to be playing better. No matter how long we kept winning, they seemed as if they would never lose. It got to the stage where we could not see them losing a game. Defeat was something they seemed to have become immune to.

That is how it felt until they played United at Old Trafford at the end of October – and lost 2–0. They went down in flames that night, raging against all kinds of injustices, especially what they claimed was a dive by Wayne Rooney that won United a crucial penalty. One of their players even threw a piece of pizza at Ferguson in the changing rooms after the game. They seemed to be totally shattered by their defeat as if losing was something that they found incomprehensible after so long not having to deal with it. They began to fold after that and we really began to believe it was going to be our year.

It also put our result against United on the opening day into its proper context. Because even if they were a team that could be said to be in transition, they were still the team that ended up posing the most serious threat to us as the season wore on. It was only in the final days of the season that they slipped back behind Arsenal and if we had not beaten them on that opening day, they would have been a lot, lot closer to us. That opening day set the tone.

Six players made their Chelsea debuts that day: Petr Cech, Paolo Ferreira, Ricardo Carvalho, Alexei Smertin, Mateja Kezman and Didier Drogba. All quality players. But normally, you'd expect a new team to spend a bit of time getting used to each other's runs and styles. We didn't have that luxury. We knew we had to hit the ground running and we took the game to United.

It wasn't the best game, to be honest. We had Damien Duff and Arjen Robben missing but United were hit by injuries, too. Rooney hadn't recovered from his Euro 2004 injury yet and Rio Ferdinand was still suspended. Roy Keane was playing in the centre of defence and Eric Djemba-Djemba and Kleberson, who were both struggling to adapt to life at Old Trafford, were in the centre of their midfield.

In the absence of Ruud van Nistelrooy, I was up against Alan Smith. I have always had good battles with Smithy. I knew going into the game that he would fight for everything and chase everything. I reminded William that Smithy would fight him. I told Gallas to make sure that in the first 15 minutes, Smithy knew he was up for a fight, too, and that he was ready to match him physically, that he would not be intimidated. Smithy is one of the best at winding defenders up. One year, he almost single-handedly deprived Arsenal of the title when he drove Tony Adams and Martin Keown to distraction when he was playing against them for Leeds at Elland Road. Arsenal lost the game, United won the title.

When you're playing against Smithy, you need to put a couple of early tackles in or go up for a couple of big headers. Smithy knows that I'm always going to do that. I know he's going to do it, too. We both like that side of the game and then when we have finished, we come off and we shake hands. He's got in trouble sometimes for overstepping the boundaries but I wouldn't have him any other way if he was in my team. Smithy chases you down and does not give you any time on the ball and, for a defender, that is a nightmare. It's a bit like it used to be against Mark Hughes, I suppose. As a defender, you know you've been in a game when you've played against Smithy.

Smithy got an early half-chance with a header but he put it over the bar and after quarter of an hour we took the lead. Geremi pounced on a mistake by Quinton Fortune and took the ball down the right wing before he aimed a cross towards Didier. Didier rose head and shoulders above his markers and nodded the ball down for Eidur who was unmarked as he raced into the six-yard box.

Tim Howard came out to try to intercept the knock-down but Eidur got to the ball first and lifted it past him. He still had quite a lot to do, though. As the ball bounced, Keane bore down on him and tried to clear it. It takes a bit of bottle to keep your nerve and your eye on the ball when Roy Keane is launching himself at you but Eidur managed it and he bundled the ball into the back of the net.

We survived a couple of minor scares. Paul Scholes hit a free-kick wide and mishit a half-chance but that was about it. They didn't really threaten us that much and we were happy to soak up what little they threw at us and make sure we didn't get caught out by pushing too hard for a second goal. We were criticized afterwards for being too cautious but we knew that the three points were more important than anything else on that day more than any other.

Their squad was a bit threadbare so they didn't have much to hit us with late on. Diego Forlan came on for Djemba-Djemba but fortunately he hadn't undergone the transformation to winner of the Golden Boot, for top European goalscorer, that happened when he left United for Villarreal later in the season. He hardly got a kick.

The victory was the perfect introduction for our new players. It breathed confidence into them, if they needed it. It gave them an early taste of a big occasion in the Premiership. It whetted their appetite for what lay ahead. People didn't know what to expect of us up until then and, up to a point, we didn't know what to expect of ourselves. So the result gave us a big lift. The manager had stressed all that week that Stamford Bridge had to be a fortress and that teams had to hate the thought of going there to play us. I felt we set a pattern that day against United.

After the United game, the manager said, 'Listen, I told you we were going to beat them.' Everything he predicted happened. From then on, there was a belief that we were going to win the league. We struck a big psychological blow that day. And I think the result made Ferguson sit up and take notice, too. Suddenly, we knew that we could beat the team that we thought was going to be one of our two biggest rivals for the title.

On the bus going to the next game at Birmingham, a couple of the lads were sitting there saying, 'Bloody hell, we're going to win the league.' We didn't know then what a tumultuous, controversial match it was going to be. But that belief was there already. Already there was a sense that Mourinho could do no wrong in our eyes. What he told us all came true. Even by then, we were all ready to walk through walls for him.

Everything felt very positive. I liked the look of the new sign-
ings, too. The last time I'd seen Paolo Ferreira kick a ball in
anger was when he made a mistake in Portugal's first game in
Euro 2004 against Greece. It was a defender's worst nightmare,
a pass that went astray and led to a goal for the opposition. To
highlight that mistake even more, Felipe Scolari dropped him
after that game.

But what a player he turned out to be for us this season.
He is consistency itself, nine out of ten every single week. As a
bloke, he keeps himself to himself and his football is no non-
sense, too. He does not over-complicate things and that's what
makes him such a good defender. He's safe and reliable and
his concentration never wavers. He knows how to keep the ball
and he knows how to protect a lead. He's still underrated but
I don't think that will last for much longer.

Ricky Carvalho only came on for a couple of minutes at
the end of the United game because he was recovering from
an injury but I'd been impressed by what I'd seen of him
in Portugal. I knew he was class and anyway I trusted the
manager's judgement in buying him. He was a good judge, too.
Carvalho is one of the best readers of the game I've ever seen.

He's a crazy lad, Ricky. A bit off his head. In a nice way,
obviously. He's got this mad sense of humour that stems
from the fact that he doesn't seem to have a care in the world.
He spent some of his career playing in the lower leagues in
Portugal and his attitude seems to be that now he is here in the
big time he is going to enjoy every minute of it.

He's a brilliant professional. He's not slack or anything
like that. It's just that he has fun in training. He likes to make

people laugh. Sometimes, we will be playing a training game and he will suddenly stand stock still on the pitch and point his finger at something in the distance. Everyone will stop and look and then he will look at his hand and brush something off his fingernail as if that was the only reason why he'd held his finger up in the first place. I don't know, maybe you have to be there.

And as for Petr Cech, I could write pages and pages about the miracle saves he made for us in his first season at Chelsea. I don't think he was properly tested against United but even in pre-season in America, he had proved to the rest of us that he was going to be incredibly hard to beat.

We would have these long practice matches in the States with Big Pete in goal at one end and Carlo Cudicini in goal at the other and we would come off after 40 or 50 minutes and the scores would still be locked at 0–0. We got an idea then that it was going to be incredibly hard to beat this guy in a match situation. It wasn't a surprise to me that he went on to smash Peter Schmeichel's Premiership record for the amount of time without conceding a goal.

Later in the season, it got to the stage where he was making amazing saves so regularly that they stopped making an impact on me during games. Think of the save from Robbie Keane's header against Spurs at the Bridge, the save from Geremi's inadvertent back header at Bolton, the dive and save on the line to stop the header from Carlos Puyol in the second leg against Barcelona.

I could go on and on and on. Sometimes, I would get home and watch the highlights of a game we had just played on the telly and realize that he had made another miraculous save and, because I'd got used to his standards, I hadn't really thought anything of it at the time. On several occasions I texted him and said, 'Sorry, mate, that was an awesome save, should have mentioned it at the time.'

His command of the box is amazing, too. If there's a ball going over my head, I know he's coming to gather it. He fills our back four with confidence. If we ever get a penalty against us, I always fancy Pete to save it. He's a great bloke, too. I think a lot of him.

We needed him against Birmingham. We got battered for much of the game at St Andrew's and Pete made a couple of brilliant blocks from Emile Heskey. I felt disappointed with my performance up there because they bullied us out of it for a lot of the first half and I couldn't get to grips with Heskey at all.

I know Heskey gets a lot of stick from fans and people who bang on about how he shouldn't be anywhere near the England team but he's one of the strikers who has given me the most amount of problems. He's probably the guy I like playing against least. I have to be honest and say he got the better of me both times we played Birmingham this season.

He's got everything a striker needs to make you very wary as a defender. He's as strong as a bull, he's great in the air and he's quick. At St Andrew's, I couldn't get near him. I didn't win anything at all. Physically, he was very tough. His work rate was first class, too. The only consolations were that he never got in behind the defence and he didn't score.

But Birmingham probably deserved to score. Robbie Savage was still with them then and he was working hard as usual. He is a pest but if he was playing in my team and I was playing alongside him, I'd love the way he plays. I know the Birmingham midfielder David Dunn well and he says he's actually not a bad bloke, either.

Savage was good in the first half and we didn't get much of a look-in. Didier had an isolated chance that he stabbed wide but Heskey got a better chance when he intercepted a back pass from Wayne Bridge and bore down on Pete. He hit his shot on target but Pete deflected it to safety with his legs.

In first-half injury-time, they came even closer to taking the lead. I blocked a drive from Damien Johnson but it rebounded to Julian Gray and he hit a crisp, clean shot past Pete and against the post. The ball came back out to him but he couldn't control it and skied it over the bar.

At half time, the manager made a couple of changes. Eidur and Smertin went off and Tiago and Kezman came on, and it steadied us. Geremi had a shot tipped away by Maik Taylor and then when he went off for Coley midway through the second half, Coley got the breakthrough. Six minutes after he came on, he lashed a shot against Martin Taylor's legs and it wrong-footed the keeper and spun in. That deflated them and they never really threatened us again.

We felt like we had cleared another important hurdle with that victory at Birmingham. They always say that it is a knack to be able to play poorly and still win, and we had never really perfected that knack before. But we had rode our luck at St Andrews. We had stayed solid and we hadn't panicked and we had ground out a result. And when we got ahead, we never looked like surrendering our lead, not even for a second. From my point of view, for the team to keep two clean sheets in the first two games was the perfect start.

In the later stages of that game, we moved to the 4–3–3 formation that we were to stick with for most of the season even though Duffa and Robben still weren't available. We went to Palace next, determined to keep the run going. And we closed them out, too. Didier scored his first goal for the club with a great back-post header and Tiago finished it off in the second half. We still hadn't conceded a goal and it meant we had made our best start to a season for ten years.

But when I got home from that game and turned the telly on, there were still people moaning that we were too defensive and that we should have gone on and won by four or five. I think there was a bit of a culture clash in those early days. Some of the new lads who had come in were just happy to keep the ball when we were ahead. That was the way they played. They didn't see the need to force the game or take chances when we already had the game won. It's the continental way, I think, and it's hard to argue with it. It's just that in England, the supporters expect a team to be gung-ho for 90 minutes and to be busting a gut to score again even if you're 6–0 up.

Coley was a huge influence on the Palace game as well and it looked like he was really on the verge of forcing himself into the forefront of the manager's plans. I was pleased for Didier, too, because there was a lot of pressure on him. The club had paid £24 million for him from Marseilles and, as the season went on, some criticism was levelled at him for his contribution. I didn't think that was fair and I only realized early in the campaign that Didier had hardly had a rest all summer.

He'd been involved with Marseilles until late in May because they had got to the UEFA Cup final against Valencia, and then he had played some matches for the Ivory Coast after that. I think he only had about ten days' rest before he joined up with Chelsea for pre-season training. He looked incredibly sharp on that trip to the States but that was probably because his fitness levels were still high from the previous season. And if his standards dipped a tiny bit later in the campaign, it was because the tiredness from playing two seasons on the trot started to catch up with him and he started picking up injuries.

I was particularly pleased we kept a clean sheet against Palace because I really rate Andy Johnson. That was the first time I had played against him and I was extremely impressed. His movement was terrific and he never stopped trying. Even when we went 2–0 up and a few heads went down in the Palace side, he was still chasing everything for all he was worth and doing his best to close us down. His attitude was absolutely first class.

I thought he had a great season with Palace and I voted for him in my PFA team of the season. Actually, I voted for him as my Player of the Year. I had him up front with Thierry Henry. The rest of my team, by the way (and of course I couldn't vote for any Chelsea players!), was Nigel Martyn in goal, Gary Neville at right-back, Jamie Carragher and Rio Ferdinand in central defence, Gabriel Heinze at left-back, Shaun Wright-Phillips (who was my Young Player of the Year) on the right side of midfield, Steven Gerrard and Papa Bouba Diop in the centre of midfield, and Cristiano Ronaldo on the left.

After the Palace game, I was rooting for Johnson throughout

the rest of the season because it was good to see an English guy in the scoring charts right up there with Thierry. I didn't want to see Henry running away with it and I thought for Johnson to score so many goals in a struggling team said a lot for his ability and his persistence.

Adrian Mutu came on briefly in that game, too. He had a real talent and he wasted it. Towards the end of October the news was to break that he had failed a drugs test which had shown traces of cocaine in his system. And I felt bad about it because it had honestly never occurred to me that he might have some sort of problem like that. It never crossed my mind that he might be doing drugs.

After Palace, we didn't extend our run without conceding a goal much longer. Just 12 seconds actually. That was how long it took James Beattie to score for Southampton against us at the Bridge. I knew it would have to be a special goal to beat Pete and it was. Coley tried a back pass straight from the kick-off and gave the ball away to Beattie about 35 yards out. Beattie turned on it and half-lobbed it and half-volleyed it over Pete's head into the net. Pete was caught slightly by surprise because it was straight from the kick-off and he was marginally off his line. 'Don't concede early,' the manager had told us just before the game. He can't have been too impressed with the response. It was only two seconds slower than the fastest ever Premiership goal, scored by Ledley King in 2000.

Beattie didn't get to enjoy it for very long, though. When Eidur flicked on a corner from Lamps, Beattie couldn't get out of the way of the ball and it hit him on the thigh and bounced off him over the line despite a desperate attempt to clear it.

Graeme Le Saux flung himself at it but he could only crash it against the underside of the bar and into the goal. Lamps put us ahead four minutes before half time with a penalty, even though he slipped while he was taking it. And that was enough for us.

We could have increased the lead in the second half. Eidur deflected a shot from Paolo just past the post, Didier missed with a header and Duffa finally got his first action of the season when he came on to give us a bit of width. But at the back, we closed things down in the second half and Southampton faded fast. It was the first time Chelsea had ever won the first four games of any season and we were already eight points clear of United. But still behind Arsenal.

But there were other little victories in that match against the Saints. It was the first time we had fallen behind under the new manager and we had still shown the resolve and the spirit to come back and win. Southampton were still being managed by Steve Wigley back then and I know they were hardly a model of defensive excellence last season but we still took some satisfaction from overhauling them. It would have been disappointing to drop points at home so early in the season.

After the international break for the England games in Austria and Poland, we came back to play Villa at Villa Park. We were about to go into the first and probably the only shaky period of the whole season, a spell when we had two goalless draws on the bounce and even more people accusing us of being boring. But we were unlucky at Villa. Didier curled a beautiful shot against the underside of the crossbar and then got booked when Ulises de la Cruz hacked him down in the box. It was a clear, clear penalty but Rob Styles was adamant it was a dive. When he saw the incident again, he admitted he had made a mistake and rescinded the card. But it was a bit late by then.

Juan Pablo Angel was lively for them that day. He was at the heart of most of what they created. But Pete had to punch away a fierce free-kick from Thomas Hitzlsperger's cannon of a left foot after about three minutes. They started to come on strong then. I misplaced a back pass which created a bit of panic and Pete had to scramble it away. I made amends just before half time when I blocked a goal-bound shot from Nolberto Solano but we were happy when the half-time whistle went because they had had the best of the opening 45 minutes.

We got a bit of luck quarter of an hour from the end when Darius Vassell shot wide after Luke Moore had set him up with a nice lay-off. But we had chances to win it at the death, too. Mutu went close with a lob that was headed off the line by Mark Delaney and Eidur blazed a shot over the bar from a tight angle. I pushed up, too, and powered in a header. I thought it was in but Thomas Sorensen clutched it at full stretch.

I was all right with a 0–0 draw. It was a decent result at Villa. They were playing well at that stage of the season even if they tailed off later on. But when we failed to score again at home to Tottenham a week later, the frustration started to build. It was after that game that the manager said Spurs might as well have parked a double-decker bus in front of their goal just so they could avoid any pretence that they were trying to play football. 'They did not play football,' he said. 'That was not football. They did not lose but nobody should give them credit for that.'

Spurs were under siege for the vast majority of the 90 minutes but we couldn't quite break them down. They were still being managed by Jacques Santini then and their priority was overwhelmingly defence. At that stage, they had only conceded two goals in their six league games, a record second only to ours.

Paul Robinson had an excellent game in their goal. He made a superb save from Didier early on and dived at his feet to snuff out another chance. Coley was playing well again and he played one crisp through-ball to Eidur that looked like it would lead to a goal until Ledley King intervened with a last-ditch tackle.

Given that we spent almost the entire game in their half, it seemed strange that the best save of the day came from our goalkeeper. Ten minutes after half-time, Simon Davies swung a cross in from the right, it flew over Ricky's head and Robbie Keane met it about six yards out. He met it on the full and it went off his head like a rocket but somehow Pete managed to hurl himself to his right and beat it away with his palms. It was a magnificent reaction save.

But that's what makes great goalkeepers great. Pete hadn't had a single thing to do. At the other end, Robinson had been hurling himself around and acting like a one-man wall to keep us out. He had plenty to keep him warm. And then the first time Pete gets called into action, he's more than equal to it. That's a special talent.

Lamps, who had made his 114th consecutive Premiership

start and broken Bridgey's record in the process, was becoming more and more influential and Robinson made another sharp save to tip his free-kick round the post. By then, we were camped in their penalty area and Eidur hit a post with a lovely volley. Duffa flashed a pass across goal that Didier couldn't quite reach and when the final whistle went, we were in disbelief. Arsenal were still only two points ahead of us but we felt we'd just wasted those two points in a match we had dominated overwhelmingly.

When we went up to Middlesbrough for the next game, it looked for 80 minutes as though we were going to get another goalless draw. That probably would have been some sort of record, too. The critics would have loved that. They were on our back now about the lack of entertainment that Chelsea were providing but we knew we were just feeling our way into the season.

We had them on the rack for most of the first half. Didier came close a few times. He headed over and hit a great shot on to the underside of the bar. We even had a period of about ten minutes when they were down to ten men because I caught Jimmy Floyd Hasselbaink with my studs as he stooped to head a bouncing ball. It was totally accidental but Jimmy didn't want to know when I offered him my hand in apology. He went off, got the wound stitched and came back on. And he still had the hump with me even then. He was shaking his head in that way that he does and staring at me as if I had done him wrong.

I always got on well with Jimmy when we were at Chelsea together. He's a fighter and a winner and he would give everything in every training session and in every game. We had a lot of clashes on the training ground because we were both so committed and the idea of holding back and not being full-on was foreign to us. They were never serious disagreements, though. Occasionally, one of us would launch into a tackle and the other would get upset. 'Fucking hell, it's only training,' Jimmy would say, and then a few minutes later he'd hurl himself into a challenge against me when I wasn't expecting it and I'd have a go at him. He was always the one telling me to calm down but he was just the same. He just couldn't see it.

I didn't mean to catch him at the Riverside. I knew he was extra-keen to do well because it was his first game against his old side and he felt he had something to prove after the club had let him go. Maybe he thought I was trying to be the big man and asserting my authority over him as the captain of his old team. I don't know. But when I went to get him up off the floor, he slapped my hand away. I went to try and help him again but the other lads just said, 'If he won't accept your apology, fuck him.' So I left him. I tried again a couple of times during the game. 'Jimmy,' I said, 'you know me, I wouldn't try and do you like that, I wouldn't do that.' He just kept telling me to fuck off. After the game, I went into their changing room and offered him my hand and he took it. We're friends again now. That's just the way it's always been with me and Jimmy. When we played them in the return game at the Bridge, Jimmy kicked me in the calf late on. 'Now we're even,' he said.

At half-time at the Riverside, the ref, Mark Halsey, had told Jimmy to go back to the dressing room and change his shirt because it was so heavily bloodstained and he came back out wearing Ugo Ehiogu's jersey. I never thought I'd spend 45 minutes trying to mark Ugo out of a game. It felt strange chasing that jersey around with Jimmy inside it.

They had claims for a penalty turned down when I got in the way of a Stuart Parnaby shot. They said it was handball but it hit me on the top of the shoulder and Halsey waved play on. We got the reward our dominance deserved ten minutes from the end when Lamps and Didier worked a routine. Lamps had a free-kick on the right side of their box and when Didier checked his run into the area and pulled back out to the edge, Lamps rolled it to him. Didier met it perfectly and side-footed it through a cluster of players and under the dive of Mark Schwarzer. We did a funny little celebration after that where we flapped our hands around our ears. I'd seen Didier do it a couple of games earlier when he scored. To this day, I still haven't got a clue what the hell it's supposed to mean.

And that was enough. It took us to the top of the table briefly, until Arsenal played again later in the weekend, but it felt as though we had lifted the gloom by getting that goal. It was an important breakthrough for us. We could feel we were starting to click and we knew that soon we were going to start cutting loose in the Premiership.

We'd already done that in the Champions League. We opened the campaign that we were sure was going to take us all the way to Istanbul with two convincing victories. The first was in Paris. The second was against the European champions. And I scored in both of them. It was great to get off the mark for the season. I was buzzing about that.

I think the only person more delighted than me after we

had beaten Paris St Germain at the Parc des Princes was Didier. The fans there gave him dog's abuse because he used to be a favourite at Marseilles, their arch rivals, and he responded by scoring two goals in a crushing 3–0 win. After he got the first, he ran along in front of the PSG fans cupping his hands to his ears. That must have felt sweet.

I'd felt nervous before the game. I think maybe because it was our first game for the manager in the Champions League and we were aware that he had won the competition with Porto the season before. He was the manager in possession of the Cup and we didn't want to let him down. That's how it felt. The first time I got the ball, I tried to play a simple pass to Bridgey and I stuck it straight into touch. I just felt edgy. It was a relief when we opened the scoring after half an hour.

That settled us down. It settled me down, in particular, because I scored it. By then, Eidur had been taken off after having eight stitches inserted in a nasty gash in his head. We thought the referee was going to stop play when Eidur was down, clearly badly hurt, but to our astonishment, he allowed it to continue and Charles-Edouard Coridon hooked his shot past the post. There would have been an 11-man uprising if that had gone in. I got my goal when Lamps floated a corner in from the left and their keeper missed it completely. It dropped over his flailing arms and I just kept my eyes on the ball and nodded it over the line into the empty net.

On the stroke of half-time, we went further ahead. Coley played a slide-rule pass to Kezman and when the keeper blocked his shot with his legs, the ball rebounded to Didier and he steered it into the empty goal. It looked simple but he had to take it first time and he did well to keep it low and on target.

Didier was chuffed with that and he killed the game off near the end. Kezman won a free-kick on the edge of the box and, as Geremi stood over the ball, Didier ran up and curled it over the wall and into the back of the net. The keeper stayed rooted to the spot. He wasn't having a great night. Didier, though, got the chance to milk the occasion for all it was worth. The manager substituted him after 80 minutes and he swaggered slowly off, drinking in all the abuse from the PSG supporters.

It was the manager's turn to get some stick in our second group game. We played his former club, FC Porto, at Stamford Bridge. I thought their supporters would give him a hero's welcome. After all, he had taken their team to the biggest prize in European football a few months earlier. After that, surely they were resigned to losing him. Surely they knew he was going to move on. I can understand that they might have been upset if he had moved to another club in Portugal, one of their sworn enemies, but I had imagined that even football fans, with their fierce tribal loyalties, would have wished him well in a situation like Jose's. To be fair to the Porto fans, some of them clapped him when he wandered round the pitch during the warm-up. But someone in the travelling contingent spat at him, which was stupid and soured the evening.

No wonder he was keen we played well against them. He knew so much about them that our team meetings lasted longer than usual that week. He had so much information to give. They weren't the same team as when he was there. Most of their best players had gone. Deco had moved to Barcelona and Ricky and Paolo had come to Stamford Bridge. But he still knew every little detail about how they would play and he wanted to impart them all to us. As usual, he was absolutely spot on. He even predicted the minute when Benni McCarthy would get off the bench. He was right within two or three minutes.

We were so well prepared, they held no surprises for us at all and we played well. Smertin put us ahead after six minutes when Eidur hoisted a cross to the far post. Lamps was there, too, but Smertin called for it and when he mishit his volley into the ground, it deceived Vitor Baia and bounced into the net. Four minutes into the second half, we went 2–0 up. Duffa swung a quick free-kick high into the box and Didier leapt head and shoulders above the defence and back-headed it past the keeper.

We conceded a goal when Pete parried a shot from Carlos Alberto that had brushed off my head and Benni McCarthy followed up and forced it in. The best was still to come, though. Two minutes later, Lamps drilled a free-kick into the box and I flung myself at it and scored with a flying header. I was pleased with that. I had scored two goals in two games in European competition.

When we played CSKA Moscow at the Bridge at the end of October, some of my family came along. They said to me that they fancied putting a bet on me to get another goal. I put them off a bit. I said I'd scored in the previous two Champions League games and a hat-trick might be a bit too much to ask. They didn't place the bet. I scored. They weren't happy.

3 Stretching Our Legs

I remember hearing stories about Joe Cole when he was a 14-year-old kid. He was a legend before he'd even played for the West Ham youth team. The word about him spread around football like wildfire. Everyone said he was the next great talent in English football. There was a story about Sir Alex Ferguson bumping into the West Ham manager Harry Redknapp and, before he said anything else, blurting out 'How's Joe Cole?'

When he was 16, Harry let him train with the first team now and then. And again there were stories doing the rounds about how the senior players used to watch open-mouthed at the some of the tricks he could do. He was a boy genius, people said, and it was only a matter of time until he was unleashed on the Premiership. By the time he actually made his West Ham debut, people were talking about him as if he was going to be the next Pele.

It was an incredible amount of pressure for a young kid and he coped with it pretty well. But it was impossible to live up to the expectations and when Claudio Ranieri first brought him to Chelsea, he spent a lot of time on the bench. He was getting increasingly frustrated by the time Mourinho arrived at the club and, to begin with, it seemed as if he was destined for another season kicking his heels and fretting about when he was going to get his chance.

Even when he came on and scored against Birmingham and made a few consecutive starts, the manager wasn't happy with his contribution. There were times, to be honest, when I feared for him. Like everybody else I loved his tricks, but I caught myself wishing that there was more end product. I know that wasn't fair because everybody who saw him play at West Ham in the season they went down knows that he played his heart out for them. He wasn't all fancy and frilly then. He was solid as a rock.

Under Jose Mourinho, by the time we got to the beginning of October, Coley had played a few times, come on as sub a few times and made winning contributions, but he was still being dug out by the manager in team meetings. The manager kept stressing to him that he had to improve the defensive side of his game and that, until he did, he was going to have to regard him as a liability. He was candid about the fact that he didn't really trust him as a player.

When our home game against Liverpool came around, he was on the bench again. The match was live on Sky and Coley got a break when Didier got injured before half-time and Coley replaced him. It hadn't been a great game until then but Coley lit it up. He made an immediate impact, setting Paolo free down the right flank to cut inside and produce a pinpoint cross that Lamps flung himself at but headed wide. After the break, Coley nearly got on the scoresheet when Chris Kirkland couldn't hold his half-volley and Harry Kewell headed it off the line.

But midway through the second half, Coley put us ahead. Lamps played a free-kick low across goal and Coley burst ahead of his marker and clipped the ball first time past Kirkland. He almost scored again when he lobbed Kirkland but the keeper just managed to push it past the post. When the final whistle went, most observers had Coley down as their man of the match. But the manager didn't. When the television interviewers asked him about Coley's performance, expecting plenty of praise, the manager wasn't exactly complimentary. He said Joe hadn't worked hard enough for the team and that his concentration had wavered after he scored.

That was hard for Coley. Everyone else was raving about him and saying that his performance had probably secured him a place in the England first team for the World Cup qualifiers against Wales and Azerbaijan that were coming up. Everyone else was saying that he was finally coming of age. And yet the man who mattered most, the man whose approval he craved more than anybody else's, was still saying that he wanted more.

The manager dug him out in the team meeting after we got back from international duty, too. He reiterated that he couldn't trust him to play in the team if he wasn't going to make an effort to improve the defensive side of his game. I know that was frustrating for Coley. The thing with Coley is that he is such a terrific lad that all he wants to do is play football. That's it. If for some reason he couldn't be a professional player, he'd rock up and turn out for a Sunday-league side. He just loves the game. But he also feels he can be the best and I admire that desire he has.

I think the manager's reaction to that Liverpool performance made a massive impression on him. He buckled down and started working even harder. He was obsessed with proving to the manager that he could be the player he wanted to be. And he succeeded. He succeeded to such an extent that I think he turned into one of the Premiership players of the season. From Christmas and beyond, he was a different class. He got more and more chances to play once Robben got injured at Blackburn at the beginning of February. He started to be noticed for his tackles and his tracking back as much as his creativity. Remember the goal against Norwich in March when he broke a couple of tackles and struck a left-foot shot into the roof of the net. Remember the way he played in Barcelona. And most of all the way he played in the second leg against Bayern Munich in the Olympic Stadium.

It was great to see the change in him. Against Bayern, he was unbelievable. He made more tackles in that game than he had made all season up to that point. And once he started doing it, he didn't stop. Everyone was buzzing for him. He has become a team player without losing any of that spontaneity and creativity that makes him so special, and by the end of the season he wasn't only one of our most dangerous players, he was one of our most reliable players, too.

I think that's an incredible achievement. And I feel proud of him for all the work he put in to succeed. A lot of other players would have given up. Particularly players of his talent. They would have tried for a while and then when they kept being criticized, they would have thrown their toys out of the pram and put in a transfer request. But Coley didn't do that. He stuck at it and I'll always have the greatest of respect for him for doing that. It feels like he can go on and be anything he wants to be now. He's found the secret. He has seen the path forward. By helping him change, the manager has also made a problem for himself because it's going to be awfully hard to drop Coley now.

It turned out the victory over Liverpool didn't mean an awful lot other than the three points. It was the first of our five matches against them that season but Stevie Gerrard wasn't in the team that played at Stamford Bridge and he is so important to them. Still, to beat them at home and then away on New Year's Day gave us plenty of confidence when we met them in the Carling Cup Final and even more when we were preparing to play them in the Champions League.

We thought our first match against them might kick-start our season but instead we went to Manchester City a fortnight later after the international break and ran into a nasty surprise from Kevin Keegan's side. If someone had told me we would lose one game all season, I think the last fixture I would have picked would have been that one. But it turned out that was to be the solitary stain on our otherwise unbeaten league season.

We lost to an 11th-minute penalty from Nicolas Anelka after the referee decided the Frenchman had been brought down by Paolo in the box. William had slipped on the wet surface and Paul Bosvelt had played a long ball over the top to Anelka. Replays suggested that the initial contact between him and Paolo was outside the box and that it was doubtful whether it was a foul at all. But Anelka got up from the tangle and put the ball past Pete.

It was doubly ironic that we should be beaten by a goal from him. As a young player, Anelka had brilliant pace and he played on people's shoulders. He was in his prime when he was a raw kid in the Arsenal team that won the double in 1998. He was dynamite then but as soon as he left Arsenal, his career nose-dived. I played against him a number of times and I got absolutely nothing from him. No trouble at all. With his pace, I thought he might try and get in behind us. But he had no heart. He didn't want to know. I'd give him a kick now and again and there would be no response from him. There would be times through the game where he would get the ball and do something lovely and then he would go missing again. It seemed like a waste of a talent.

It never stopped surprising me that someone with his skill could play such a minor part in a game. Sometimes, he'd produce a great touch midway inside our half and lay it off but he never did anything to suggest he was going to hurt the Chelsea sides I played in. And then suddenly there he was sprawling on the floor, winning a penalty, scoring it and condemning us to our only defeat of the season.

Keegan was hopping mad on the touchline after the penalty award because he thought Paolo should have been sent off for a professional foul. He was screaming at the fourth official. City would have been playing against ten men for 79 minutes if that had happened but in the end it didn't make any difference anyway.

At half-time, the manager was livid. It was one of the few

times I saw him really angry. The England lads had just come back from two qualifiers against Wales and Azerbaijan and most of the other boys had been away to play for their countries, too. Quite a few of us had scored goals and the manager lit into us. He said it was all very well us performing heroically on the international stage but we had to reproduce that form when we came back home: 'What about a couple of goals for your club, too?'

We made plenty of chances in the second half even though the injury Didier got against Liverpool was going to keep him out for six weeks. But City, who aren't exactly famed for their defensive solidity, were rock solid at the back and Sylvain Distin and Richard Dunne did everything they could to hold back the blue tide.

They needed a little bit of help. Lamps hit the post with a volley that skidded off the surface and Eidur missed a clear chance late on. The ball was played square to him about ten yards out, he peeled away from his marker and opened his body to take the free shot at David James and then sliced his shot horribly wide as he stumbled backwards.

We looked like we were stumbling backwards, too. The defeat left us five points behind Arsenal and our critics were making great play of the fact that Arsenal had scored 29 goals as they continued on their free-flowing path towards what seemed like another title. And we had only scored eight as we struggled to keep up.

Roman Abramovich was gutted after the game. I don't think he expected something like that so early in the season. The manager was fuming after the game, too. Roman was puzzled more than anything. He came into the dressing room and just said 'Why?' There was silence from the players and the staff. It was pretty uncomfortable. I thought then that I didn't really want to experience that again.

After every game, Roman makes a point of coming down into the dressing room. He goes round every player and shakes everyone's hand. Thankfully, most of the time he has been saying 'well done'.

In a way, it was a relief to return to Champions League action four days later, beat CSKA Moscow and know that we were virtually certain of qualifying for the first knockout stage of the competition even though we had only played three games. It was an important win for us because the news about Mutu's drug-test failure was beginning to break and the club felt like it was under siege. Not for the first time in the season and not for the last.

I got my third goal in successive games in the competition when Eidur nodded a corner back across goal and I headed it over the line. Three matches, three headed goals. It makes it seem as if European defences don't attack the ball at set-pieces quite as well as their English counterparts but I think it was more down to coincidence.

Still, it gave me a lot of confidence. I suddenly started thinking I was Andrei Shevchenko and I nearly scored again with a left-foot drive from about 20 yards that skimmed just over the bar. And eight minutes before the interval, I had another chance with a header that was going in until their keeper clutched it diving full length.

We put the game out of their reach on the stroke of

half-time. Smertin passed to Lamps who took the ball out wide and was brought down by Evgeny Aldonin. Duffa swung the free-kick in and Eidur, who had been left unmarked, finished it off from close range.

That victory was a real boost for us and it sent us back into Premiership action filled with confidence again. It's funny sometimes how the different competitions can rub off on each other like that. I've seen it happen to other clubs so many times down the years. People rubbish the Carling Cup but so often you see a team that might be struggling in the league get a great result in the Carling Cup and suddenly it has a knock-on effect on their league form and they start to climb the table. At last, we were ready to roll in the Premiership.

But not before I gave myself and a few of the other lads a huge scare before the home game with Blackburn the following Saturday. Ranieri had always asked us to arrive at Stamford Bridge at 11.45 prior to a 3 o'clock kick-off on a Saturday afternoon. But the new manager brought that forward an hour and asked us to report by 10.45.

On the day before the Blackburn game, Scottie and Johnno phoned me to check what we were supposed to be wearing in terms of the team uniform for the day and what time we were supposed to be getting there. I had a brainstorm and said 11.45. I don't know why they were asking me, really. Scottie and Johnno were due to be making their first starts of the season so they were a bit unsure about the drill. And I suppose I've got a bit of a reputation for being the organizer. When we arrive at a team hotel on an away trip, I always lay my sheet of instructions for match day out on my desk neatly in my hotel room so I've got it to hand if I need to check stuff the next morning.

I arranged to pick Bridgey up about 10.15 because it only takes about half an hour from our houses to get to the ground so I thought we'd be nice and early. I thought it was a bit weird that when I was a few minutes late, he started texting me asking me where I was. It was unusually twitchy for him given that we weren't in a rush.

I picked him up and we started driving into London and he said something about me needing to put my foot down. 'What is the matter with you?' I asked. 'We've got ages.' When he said we had to be there in ten minutes, it suddenly clicked in my mind. We were still about 20 minutes away. I put my foot to the floor and got there in record time but we were still late.

Bridgey phoned Johnno and Scottie and told them I'd made a mistake and they thought it was a wind-up. When they realized we weren't joking they started to panic. 'It's my first start and I'm going to get fucking bombed for being late,' Scottie said. He wasn't impressed.

So we all panted in about ten or 15 minutes late. The manager wasn't impressed either. I held my hands up and said it was my fault and that I had told the boys who had phoned me the wrong time. The manager said that if it ever happened again, he was not going to stand for it, which left it open-ended about what the punishment would be. It sent a bit of a shiver through all of us. And it made us think we'd better play well against Blackburn.

And we did. It was probably our best attacking performance of the season so far. Kezman was dropped, Duffa started up front alongside Eidur and Robben was fit for the first time and took his place on the bench. Right from the kick-off, we ripped Blackburn apart.

Paul Dickov was a bundle of trouble for them up front as usual but apart from him, we attacked almost at will. The only surprise was that we didn't score until seven minutes before half-time but it was a goal that was worth waiting for. Coley dinked a brilliant pass over the top of the Blackburn defence and Eidur ran on to it and side-footed it past Brad Friedel on the volley.

Eidur got another two minutes later when he ran on to a long ball from Lamps and lashed a shot that was still rising when it hit the back of the net past Friedel. We were flying now and Coley and Scottie were dominating midfield. Coley and Eidur played a lovely exchange of passes before Coley blasted another shot just over the bar from 20 yards.

Four minutes into the second half, with the rain pouring down, Eidur burst into the box and was chopped down by Craig Short for a penalty. He got up and looked at Lamps, who is the normal penalty taker, with pleading in his eyes. Lamps knew Eidur had never got a hat-trick before so he stepped aside without an argument. Eidur sent Friedel the wrong way. I was delighted for him. He deserved that.

And then, in the 63rd minute, an important moment in Chelsea's season unfolded. Robben got off the bench and came on for Coley and even our fiercest critics began to realize that, with a guy like that in the team, there was no way we could be called boring. I mean, how many other sides played with two wingers like Duffa and Robbie? How many teams were as exciting to watch going forward as Chelsea with those two in the team?

It was clear from watching Robbie in that game that he was a special talent. We'd seen that in training, obviously, but somehow it never seems real until you see it happening in a competitive environment. He ran with the ball as if it was glued to his foot. One thought flashed through my mind as I watched him. 'Oh, my God,' I said to myself. 'He has got to be on from the start in the next game.'

Robbie terrorized the Blackburn defence. You had to feel sorry for them. They were 3–0 down and then they've got this guy running at them when they're already knackered and dejected. He nearly scored with his first run, weaving in and out of defenders on the left and then driving a shot across goal and just past the far post.

Duffa got the fourth goal in the 74th minute, cutting inside from the right and firing a left-foot shot low past Friedel's left hand from the edge of the box. He was chuffed to score against his old club. And it should have been five when Robbie played a beautiful one–two to get to the byline and lay the ball on a plate for Kezman in the middle. Kezman made a good first-time contact with it but his shot hit the face of the bar and bounced away to safety.

Now there was no stopping us. The next day, Arsenal lost their unbeaten record when they lost 2–0 at Old Trafford and the Premiership picture started to change radically. Their confidence evaporated just as we were beginning to hit our stride. We went up to West Brom knowing that the momentum was swinging our way.

West Brom were struggling. They had just sacked Gary Megson and they looked dead certs for relegation. They hadn't appointed Bryan Robson to replace him at that stage so caretaker boss Frank Burrows was in charge. We didn't help their cause much because we routed them. Not in the first half, when we were lucky to go in a goal up. But in the second half, we were unstoppable.

I was pleased with our first goal. Lamps swung a corner over just before half-time and I got in a bit of a tangle with Darren Moore. But I didn't give up on it and when I had struggled to get free, I flung myself at the ball and headed it goalwards. William was standing a few yards out and deflected it into the net. I felt that goal was a victory for perseverance.

Robbie came on at half-time but it was Duffa who provided the cross for the second goal, curling in a ball from the left that Eidur buried from six yards with a diving header. Zoltan Gera got one back for them but then when he lost the ball on the edge of our box, Lamps raced the length of the pitch and slid the ball wide for Duffa who clipped it past Russell Hoult. Lamps got his first goal of the season from outfield play eight minutes from the end with one of his trademark low drives from distance that fizzed inside the near post.

Suddenly, boring Chelsea seemed to be a long way in the past. The victory at the Hawthorns put us level with Arsenal at the top and it sent a thrill through me when I heard our fans standing up in the away section singing about us being top of the league. Arsenal drew at home to Southampton that Saturday. They were starting to fold.

We were going from strength to strength. We qualified for

the knockout stages of the Champions League next by winning at CSKA Moscow. Robbie scored his first goal for the club with a strike midway through the first half. He took it so casually that it was obvious again what a special talent he was. The goal moved us out of reach at the top of Group H.

Robbie had switched to the right flank just before he scored. He played a series of passes with Eidur and Duffa that sliced the CSKA defence open and then placed his shot across the goalkeeper. He didn't hit it with great power or anything. He just passed it into the net, confident that he'd wrong-footed the keeper by dragging it back across him, so that he didn't need to hit it hard. It was a great lesson in finishing.

Robbie tortured the Moscow defence just like he had tortured Blackburn and West Brom. He nearly burst clean through after another mesmerizing dribble but a last-ditch tackle stopped him. After half an hour, he played Eidur through. Eidur took the ball round the keeper and tried to slide it over the line from a tight angle but Semak hacked it clear.

Their Brazilian striker, Vagner Love, blasted a penalty high over the bar in the second half and that was their last chance. I got my only nasty surprise of the evening when I came out of the showers after the game. For some reason, Robbie and Kezman, who you wouldn't pick as the two practical jokers of the team, had cut up the shirts and socks belonging to me and Lamps and put shampoo in our pants.

So when they got changed into their suits, Lamps and I soaked them with shampoo to repay the favour. They went back in the shower and me and Lamps got changed into our suits. We thought it was over then but suddenly they popped out of nowhere and soaked us again. In the end, the four of us were sitting on the team bus sodden and regretting all the silliness.

We were both a bit surprised by that. There isn't as much practical joking as there used to be at the club so it caught me unawares. Lamps and I haven't got them back yet. We were thinking about putting a couple of snakes in their cars but then we got this vision of them driving down the A3 and seeing a snake and swerving off the road. That wouldn't have looked very smart. We decided it was a bad idea. I bet the Crazy Gang from the old Wimbledon days would have done it though.

I forgave Robbie everything when we played Everton at Stamford Bridge the following weekend. Everton were in third place in the Premiership, astonishing everyone with how well they were doing. I confess that I didn't think they would keep it going to the end of the season. I thought they would fade away and finish mid-table. But they didn't. They stayed up there all the way and in Tim Cahill and Marcus Bent they had two players who impressed me very much. They gave us two very difficult games.

Cahill might have scored with a header early on but he was denied by a great diving save from Pete. Then Robbie produced one of the best bits of skill of the season so far, flicking the ball over his marker on the edge of the box and volleying a shot that was heading for the roof of the net until Nigel Martyn tipped it onto the crossbar. We were pressing hard and Eidur had a shot kicked off the line by Tony Hibbert. In the second half, Eidur went close again and Alan Stubbs put a header over the bar for them and I began to think that despite all the chances we might be heading for another goalless draw.

But I had reckoned without Robbie, who was playing like a man possessed. It was his home league debut and he introduced himself to the fans in the best possible way. With just over 70 minutes gone, Eidur got the ball in midfield and played one of those balls over the top of the defence that are his speciality. He has got a wonderful knack of weighting them just right. He reads the game beautifully and sees things other players don't see. He's got a brilliant football brain for anticipating the movement of others. It's a real gift and this time his pass sent Robbie scorching free of the Everton defence.

Robbie's pace took him clear but as he bore down on Martyn, David Weir made one last desperate attempt to pull him back. Robbie just shrugged him off and as Martyn came out to try and block his shot, Robbie lifted it over his shoulder as he tried to spread himself and the ball bounced into the net. We held on fairly comfortably for the win. It was their first away defeat of the season but more importantly it put us two points clear at the top of the table because Arsenal drew at Crystal Palace. Once we hit the top, nobody was going to knock us off.

Next up was Fulham, our nearest neighbours. They might consider us their biggest rivals but it's a one-way thing because we look at Arsenal and Spurs as the real London derbies. I haven't got an awful lot of fondness for Fulham, really. I was asked once whether we would mind sharing Stamford Bridge with them if they moved away from Craven Cottage and I said that, actually, yes we would. I said it was our ground and we wanted to keep it that way. Chris Coleman had a bit of a pop at me in the papers after that and said I was being big time.

So it would have been nice if I'd finished off a run I started in my own half with a goal. I kept going and kept going and forced a way through their defence until there was just Mark Crossley to beat. I'd gone 50 yards by then and I thought I'd done the hard part but I couldn't finish. I think I was thinking about it bulging the net before I'd hit it. I suppose that's why I'm not an attacker. It was a shame. It would have been some goal.

Crossley saved well with his feet from Robbie in the 13th minute after he tore past Zak Knight, and then the former Forest goalkeeper had luck on his side two minutes later when he totally misjudged Robbie's swerving effort but the ball bounced away off his shoulder. Smertin shot wide after William and Robbie had combined down the left, and after 19 minutes Eidur put one wide when he should have scored after Robbie had set him up eight yards out.

We were playing well and we got the lead we deserved when Steed Malbranque fouled Makelele on the edge of the box. Eidur touched the free-kick to Duffa, he stopped it and Lamps bent it with the outside of his foot so that it swerved away from Crossley and into the corner of the net. I nearly scored with a header across goal but Papa Bouba Diop made a great clearance. Then, in first-half stoppage time, Lamps was tripped in the area by Moritz Volz and the ref, Uriah Rennie, decided Lamps had dived and booked him.

Now everyone in the game knows that Lamps is not a diver. That is not his style. He doesn't do it. I think Rennie at least had the guts to rescind Lamps's yellow card after he had seen the replay but that didn't get us our penalty back.

Ten minutes after the interval and very much against the run of play, Fulham were level. There wasn't a lot we could do about it really. It was one of those goals that you just can't legislate for. Tomas Radzinski had put a cross in from the right wing. I got a good head on it but it dropped for Papa Bouba Diop about 30 yards out. We started to move to cover his intentions, thinking he might bring it down and play it wide, but he shaped himself for a volley and struck a fantastic shot arrowing into the bottom right-hand corner past Pete's outstretched right hand.

They were only level for two minutes until Robbie scored with a goal that was just as much a candidate for goal of the season as Bouba Diop's had been. Robbie's, of course, involved a mazy dribble. It was fantastic to watch. He left two defenders on their backside with a clever turn and then jinked past two more in the box. The ball ran away from him a little bit and Lamps closed in, anticipating finishing things off. He even drew his leg back and brought it down to shoot. But Robbie wasn't having any of that. Somehow, he stretched out his left foot and got enough power in his shot to rifle it past Crossley. It was a mesmerizing piece of skill and his fourth goal in four games.

We went 3–1 up in the 72nd minute. Lamps angled a free-kick across the box with pace and when Bouba Diop slashed at it and missed, William stooped at the back post to score. That was bad news for me. William and I have a bet every season about who is going to score the most goals. Marcel Desailly was in on it the season before and I won it. But William still hasn't paid me from then. Anyone who sees him, tell him he owes me £500.

Robbie had one more piece of genius left in him before the end. Tiago played a ball for him to chase towards the byline but Robben surprised his marker by back-heeling it into the path of Tiago, who had continued his run. Tiago cut inside on to his right foot and drove his shot past Crossley. We were two points in front at the top of the Premiership again and feeling like we were on an unstoppable roll.

That didn't last long. A week later, Bolton did a pretty good job of stopping us at the Bridge. The kick-off was delayed for half an hour because of some horrific car crash on the A4 coming into London but when the match started we picked up where we had left off at Fulham. The game was only 36 seconds old when Duffa ran on to a great through ball from Lamps, took it round Jussi Jaaskelainen and slid it into the open net. I thought Duffa had overrun it at first because the pitch was slick from the rain that was falling but his pace allowed him to catch up with it and thread it home from a narrow angle.

We went two up just after the break. Lamps won a corner on the right, Robbie took it and when Duffa played the ball back to Robbie, Tiago got to his cross first and clipped it into the roof of the net from close range. We thought it was game over then. Throughout the season, we were good at shutting up shop when we needed to. But the way we conceded two goals against Bolton was the sole example of us blowing a decent lead.

The manager was particularly annoyed with us because both

the Bolton goals came from set-pieces. We are prepared so well for opposition set-pieces that we've got no excuses if we let one in. The first one, ten minutes after the interval, was a scramble. Pete came to try to claim a free-kick from Gary Speed but lost the ball in the melee of bodies that were packed into the box. The ball got jolted free and Kevin Davies bundled it over the line from a couple of yards out. We nearly sealed it 12 minutes from the end but Eidur's shot cannoned back off the crossbar even though it had beaten Jaaskelainen all ends up.

There were only four minutes left when they got the equalizer. I got a bit of grief from the manager about it afterwards because I left my man, Rahdi Jaidi, and he scored the goal. It was another free-kick. This time, Bruno N'Gotty took it and because Jaidi, who is a giant of a man, hung back, I thought I would go and try and help out on the line. But we couldn't clear the ball properly and when it broke clear, it fell to Jaidi about ten yards out and he volleyed it through our lunging attempts to block it and wheeled away to celebrate. I couldn't believe it. I was gutted.

A week later, though, we bounced back in style at Charlton. That was the day I had the three bananas for the pre-match meal and thought it had brought me good luck. After all, we needed to change our luck at The Valley. The previous year, we had had a miserable Boxing Day there when we got humiliated 4–2. I remember one goal from Matty Holland in particular that didn't leave me feeling particularly proud of our defending. I left Charlton that day feeling I had let down the supporters who had made the journey to south London.

There wasn't going to be a repeat of that this time. Bolton's fightback had left us feeling angry and determined to banish it from our minds at the first opportunity. Duffa got us off to the perfect start when he ran on to another of Eidur's brilliant through balls, cut in front of Paul Konchesky and slipped his shot past Dean Kiely from an acute angle.

We kept that lead until the interval and then two minutes into the second half, I headed in Duffa's corner to put us 2–0 up. Two minutes later, after Tiago had been denied a clear penalty when he was held back in the box, Duffa took the resulting corner and Ricky headed it back across the six-yard box. Charlton couldn't clear it and one of their defenders nodded it on to me inadvertently. It came to me at a difficult height but I managed to twist my body so that I side-footed it down into the ground. I didn't get much on it really but Dean Kiely was expecting a fiercer shot so he had gone to ground. The ball bounced over him and even though he flapped his hand at it, he couldn't stop it going in. William was there, too, and he belted it into the net after it had crossed the line. I wondered if he might try and pull a fast one and claim it to gain a bit of ground on me in our scoring race but even he didn't have the nerve to try to pull that one. For the rest of the game the Chelsea fans were singing, 'Terry's on a hat-trick!' Eidur got a fourth after 58 minutes and with the previous season's defeat properly avenged, we got back on the coach happy. We were five points clear at the top again.

Bolton was forgotten and we were in the mood to stretch our legs at the top and try and move away from the pack. That was our mindset all along. We didn't want to start worrying about when the rest might close the gap. We wanted to concentrate on pulling further and further away from the teams trailing in our wake. Newcastle were next up and we fancied our chances against them, especially because they were without Alan Shearer.

But they played really well in the first half. Their movement was excellent and Kieron Dyer and Jermaine Jenas had a great first 45 minutes. Pete needed to be at his best to push away a dipping, swerving free-kick from Laurent Robert and we were grateful to him again midway through the half when a through ball from Dyer put Craig Bellamy through. Bellamy was one on one with Pete but he couldn't squeeze his shot past him and the ball rebounded to safety off his legs.

We punished them for missing their chances after the break. Lamps got the first after a nice knock-down from Didier in the 63rd minute. Lamps took it on the chest and then volleyed it past Shay Given. It was a bit like his goal against Bayern Munich at the Bridge later on in the season. Not quite as good but similar. And then Didier got the second himself. I knocked a long ball forward for him to chase but he really had no right to get to it before Titus Bramble. But Bramble let it bounce and then Didier went to work. He muscled Bramble out of the way, controlled it beautifully then took it into the box and curled it past Given with the inside of his left foot. It was the kind of individual goal out of nothing that the club had paid so much money for.

Kezman should have scored 20 minutes from time but he hit the post with the goal at his mercy after Duffa had squared it to him. Robben did score a third two minutes from the end, starting the move in his own half and running like lightning into their box. The bit I liked best was when Lee Bowyer came to challenge him and Robben just dumped him on his backside with a little shoulder barge. That showed you what a competitor Robben is, too. As Bowyer was dragging himself up off the floor, Robben checked inside the last defender and slid his shot past Given. In injury-time, Given brought Duffa down in the box and Kezman stepped up to take it. Once again, Lamps was supposed to be the penalty taker but all the lads knew how much it had been getting Kezman down that he hadn't scored for Chesea yet and this seemed like the ideal opportunity for him to get the monkey off his back. From the bench, the manager was gesturing he wanted Kezman to take it.

What Kezman did next took some real guts. He ran up and down on the spot for a few seconds before he began his run-up as though he was really, really nervous. But then as he got to the ball and Given dived to his left, Kezman just lifted the ball gently into the air and watched it float over the line and into the back of the net. My heart was in my mouth in the split second when I realized what he was going to do. If Given had just stood there and caught the ball, I don't know how Kezman would ever have recovered from it. I suppose that's a striker's instinct for you.

That victory moved us eight points clear at the top of the Premiership. Arsenal had fallen apart since they lost to United. They had taken nine points from six games and their challenge seemed holed below the water line. Belief was coursing through us. We had come through our shaky patch with minimal damage and now we were putting our foot to the floor. I felt already that no one was going to catch us.

4 England

I knew it was a big year for me with England as well as Chelsea. The World Cup finals in Germany are approaching fast and I've made no secret of how desperate I am to have nailed down a place in the first-choice England line-up by then. I hoped that the way I played for my club would force me into the first-choice starting eleven for my country. I'm not quite there yet but I'm getting closer. And I am the man in possession which is always supposed to count for something.

In some ways, I was lucky with the chances I was given in the last 12 months. Because of Rio Ferdinand's eight-month suspension, I had moved into pole position alongside Sol Campbell for Euro 2004. Rio was still absent for the first two qualifying games of this season away in Austria and Poland and because Sol had a bad year with injuries, I also played in the home games against Northern Ireland and Azerbaijan at Old Trafford and St James' Park in March.

But when Sol and Rio were both available, for the October qualifiers at home to Wales and away to Azerbaijan, Sven-Goran Eriksson still decided he wanted to stick with them. So

I was dropped. I wasn't expecting it. I knew it would be tight and I knew it was a tough choice but I thought I deserved my place in the side. I was in excellent form for my club who were flying along at the top of the Premiership and I didn't think anyone deserved to be in front of me.

I'm not being arrogant. I'm just trying to be honest. I believe in my own ability and I believe I am good enough to be starting for England. I know I have still got a lot to prove at international level and I know that maybe I have never shown Mr Eriksson my best form so far, but I still think I deserved to keep my place against Wales.

Mr Eriksson came and sat down with me on the bus on the way to training the day before the game, which was at Old Trafford. He just told me straight out that I wasn't going to play. 'But we will see for the future,' he said. I was desperately disappointed. I certainly wasn't going to have a flare-up with him about it because that wouldn't have done anyone any favours, least of all me. But it still hurt.

I thought I'd done enough in Austria and Poland at the beginning of September to get the nod and keep my place. We had started the game in Vienna well and opened the scoring with a clever goal in the 25th minute. The former Arsenal keeper Alex Manninger pushed out a low cross from Gary Neville but their defender Martin Stranzl passed the ball back to the keeper even though the box was crowded with England players. Manninger panicked and dived on the ball and we were given an indirect free-kick 15 yards out.

Instead of just trying to blast it through the wall, though, the lads worked a brilliant free-kick. Alan Smith touched the ball to David Beckham and everybody was expecting him to shoot. But instead, Becks passed to Lamps who was standing unmarked by the side of the wall and he just swept the ball into the back of the net.

It was an ingenious move but the fact that Lamps wasn't picked up and that Michael Owen was left all on his own, too, and could have been played in just as easily, exposed the difference in quality between the two teams. They gave us a bit of a scare when one of their forwards got to the ball in front of David James, who had come racing off his line. Jamo was caught in no man's land and the geezer clipped the ball towards goal but I had got back in time to clear it off the line.

I thought that was going to be our only brush with trouble. Midway through the second half, Smithy won possession with a mixture of his usual work rate and aggression, and Owen laid the ball off to Stevie G. Stevie hit it as sweetly as ever, from about 20 yards, and never gave Manninger a chance. We were three-quarters of the way to getting the job done.

But with 19 minutes left, they got a free-kick on the edge of our box and their substitute Roland Kollmann curled the shot round the wall and into the net. Two minutes after that, a speculative shot from Andreas Ivanschitz skidded on the wet surface and squirmed under Jamo's body as he dived to smother it. It was a mistake but nobody needed to tell Jamo that. In moments like that, being a goalkeeper must be the loneliest job in the world.

That was how it finished. To throw it away like that felt appalling for all of us. I also knew that it had represented one of my chances to stake a real claim to a spot in the starting line-up and I felt that my presence was going to be associated with the night we gave away a two-goal lead against a team as ordinary as Austria. If the team is doing well, I'd be doing well. But when the team is under the spotlight for the wrong reasons, people start to ask questions about your influence and your suitability for the job.

In the next couple of days, the press went to town on poor Jamo. They didn't exactly spare the rest of us, either, but they made Jamo the scapegoat. In fact, the *Sun* made Jamo into a donkey. They started a campaign to humiliate him and told their readers they were going to send a donkey out to the next game in Poland because they were sure the donkey could do a better job in goal.

The other papers weren't far behind. It was cruel stuff. Jamo's a strong character because if I had made a mistake and the papers were crucifying me like that, it would destroy me. It would have absolutely shattered my confidence, particularly when you are away from home and your friends and family.

We all thought the treatment of Jamo in those couple of days after the Austria game had overstepped the mark. You want to feel fully supported when you are playing for England and giving your best for your country. And then you make a mistake and you end up being vilified. I know this isn't how newspapers work but if only they could wait until we got home and did it then, even that might feel more acceptable. It's the combination of being away from home and being slagged into the ground by the press that seems so hard. And as far as we were all concerned, the donkey thing with Jamo went miles too far.

I know it's a cliché but when stuff like that gets written, it just brings you all closer together. Katowice, in Poland, isn't the best place to go on the back of a bad result. It's in Polish coal-mining country, down in Silesia in the south near the Auschwitz concentration camp. It's a hostile, desolate part of Poland, which is why they play so many of their big games down there. They know the crowd can be guaranteed to give visiting teams some serious stick.

We paid a visit to Auschwitz a couple of days before the game. To my shame, I didn't know an awful lot about it before we went. I'd heard of it and I knew it was a concentration camp but I wasn't aware of the full horrors that had gone on there. I spoke to Jamo about it a bit before we went and he told me some of the facts.

Most of the lads went. I was impressed with that. Footballers get stick for existing in their own bubbles of luxury all the time but most of us made the effort to get out there. I was glad I went. It was a sad, sad place that made you realize what people are capable of doing to each other and how low humanity can sink. I found it very eerie. Some people say the birds don't sing there and even now, more than 60 years on from when it was liberated, there is an air of grief hanging over the whole place.

The guide took us into the building that used to be the gas chamber. There were about 30 of us in there and it felt fairly cramped. The guide said the camp guards would herd more than a thousand people at a time into those chambers and then turn the gas on and kill them all. It was so horrific it was hard to believe.

We were shown around the brick buildings where the camp inmates slept. It's like a museum now and the exhibits make you shiver. In one of the display cases, there are huge mounds of human hair that the Nazis cut off their victims. They were all shaved when they entered the camp. We saw the place where the trains that brought the Jews from the ghettos stopped to unload their cargo before the guards decided who lived and who died immediately. And we saw the main gate and the motto over it that said '*Arbeit Macht Frei*', or 'Work Sets You Free'.

That sent another chill through me. I had had no idea what it was like. So often, we go to other countries as footballers and see nothing of them except a stadium and the inside of a hotel room. But this felt as though it had been incredibly worthwhile. I'd learned something. I'd seen something I would never forget.

Some people said they thought it was a bad idea to take us somewhere like Auschwitz so close to an important game. But nothing that helps you put your occasional problems in context a bit can be a bad thing. And even though we all talked about what we had seen at the concentration camp and all felt deeply affected by it, we knew we had to focus on the game ahead.

We expected the occasion to be hostile and difficult. We knew we would have to try to silence the crowd as soon as we could. The Slaski Stadium in Katowice is a doghouse when it comes to venues. The changing rooms are terrible. The pitch is bad. The fans are booing and yelling and screaming, and the weather was bitterly cold. But we were in a rage about the result in Austria and we were in a rage about the treatment of

Jamo, and it was Poland who suffered. We took the rage out on them, got a good result and came home with our pride restored.

Jamo was dropped for the game in Katowice and so was Smithy. Paul Robinson took over in goal and Jermain Defoe was drafted in to the attack. It was Jermain's first England start and he put us ahead nine minutes before half-time with a great turn and a clinical finish after Becks had played the ball to him.

We had lost Gary Neville because of an injury after half an hour. I like playing alongside him. He's a great organizer and a great talker. I even like watching him in training. Every day after every training session, him and his brother, Phil, stay behind to do extra work. They never stop wanting to learn. They never stop wanting to get better, even after everything they have both achieved. They're a model for anybody to try to copy.

Jamie Carragher came on for Gary and I managed my second goal-line clearance in successive games before they nicked an equalizer two minutes after the break. Kamil Kosowski drove forward through the centre and split our defence with a pass to Zurawski, who lashed his shot into the top corner past Paul Robinson.

But this time, we were determined we wouldn't fold like we had in Vienna. Less than an hour had gone when we took the lead again. Ashley Cole crossed a ball in from the left and, as Owen pressured their defence, Glowacki slashed at the ball and diverted it past Jerzy Dudek. We had the best of the remainder of the game and we never looked like losing our lead again.

Afterwards, of course, the press boys wanted to speak to us.

But we took a decision that we didn't want to speak to them. We were still upset about the treatment meted out to Jamo. You don't forget about that kind of thing just because of one victory. You don't just forget about what one of your colleagues has been put through at a time when he is already down on himself for making a mistake.

The idea of what the press called a vow of silence the next day came from quite a few of the players. When it was put forward, we all decided we needed to stick together. And so we walked out of the changing room and down the corridor and none of us spoke to them. It was nothing personal. I did a lot of press last season and I get on well with the vast majority of the sports reporters. A lot of them are good lads. But we just felt enough was enough and that there comes a time when you have to make a stand and say you are not putting up with that kind of treatment.

We were heavily criticized for it, of course. We expected that. Becks took most of the flak because he was the captain and people assumed he had been the ringleader. Well, that wasn't true. We were all in on it together. I still think it was the right thing to do.

We were called 'childish' and 'petulant' and 'spoilt' but at least we were standing up for what we believed in. It felt good to be part of an England squad that was sticking together and behaving a bit like a club side with proper camaraderie. That was one of the incidents that brought us a lot closer together as a group and which has contributed to the brilliant team spirit this England side has developed.

I desperately wanted to be part of that group and stay in

that first team and a month later, we were getting ready to play Wales when Mr Eriksson came and sat next to me on the team bus and gave me the news I had been dreading. I was disappointed but Rio and Sol had been his first-choice pairing for a while and he wanted to stay loyal to them. All I could do was keep giving 100% in training every day and impress him that way. And then if I got another chance, it would be down to me to prove myself again.

The England coaches Steve McClaren and Sammy Lee were really good to me at that time. They made a point of coming to speak to me. They were very positive. I've been impressed with both of them when I've been on England duty. Some of the sessions they put on are superb and Steve was very reassuring about Mr Eriksson's decision.

I knew I had to accept it anyway. There was never any chance of me throwing my toys out of my pram. I'm not that kind of bloke. I've got a lot of respect for Sol and Rio anyway. That's the first thing. I know they are both brilliant defenders and I know I can't expect just to heave one of them out of the first team without a hell of a fight. So I sat on the bench against Wales when we got a comfortable 2–0 win, and then I got on the flight to Baku for the qualifier against Azerbaijan.

We had all been warned about how inhospitable Baku was going to be, too, but the hotel where the squad stayed was lovely. It was a Hilton or a Marriott, I forget which, and it would not have been out of place in any affluent European capital. There's a lot of oil money in Baku, apparently, because it's on the Black Sea so even though there's plenty of poverty there, there's plenty of wealth alongside it.

I enjoy travelling with the England squad. It helps if you think you're going to be playing and I knew I would almost certainly be on the bench again in Azerbaijan. But I'm only a young lad and it's a privilege for me to be with England in any capacity. It still gives me a big thrill to be involved. I'm impatient to be in the first-choice eleven, of course I am, and maybe if I'm still not being picked two or three years down the line, I'll feel differently. But at the moment, I'm still doing something I've always dreamed of doing. I feel I deserve to be in the team but I'm still happy to be in the squad. I'm on the brink of being in the squad that goes to a World Cup Finals, which is every footballer's ultimate goal as far as international football is concerned.

What I have to do is keep my form and keep pressing for a place. I have to force Mr Eriksson's hand. I have to keep playing at the highest standard for my club and trust that that will eventually win my case for me. The stakes are very high but you don't win a prize like this with dramatic gestures or confident statements. You win it by playing consistently well to the point where you can't be left out any longer.

I didn't feel as if I'd been disconcerted by being dropped for the Wales and Azerbaijan games but my first match back for Chelsea was our defeat by Manchester City at the City of Manchester Stadium, our only league loss of the season. After that shock, though, we started to motor and when England travelled to Spain in mid-November for a friendly at the Bernabeu in Madrid, Sol was injured again and I was back in the starting line-up.

The game felt as if it was cursed from start to finish. It was one of the most unpleasant, sickening atmospheres I have ever experienced at a football match. I was impressed with the stadium and its steep, steep sides. It was a brilliant football arena and you could sense all the history of Real Madrid about the place. But the racist abuse the fans dished out to our black players stunned me and the rest of the squad.

We played badly, too. We hardly got a touch in the first half. Spain were passing us to death. They were playing around us and we were chasing shadows. It made us all feel stupid and a little bit powerless. And when the racist chanting started as well, tempers began to fray.

They had taken the lead after nine minutes when Asier del Horno, the left-back we have just signed from Athletic Bilbao, looped a header over Paul Robinson from about 12 yards out as Raul tried to deflect it in. It was a bit of a soft goal for us to concede from a set-piece and it just increased the anger that was raging through us.

Jose Antonio Reyes and Joaquin were tearing us apart on the flanks and Xavi was dictating things in the middle and all around us we were aware of these monkey chants coming from the stands. There were 48,000 people in there and the noise was deafening. I heard afterwards some observers trying to say that it was only a very small minority of fans making the monkey noises. But that wasn't true.

From down on the pitch, I could hear the racist abuse coming from all around. I could see some of the people making the monkey noises and they had expressions on their faces that seemed to be a mixture of hate and amusement. They found it funny what they were doing to Ashley Cole and later to Shaun

Wright-Phillips and Jermaine Jenas. I had never heard or seen anything like it. It was a real shock to my system. It was my first real experience of racism at a football ground.

I know we still have problems at English grounds but it is nothing like the way it is in Spain and Italy any more. We still have work to do but at least we can take some satisfaction in the fact that countries like Spain and Italy have got far worse problems than we have. We still need to be vigilant but we are making progress. In Spain, though, it seems like racism at football grounds is acceptable.

In that poisoned atmosphere, it wasn't a surprise to me that the match boiled over. I was so angry about how badly we were playing and the monkey chants topped it off. Wayne Rooney got involved in a few rucks with Spanish players. He fouled Joaquin and nudged their keeper, Iker Casillas, who made a big drama out of it and fell theatrically into the crowd. Wayne got a yellow card for that and Mr Eriksson took him off a couple of minutes before half-time.

Wayne got heavily criticized for his behaviour that night and for taking off the black armband we were all wearing as a tribute to Emlyn Hughes, who had just died. But he's under a lot of pressure for a young lad and most of the time he deals with it very well. I love the way he is on the pitch anyway. So what if sometimes he gets a bit angry with himself or with a referee or an opponent. Everyone needs a bit of fire in their belly. At least he cares. And his talent is frightening. Some of the goals he scored for United were breathtaking, particularly that volley against Newcastle at Old Trafford. If he does something like that, you can't defend against him. Even when he's training

Me in some England gear. I'm so proud to represent my country.

Two of the manager's back-up team, assistant manager Baltemar Brito and fitness coach Rui Faria, on the pre-season tour of the States.

Eidur gets in front of Roy Keane to score the winner against Man U on the opening day. Big goal.

LEFT: Playing quarterback on the US tour. I think I'll stick to the day job.

RIGHT: Coley's happy after his goal wins the game for us at St Andrews.

RIGHT: Putting in the hard yards on the pre-season tour with Scottie Parker leading the way.

LEFT: The boss discussing tactics with Clarkey during the Birmingham league game.

RIGHT: Didier celebrates scoring his first goal for the club in the away win at Selhurst Park last August.

In action for England against Ukraine in the World Cup qualifier in August.

ABOVE: Trying to cool down on the fields of Philadelphia during the pre-season tour.

BELOW: Lining up before our opening World Cup 2006 qualifying game in Vienna, where two late goals gave Austria a 2–2 draw.

ABOVE: Making a tackle against Poland in Katowice when we got things back on track with a win.

LEFT: Scoring in Europe against PSG in Paris in our opening Group H Champions League game and celebrating with Maka.

ABOVE RIGHT: Joy with Didier and the supporters after my goal against Porto, in front of over 39,000 fans.

RIGHT: I got a lot of satisfaction from scoring this diving header down among the feet of the Porto defence. The 3–1 result was a good one.

ABOVE: Observing a minute's silence for children murdered in the Russian school massacre.

BELOW: Chris Kirkland pulls off a spectacular save during our victory over Liverpool at the Bridge in October.

with the England squad or playing on the biggest stage, it looks like he's treating it as if it's a kick-about in the park.

For once, he was powerless to help us that night in the Bernabeu. We could have gone 2–0 down but Robbo made a brilliant save from Raul's penalty kick. In the second half, the racist abuse got even worse. Ashley had a bit of a dust-up with Aragones on the touchline which I'm sure was rooted in what Aragones had said about Henry. And when Shaun came on for Becks after an hour and Jermaine Jenas came on for Lamps at the same time, the crowd pumped up the volume on the monkey chants.

I came off after about an hour and watched and listened as the match petered out in a rash of substitutions. I still couldn't believe what I was hearing from the stands. When we got back to the dressing room afterwards, I didn't really know what to say to the lads who had been the subject of all the abuse. It was clear that they were devastated. We were lucky that we had someone like Jamo in there who lifted the mood a bit with a few jokes. But even they were laced with bitterness at the Spanish crowd. It was an awkward situation. I'd never experienced that kind of abuse so I didn't want to make it any worse for Shaun and Ashley and Jermaine by going over to them and asking them how they felt. I just tried to stay out of it.

The Spanish Football Federation were fined a few thousand quid a couple of weeks after the game, which was a joke. I heard Gary Neville saying after the match that if it had been an English crowd who had behaved that way, they would have been heavily punished for their behaviour. But the Spanish just got a tiny little slap on the wrist and that was it.

I wasn't involved in the next friendly, a goalless draw with Holland at Villa Park in February, because of my toe injury but I was back in the squad for the qualifier against Northern Ireland at Old Trafford at the end of March. My confidence was sky high by then. We were flying in the Premiership and still involved in the Champions League. Sol was still injured and so I was back in the first team in central defence alongside Rio.

I was pleased with the way I played at Old Trafford. Once I got my chance again after being left out of the previous two competitive matches, I knew I had to take it. And I felt I played as well as I could. I carried my club form forward to the international stage and what danger there was, Rio and I coped with comfortably.

We had a few chances in the first half. Lamps put Michael Owen through but Maik Taylor saved his shot after he tried to slide it past him. Wayne was playing brilliantly and Taylor tipped a long shot from him round the post and then kept out a free-kick from Becks. Wayne hit the post with a header and even though we went in at the interval without having scored, we were confident we'd soon put that right.

Coley made the breakthrough two minutes after half-time when he intercepted a poor pass from Tony Capaldi on the edge of the Northern Ireland box. Coley stepped inside his man and then curled a shot inside the far post. Five minutes later, Lamps spread panic in the Northern Ireland defence when he swapped passes with Wayne and surged into their box. The ball broke to Michael and he swept it home from close range. A minute later, we were three up when Wayne tormented Colin Murdock near the byline and then drove over a low cross that Chris Baird inadvertently turned into his own net. Lamps got the fourth with a long shot that was deflected past Taylor by Murdock's head. We moved on to the game against Azerbaijan at St James' Park the following Wednesday happy that qualification was going so smoothly.

I felt great about how well things had gone at Old Trafford but I spoiled it a bit by making an early mistake against the Azeris. All the hype before the game was about how many goals we would score against the group whipping boys. People were talking about eight–nil and ten–nil. We knew that wouldn't be the case because that hardly ever happens in international football any more and they were bound to pull all their players back behind the ball.

Even so, it wasn't the kind of game where you wanted to make an error. And I made one. I let a pass get past me and it went to their forward Gurban Gurbanov. The game was only a few minutes old and we were left exposed. He was in a great position but he put his shot a few inches wide of the post. I was very relieved about that. That could have been a moment like the game when San Marino scored against us after seven seconds under Graham Taylor. I didn't want to be associated with an embarrassment like that.

The rest of the game went smoothly enough but I felt annoyed with myself about that slip. I didn't let it play on my mind during the game but it nagged at me a bit. At least we kept a clean sheet. And even if the avalanche of goals never arrived, Becks lit the game up with our second goal when he ran on to Lamps's through-ball, cushioned it on his chest and then sent the keeper the wrong way by pretending he was going to curl it one way before actually drilling it the other.

We had been booed off at half-time because the score was goalless and the crowd had been expecting a rout. But we had done everything but score. Michael's close-range header had struck their keeper and then rebounded off Becks and on to a post and Lamps had lashed a shot into the side-netting. But we just couldn't break through in the first half and Becks even picked up a bizarre booking when he was shown the yellow card for running back on to the pitch while he was still trying to change a boot.

But six minutes after half-time, Wayne finally gave us the impetus for the breakthrough. He rode one tackle in the box rather than going down and claiming a penalty, and then pulled the ball back for Stevie G. It was a difficult chance but Stevie volleyed it down into the ground and it bounced over the keeper and the defenders on the line. Once we had gone ahead, it was game over.

There was a bit of a bizarre aftermath to the game when Carlos Alberto, the former Brazil captain and the Azerbaijan manager, lit into Michael in his press conference because someone had been winding him up about how Michael had said he was going to score five times. Carlos Alberto went nuts about that and came out with all sorts of stuff about how Michael wasn't fit to lace the boots of proper world-class players. He found out later that Michael had never said any of the things he had been told he said. And so he had to apologize.

I didn't go on the tour of America at the end of the season because I was recovering from the operation on my toe. The operation went well and I reported back for pre-season training a couple of weeks early so I could test it out. There was a little bit of stiffness at first but the medical staff said that I had to expect that. And after a couple of days, it felt fine. It was great to be playing without pain.

So now I have to aim for the qualifiers away to Wales and Northern Ireland in September and at home to Austria and Poland in October. I have to assume Sol and Rio are going to be fit. I have to assume I'm going to be fit, too. You're always tempting fate if you look too far ahead in football. I know I need to get off to a good start with Chelsea this season and start the campaign in the same way I played during the last one. I'm hoping that if I do that, I will do enough to get the nod.

Because things have been going so well at Chelsea, though, I almost feel as if it is in my hands at the moment. I know that what I did in our Premiership-winning season won't count for anything now. That will be forgotten when Mr Eriksson is picking his teams in the autumn. It will be about whether I can capitalize on what I achieved last season by carrying my form forward and playing at the same level. If I start the season badly, I won't deserve to get ahead of Sol or Rio.

Rio came back from his suspension as good as he ever was. In fact, he came back even better than he was before, which is an unbelievable achievement. And anyway he's a different type of player to me and Sol. Sol and I are more similar. I'm not saying we duplicate each other but we have similar attributes and it makes more sense to pair one of us with Rio than to play both of us at Rio's expense.

It's going to be a tough contest. It's a big year for all of us. A big season with our clubs and then the World Cup Finals waiting at the end of it. I've never had the privilege of being involved in a World Cup and I'm desperate for the chance to experience it. Those are the kind of tournaments that you play football for. Those are the tournaments where heroes are made and legends are born. We've got the talent to go all the way in Germany, too, and if I could be part of that experience, it would be the fulfilment of a lifelong dream.

I honestly believe we can win it. We have got the blend of youth and experience that is always crucial. We have got a great team spirit. The lads who have been in the team a lot longer than me say it is the best it has ever been. I just have a feeling we are going to have a glorious summer next year. And I want a piece of it.

5 Maximum Christmas

I feel like I am always concentrating to my maximum in every match. I've worked very hard on that. But when I play against Thierry Henry, I feel like I go to a higher level. Perhaps it's because I've got so much respect for him. Perhaps it's because everything he does spells danger for a defender. He's just a class act on and off the pitch and every time I go into a match against Arsenal and he's in the team, I know I'm going to have to be at my peak to have any chance of keeping him in check.

The first time I ever played against him, I felt sick with nerves the night before. But I have always done okay against him. In fact, it got to the point before Euro 2004 when other people were winding him up about the prospect of playing against me in the France v England game because the press said he was so quiet in our matches. He bit on some of that stuff, especially when the English press started digging him about it when they went up to northern Portugal to talk to him about me. His response was to win the injury-time penalty that won them the match. He's a bad man to upset.

I would never pretend that I have discovered the secret of defending against him. He's too good for that. We just tend to play a little bit deeper against Arsenal because of his pace and his skill. That has made it hard for him to get in behind us. Whenever he gets the ball, we always make sure we double up on him, too. I know without looking that if he gets past me, William or Ricky is going to be right there waiting for him, too. William grew up in the same Paris suburb as Thierry, I think, and they came through the French system together so they know each other's games inside out.

So when we went into the showdown with Arsenal at Highbury on 12 December, I felt ready for Henry. I wouldn't say I felt confident because I think it's dangerous to be confident against someone like that. You have to be on edge. You have to try to prepare yourself for the unexpected. But Arsenal were wavering in the league following their defeat by United and we had started to motor. So we felt that despite our poor league record against them, we were catching them at a vulnerable time. Our new players didn't know anything about that bad record anyway. They weren't aware of the history we had with them. The rest of us felt this was our chance to snap that league hoodoo anyway. The manager said that every year was different and if we had struggled against them in the past, this was the year we were going to change it.

Not quite the ideal start then when Henry volleyed a left-foot shot past Pete after 73 seconds. Cesc Fabregas, who was playing in the centre of midfield in the absence of Patrick Vieira, had lobbed a fairly innocuous ball forward towards Henry but we had cleared it out wide. Jose Antonio Reyes nodded it straight back in to Henry, though, and he swivelled on the ball and lashed it into the goal from about 20 yards. It was a fantastic goal, instinctive and clever. So much for him being quiet against us then. So much for him being a flat-track bully and never being able to produce it in the big games. That's why you can never relax when you're playing against Henry, whether the game's 73 seconds old or 73 minutes.

But a quarter of an hour later, we forced our way back into the match. Arsenal had been vulnerable at set-pieces and we hoped we might be able to exploit that. So when Manuel Almunia tipped a drive from Lamps over the bar, I jogged up to their penalty area with bad intentions. Robben swung the corner over and I made my run. Henry tried to track me but he got in the way of Sol Campbell who was my marker and that gave me the split second I needed to get a clear header. I made a good contact with the ball, nodded it down firmly and watched it bounce through a crowd of bodies and into the back of the net.

Confidence surged through us after that and Eidur and Tiago both went close but just when we thought we had gained the upper hand, Henry struck again. Robert Pires had won a free-kick a few yards outside our box after half an hour when he ran into Lamps and Makelele but Graham Poll gave a free-kick. It was Eidur's job to stand on the ball and make sure they didn't take a quick one. Henry was standing over the ball and I saw him say something to Poll. Poll motioned to Eidur to move away and Eidur backed off. It's easy to say this with hindsight but he should have stood his ground. He might have got a booking but that would have been better than what happened. Then at least we could have moved someone else there to protect the ball until Pete was ready.

As it was, Pete was right on his left-hand post, still trying to position the wall, when Eidur backed away. Eidur turned and tried to shout a warning to Pete but it was too late. In that instant, Henry took a couple of steps forward and clipped the ball over the wall and towards the opposite corner. Pete scrambled across his goal and he says he was still confident he might have got it but the ball took a slight deflection off Tiago that nobody picked up on and that took it the crucial couple of inches further away from Pete's dive. Henry wheeled away in delight. He was on fire in that game. We just looked at each other in disbelief.

Robbie got booked for complaining to Poll but we only had ourselves to blame. The manager was furious with us afterwards. It's always particularly frustrating to concede at a set-piece and that one could easily have been avoided. I think we protested because we were embarrassed, basically. We knew we hadn't done our jobs properly and now we were behind again, Highbury was rocking and Arsenal were sensing an end to all their recent problems.

The manager was annoyed with us at half-time but he told us to go out there and put it right in the second half. And we caught them cold after the restart just like they had done after the kick-off. Lamps hit a free-kick deep to the back post, William headed it back across goal and Eidur got to it just in front of Kolo Toure. The ball looped up off a combination of his shoulder and his head and as Almunia stood rooted to the spot, it floated into the corner of the Arsenal net. If we were upset at conceding from a set-piece, Arsenal must have felt even worse.

The chances flew about for the rest of the second half. Reyes blasted a shot over, Didier came close, Lamps put a shot wide. And then, eight minutes from time, Henry had a golden chance to finish it all off. He had been on fire all through the game. He was in one of those unplayable moods. But at least we had managed to limit the damage he had done. But then Pires got free down the right and as I frantically ran back towards the line to try to block any shot that might come in, Pires cut the ball back to Henry about eight yards out. It was perfect for him. A feeling of dread washed over me. He had been playing so well. He had started it all off and now he was going to finish it, and there wasn't going to be time for us to get back into the game.

Henry let the ball roll across his body and come on to his left foot. There were a couple of us on the line so he tried to lift it. But it just got away from him a little bit and he ended up stretching for it. The result was that he lent back too far and got under the ball. He skied it high over the bar and put his head in his hands. I looked round and some of his team-mates were looking at each other in disbelief. Henry is usually such a deadly striker, they couldn't believe he had missed one like that. I just felt this immense feeling of relief flooding through me. After the game, I was disappointed we hadn't got the win but the memory of that miss made me happy that we had at least earned a share of the points.

By the time I got back on the team coach, I was feeling much more positive. We had played better than them. We had maintained our lead over them, which was considerable now. We had come from behind twice and the only reason they had been in the game was because Henry had had an inspired night. We could live with all that. We had been to their place now and we hadn't lost. And they still had to come to Stamford Bridge. We knew after that game at Highbury that if we could have a successful Christmas, we would have one hand on the Premiership trophy.

Before we played Norwich, something happened that had a huge effect in terms of the day-to-day life of the club. We formally switched training grounds from the one at Harlington, near Heathrow, which we had occupied all my playing life, to the new headquarters out in Surrey, near Cobham. Many of the players had already moved to houses near the new ground, anyway, in anticipation of the move. Suddenly, my journey time to training every morning was cut to about ten minutes. It felt like a real luxury.

I was still sad to leave Harlington, though. I had been going there most days for the last ten years of my life and I had some happy memories of the place. When I first arrived at Harlington as a 14-year-old, Glenn Hoddle was in charge. Then there was Ruud Gullit, Gianluca Vialli and Claudio Ranieri. Some of the happiest memories were of the times when the first-team players had left for the day and just us YTS boys were left. It felt like it was our training ground then. We would have 'stupid penalty' competitions and flip-flop fights and talk about all the things we were going to achieve in the game.

The facilities weren't the best but back then it didn't seem to matter. The training ground actually belonged to Imperial

College and its students had first call on the pitches. We had to fit around them, which obviously wasn't ideal. But it was a quirky place full of character. The changing rooms were downstairs, three small rooms along a long corridor.

When Gullit was in charge, each room housed a different clique: French boys in one, Italians in another, British in another. It was all strictly divided up. Same under Vialli and Ranieri really. Then, when Mourinho arrived, he got all the walls knocked down so we just had one big changing room. That felt a lot better. It was great. They spent a lot of money on improvements even though we knew we were leaving. But it was money well spent. We were there for half the season. Those improvements helped us win the title.

The new training ground is superb. Everything a player could want is there. A fantastic covered pitch built under a kind of plastic bubble, brilliant drainage on the outside pitches, a state of the art gym, a great canteen. No stone has been left unturned in making it a great working environment for the players. Any new players thinking of joining the club are going to be impressed by what they see there.

We had known that the move was coming for a long time so it was a relief to finally arrive there. But if there was a change in the daily routine, there was no change in our form. After Arsenal, we started to lengthen our stride and our march was relentless.

In terms of its intensity, the next game after Arsenal couldn't have been more different. Norwich were in freefall before they came to Stamford Bridge the weekend before Christmas. That late-season rally they were to have was just a distant dream then, and they were struggling. We were 3–0 up with only ten minutes gone, after their defence practically invited our front men to score, and the game was dead.

It didn't help them that their top striker Mathias Svensson had to be taken off after eight minutes. He and I went for a 50–50 ball together and he injured his foot in the challenge. He signalled straight away to the bench that he would not be able to continue and they brought on Leon McKenzie in his place.

They were trying to play it about a bit at the back at the start but Thomas Helveg passed it straight to Duffa about 30 yards out. Duffa accepted the gift gratefully, ran at their defence and curled a left-foot shot low past Robert Green from 20 yards out. It was the fifth time in nine games that he had opened the scoring for us. We were flying. The only way Marc Edworthy could cope with Robbie on the Norwich right was to bring him down. We should have had a penalty when McKenzie handled in the box and it generally felt like every time we attacked we were going to score.

We got a second 12 minutes before half-time. This time, it was Gary Doherty who misplaced his pass and if there's one guy you don't want a bad pass to go to, it's Robbie. Robbie picked it up and twisted and turned past a couple of defenders. When he eventually found his path blocked, he had created such havoc in their defence that Lamps was in plenty of space on his right. Robbie slipped a simple pass to him, Lamps took a touch and then hit an unstoppable shot from 30 yards out that had wicked swerve on it, which flew high into the roof of the net past Green's left hand.

Our third goal was a classic, started and finished by Robbie.

Two minutes before the interval, he tore through the Norwich midfield and passed to Lamps. Lamps helped it on to Tiago who played a first-time back-heel into the path of Robbie. Robbie took it on and volleyed it past Green with ferocious power. It was a brilliant goal. A gem of creative football. Those 'boring Chelsea' insults had lost all their meaning now. They seemed like criticism from another age and Robben got a standing ovation when he was replaced by Kezman 12 minutes from the end. Didier completed the rout in the 82nd minute when he rose above Fleming and powered in a header from Duffa's corner.

And so we were six points clear at the top of the table at Christmas. We had some tough games coming up and we knew that this time the previous season was when our Premiership challenge had fallen apart. It had been such a miserable time that Roman actually came up to me this season and made me promise him we were going to have a better Christmas than we had the previous year. We had difficult games but we were confident that we would be able to kick on.

I think some of the lads who have families find Christmas hard. Some of them have come from leagues where they have a winter break so I think it's especially difficult for them. But I am lucky in a way in that I have been used to travelling with the team for a few years now. I'm sure I'd feel it more if I had kids but I think most players in the Premiership just accept it as part of the job anyway. It's a small price to pay for the lifestyles we lead and being able to play football for a living.

Actually, the bigger danger for footballers over the past few years appears to have been attracting bad headlines for having a laugh at the club Christmas party. Christmas, or the period immediately before it, and summer are usually the times when the behaviour of footballers comes under the spotlight because they have got some free time and they try and take the chance to relax a little bit and take a break from the pressures of the game. I've had my share of those kind of headlines in the past but it got to the point where I realized I had to do something about it and put a stop to them. I knew I had to make a few changes and keep my nose clean.

I know that I am very lucky to be in the situation I'm in. There is such a lot of hype around football, everybody wants a piece of the action and the result is that we get great wages. A lot of people think you just get loads of money and it sits in the bank. Of course, those of us in the Premiership have got nice houses and nice cars but it is only a short career. I want to try and pay off my mortgage as soon as I can because I know I am probably not going to be earning this kind of money when I stop playing football.

More than anything, I see it as a chance for me to be able to repay my family. I see it as a chance to repay my dad who worked from seven in the morning until seven at night when I was growing up. It is a chance for me to say to him that he doesn't need to work any more. It is a chance for me to buy him a house and look after him a bit. He was a forklift truck driver at a wood yard, unloading boats and loading them on to lorries, and all he ever did was work to support us.

He didn't have time for much else except eating and sleeping. At weekends, he would get up early to take my brother and I to our football because he knew that was our obsession and that we had talent. We never had any money. We even struggled for food at times. Sometimes, we went round to other people's houses for food. But the one thing we always had was new football boots when we needed them. My dad wanted to give us a chance with our football and he was determined that nothing was going to get in the way of that. We always got to our football matches even if my dad had to borrow a tenner for petrol to get us there. That was how we grew up. So I appreciate my money and I appreciate the sacrifices my dad made for me to play football and I'm happy I can pay him back.

I know the value of money. I know I have to save. Ninety per cent of my money goes into savings and investments for after my career. I hope there is life after football for me. I would like to be a manager. But I know I have to be careful. And people look out for me. If I go out and spend five hundred pounds on a jacket, my accountant's on the phone the next day wanting to know why. I get my bank manager on the phone saying I have spent too much in a particular month and that my investments that month will suffer because of it. The upshot is that I have to spend less the next month.

There is so much talk about players being out of control but most of it is wildly exaggerated. There was one occasion recently when the Chelsea players went out as a squad to a nightclub in central London and the bill at the end of the evening was £2,000 between about 20 of us. It's a good night out, I agree, but in the greater scheme of things, it's hardly wildly excessive. A couple of days later, the reports were saying that we spent £50,000 and that we were buying bottles of Cristal champagne left, right and centre. Well, just so you know, I think champagne's disgusting. I'll drink it from a magnum on a football pitch when a title's been won or a cup has been lifted but otherwise I don't want to go anywhere near it. I would never pay silly money for a drink. But people believe that kind of stuff. I even had a call from my dad about that night. I kept the bill and I showed it to him to prove how much we actually spent.

So I had no distractions during the festive period this season. Christmas and New Year were blissfully straightforward. We did have a players' party the Sunday before Christmas. We thought about going in fancy dress but that's a sure-fire way to attract attention and criticism. I remember the Leeds boys turning up to theirs in Nazi uniforms one year, which went down well. So we decided to knock that part of it on the head.

But the manager was brilliant about it. He said we could leave early after training on the Sunday and he would postpone training on the Monday to 3 pm. I asked him if there was any chance that we could have the Monday off. I said this was an English-style Christmas party we were talking about. And he was brilliant. He said that as long as it didn't finish too late and as long as it didn't get out of hand, he would agree to that. He trusts us and I like to think that we repaid that trust.

So after training on the Sunday morning, we hired our coach and its driver Derek for the day and got him to take us into Cobham for a bit of paint-balling. While we were doing that, I got the driver to go to the local McDonald's. So when we got back on the bus, there were 35 Big Mac meals waiting for us there. We went on to a little bar in Esher for a few drinks and then we got the driver to take us into London.

We hired out a nightclub in the West End. It wasn't just for the players. Everybody got a few invitations each and it was up to them who they wanted to invite. We arranged some cars to pick us up around the back of the club so that we could avoid the photographers who were at the front. Everything went really smoothly. There were no problems. No trouble. It was what a Christmas party should be like.

Actually, the most raucous event at our club in December was nearer the beginning of the month when I organized a computer-games competition at my house in Surrey. It had been an ongoing thing at the club on away trips that we competed against each other on this game called Pro Evolution Soccer. We all go to each other's rooms and play each other. If you beat someone who has been unbeaten for a couple of the trips, you're then the champion.

So I spoke to my agent Aaron Lincoln about organizing a proper tournament for all the lads round at my house. He spoke to the people at Konami, who have developed the game, and they came round to my house and put four plasma screens up in my snooker room at the top of the house. All the lads came round and the chef from the training ground came round to do the food. We put people in two big groups and then the top four from each group went into the quarter-finals. Glen Johnson was looking hot favourite at that point. Coley was second in Johnno's group. Eidur's son played as well.

So there was me, Didier, William, Carlo Cudicini, Scottie, Kezman, Big Pete, Robbie, Coley, Bridgey, Ade Mafe (one of our fitness guys), Aaron and Billy the masseur. Lamps doesn't play and neither does Duffa. Sky's *Soccer AM* programme did a preview of it and called it 'Judgment Day'. We had proper trophies made as well. We put a few posters up at the training ground and even the manager started getting into it. He let us off a little bit earlier after Sunday training and we all shot back to mine.

We watched the tape *Soccer AM* had done for us and then it was game on. Pete was humming all the way through his games. It was like a kind of nervous habit but it seemed to do the trick because it put a few people off. I got knocked out in the quarters by Coley. I was gutted. But no one took any notice. It went on for about seven hours. The quarters started about 7 pm and it was ten minutes a game.

What was particularly disappointing was that I had looked hot favourite at first. People were saying it was between me and Johnno for the title and I beat Pete 7–0 in my first game. I was thinking, 'That's it, I've won it.' Some of the players seemed more nervous than they were before a Premiership game. When someone scored during a match, we had to pause the game for people to celebrate and recuperate and calm themselves down.

The semis were Coley v Eidur. Eidur's not bad at it but you wouldn't have expected him to have got that far. He had been practising a lot before the tournament. You had to choose an international team and then that was your team and you had to stay with it. Scottie turned up in an Italian top. I was England. Coley was Brazil. Johnno beat Coley 5–2 in the final.

But that wasn't the end of it. No way. Because after that, we did a straight knockout cup competition. A few of the boys had got tired and gone by then so there were eight people in that tournament instead of 16. There was a lucky dip and whichever team you drew out was your team. Johnno drew Jamaica who were crap, so that levelled it all out. I went on to win the cup. Some of the other lads gave me plenty of stick. They said it was the earlier competition that mattered. They said that was the Premiership of computer-game competitions. But I wasn't having it. My argument was that the two previous finalists, Johnno and Coley, were still competing, so I deserved to be recognized as the champion of champions. Funnily enough, there weren't too many people agreeing with me.

Back in the real world, our real-life manager was worried that our real-life players would be exhausted by the peculiar demands of the English Christmas holiday programme. He thought the schedule was dangerous for the health of our players. He pointed out in a couple of interviews that playing so many games in such a short space of time increased the risk of injury. He said the build-up of matches was crazy. He's probably right but when you're a player and you're winning, you tend not to worry about it so much. The four matches over the holiday spell went like a dream, starting with Villa at the Bridge on Boxing Day. Last Boxing Day, we got battered by Charlton but we were so well drilled and defensively disciplined now that there was never going to be a repeat of that kind of result. Villa worked hard but we had just too much for them.

Eidur missed an early half-chance Robbie had created for him and I headed over from a free-kick. Lee Hendrie, who was having a good season, kept having a pop from range and was playing well. Villa weren't intimidated. They didn't just sit back and defend. They were going for it. Their season tailed off later but at that stage they were playing good football and spreading the ball around with confidence.

But they didn't have anyone like Duffa and Robbie and when the two of them combined after half an hour, they ripped Villa to pieces. Robbie got the ball in space near the half-way line and raced forward. He has got so much pace and such brilliant close control that he stretches defences right out of shape when he runs at them. He's one of those lucky guys who seems to be able to run faster with the ball than without it. Ryan Giggs is a bit like that, too. It's just the special players, the really classy wingers, who have got that gift.

So when he reached the edge of the box, Villa were back-pedalling furiously. Robbie could have shot but he played the ball out towards the right to Duffa instead. Duffa used his first touch to bring him inside on to his left foot and then rifled his shot low past Thomas Sorensen at his near post. It was a brilliant counter-attacking goal, great to watch, but cold and clinical as well. A brutal, destructive run by Robbie finished off by a piece of ruthless finishing from Duffa.

I should have extended our lead just before half-time when I got a free header from a Robben corner but I couldn't quite get it on target. It missed by a few inches. After the interval, a fierce shot from Mathieu Berson hit me on the arm. There was no way I could have avoided it and, even though Villa appealed loudly for a penalty, the referee waved play on. At the other end, Eidur nearly got on the scoresheet midway through the half but Sorensen pushed his shot wide after Lamps had played him in with a great ball.

We were happy to take 1–0 when the final whistle went.

Villa had given us problems before and I had them down as a useful side. And to get a win on Boxing Day was the springboard we needed. Already, it was a better Christmas than the previous one and we went down to Portsmouth with our morale high. We knew Arsenal had only scraped a win there ten days earlier when Sol Campbell had burst from deep and scored a scorching winner with a long shot, so we knew it wouldn't be easy but we were confident.

Pete kept us in the game early on with a brilliant save from Nigel Quashie. Quashie had the ball out on the left about 35 yards out but he brought it inside on to his right foot and let fly. Pete had it covered but then at the last minute, the ball swerved in the air to Pete's left and looked like it was going to dip under the bar and beat him. Somehow, though, Pete managed to arch his back and throw out his left hand and tip the ball over the crossbar. It was one of those miracle saves that we were getting blasé about him making.

There weren't many more chances in the first half for either side and it stayed tight until the last ten minutes. I was still confident we were going to score though and when Lamps found Robbie out on the right in the 80th minute, he cut inside on to his left foot and belted his cross-shot past Shaka Hislop. It was great to see Robbie's celebration and how much it meant to him. He took his shirt off and whirled it round his head as he ran back to the centre circle. He got booked, of course, which has to be one of the worst rules in football. There are so many things footballers aren't supposed to do these days but surely we should be allowed to show our delight at scoring a goal?

We knew we were going to win then. I'd heard Pete talking

to the press about the feeling there was at Chelsea now when we went a goal up. Basically, as soon as we scored, we were so confident in our ability to stop the other side scoring that we felt the game was won. We felt that once we had the advantage, we were never going to lose it. A game like Bolton was just the exception that proved the rule. That wasn't going to happen again. In fact, we ended up getting another goal to finish things off right at the death. Eidur's shot was blocked but Coley knocked the ball in on the rebound, and we went into the New Year riding high.

We had high hopes for 2005. We were now in the year that marked the 50th anniversary of the last time we won the title and we were starting to have an unshakeable belief that this was going to be a momentous year for us. The Carling Cup was first on our agenda, and of course there was the FA Cup. But we wanted the Premiership most of all. And we believed we could win the Champions League, too. Christmas and New Year gave us the base to push on towards all our goals.

Our victory at Anfield on New Year's Day felt like a massively important win. None of us knew then how much pain we would be feeling at Liverpool's ground a few months down the line. No one really thought that Liverpool would progress to the latter stages of the Champions League or that they would have much of a chance against us if they did. When we won up there on the first day of 2005, I thought that I would look back on Anfield as one of the happiest memories of a great season. Instead, it's a place I will associate now with one of my worst nightmares.

At least the game there on New Year's Day was a cause for

celebration. We knew it would be difficult because even though Liverpool had had a very inconsistent season, they still had very good players in their team. Most of all, they had Steven Gerrard.

Stevie was pushed quite far forward at Anfield and Makelele kept him reasonably quiet. But there was a lot of controversy surrounding the game. Most of it revolved around a supposed handball from Tiago that the referee, Mike Riley, didn't spot. That prompted a lot of calls for video replays to be brought in. I know that argument comes up every season and I'm against it for things like that. I think it would slow the game down too much if, every time there was a debatable decision, the referee had to stop play while the fourth official or a panel of observers in the stands pored over the replays.

But – and you won't be surprised to read this after what was to happen to us at Anfield in the Champions League semi-final – I am in favour of the use of video technology when it comes to a question of whether the ball has crossed the line. That is so fundamental to the outcome of the match that it is worth stopping the game for if there is genuine doubt. And in the case of the Champions League game in May, there was genuine doubt. Not even the various camera angles could help people decide. It was only simulation that showed Luis Garcia's effort had not crossed the line. If there was real doubt about whether it had crossed the line, the goal should not have been allowed to stand.

The New Year's Day game was also marred by an injury to Xabi Alonso. Lamps tackled him and Alonso went down in a heap and hobbled off a few minutes later. It became apparent later that Alonso had broken his ankle in the challenge and Liverpool were understandably upset about it. Lamps was upset about it, too. Nobody likes to see a fellow professional get a serious injury and no one wants to be considered responsible for something like that. But everyone knows that Lamps is just about as far away as it is possible to get from being a malicious player. Sometimes, you just have to accept that bad things are going to happen accidentally when players are utterly committed to trying to win a game of football.

It was a tight game. Liverpool could have gone ahead when Djimi Traore exchanged first-time passes with Florent Sinama-Pongolle and drilled a low shot from 12 yards that Pete blocked with his legs. We went close, too, when Tiago played a nice pass for Robben to beat the offside trap. He took the ball a little too close to Jerzy Dudek, though, and Dudek managed to scramble the ball away for a corner.

A few minutes before half-time, the Tiago handball incident erupted when a cross from Stevie G hit him on the hand. The crowd got even more irate when Sinama-Pongolle fell under a challenge from Makelele in the area and Riley gave the free-kick to us. They were going nuts about that. I thought the atmosphere was good that day but little did I know what it was going to be like that day in May when we went up there for the Champions League.

We didn't silence them until ten minutes from the end. Coley had come on for Duffa a few minutes earlier and when Johnno nodded a Robbie corner back to him, Coley fired in a lovely volley that looked technically perfect from the edge of the area. It went through a crowd of bodies and clipped Jamie

Carragher's trailing leg on the way through and Dudek had no chance. It was a brilliant strike from a guy who seemed to be telling everyone that he was tired of the criticism and was ready for some praise. His goal-scoring contribution, which we hadn't predicted at the start of the season, was becoming invaluable.

We completed our perfect Christmas on the night of 4 January when we beat Middlesbrough at the Bridge. Four wins out of four, 12 points out of 12 and a happy squad of footballers all round. I had a scare half an hour or so before the game against Boro, though, when I was forced to miss the warm-up and head back into the changing rooms. I have had a bit of a problem with a little piece of floating bone in my right ankle. At one point, I was going to get surgery on it this summer but I had to have an operation on my toe instead. It's nothing major, nothing serious, but every now and again, it gets stuck in my ankle joint.

Usually, it happens in training and the Middlesbrough game was the first time it has happened to me before a match. When I put my foot down on the ground, it feels as though my Achilles is going to snap or my ankle is going to break. It's very painful for a short period of time but a little bit of manipulation from the masseur usually sorts it out. It was the same on this occasion. It was just a bit nerve-wracking because it was so close to the start of a game. Because I had missed most of the warm-up, I didn't feel quite as sharp as I might have been when the game kicked off but after about 15 minutes I was fine.

Didier, though, looked razor sharp right from the start. In the fourth minute, he forced Schwarzer into making the first save of the night when he met Robben's corner with a firm header. Schwarzer was alive to the danger again a few minutes later when Didier controlled a long clearance from Pete and let fly with left-foot volley on the turn, which the Boro keeper just managed to hold on to.

Two minutes after that, Didier got the goal he deserved. Lamps slid a pass through to him and Didier turned and slipped the ball through Gareth Southgate's legs before slotting the ball past Schwarzer with his right foot. It was another brilliant finish. Didier was on fire and four minutes later he scored again. Lamps swung a free-kick into the box with pace and accuracy and Didier got to it before Southgate and rose to nod it past Schwarzer.

Duffa and Robbie went close to turning the first half into a rout and Lamps played Paolo Ferriera in just before half-time but he lifted his shot high over the bar. Schwarzer nearly gifted us another goal when he gave the ball straight to Duffa from a goal kick. Duffa smashed it back towards goal but it cannoned to safety off the crossbar. When the final whistle went, we were seven points clear of Arsenal. They had only drawn at home to Manchester City. Things were still going our way. We had not lost for 13 games. We were firmly in control of our own destiny.

We kept a grip on it at White Hart Lane ten days later. We'd beaten Scunthorpe United in the FA Cup 3rd round in the meantime and drawn with United in the first leg of the semi-finals of the Carling Cup. And at Spurs, we just marched on. No surprise there, really. We haven't lost against them for 30 games in the league, a record that spans 15 years. We established another record at White Hart Lane, too. It was our sixth con-secutive league victory without conceding a goal.

They were a different side to the one the manager had accused of 'parking a bus' in front of their goal at Stamford Bridge in September. Martin Jol had taken over from Jacques Santini after he walked out and they were playing much more attractive football. Jol had even won the December manager of the month award so we knew they were going to go for it.

They started brightly. Erik Edman hit a long-range shot over the top and Robbie Keane flicked a header wide. Big Pete also had to make a good save from Jermain Defoe. But Didier nearly scored when he beat the offside trap and lifted the ball over Paul Robinson only to see it bounce just past the post. We thought we might have had a penalty when when Robben was brought down in the box by Noe Pamarot but Graham Poll didn't give it.

Then Duffa chased a ball that looked like a lost cause in to the corner flag. Somehow, he slid and hooked his foot around it and stopped it going out of play. Then he leapt up, nicked the ball away from a tackle and played a pass into Smertin. Smertin arrived at speed, got to the ball first and went flying under a challenge from Ledley King. Spurs were upset when Poll gave the penalty but I didn't think Ledley got a piece of the ball and therefore it had to be a pen. Lamps stepped up and buried it. It was his 50th league goal.

Lamps got a second in injury-time when he tucked his shot away after Eidur had done brilliantly to dribble to the byline and cut the ball back for him. Just as good as the victory was the news that Arsenal had lost at Bolton. Everything was going our way.

We were rolling now. We weren't in the mood for slip-ups or

any piece of generosity or weakness that might somehow undo all the hard work we had put in and let Arsenal or United sneak back into the Premiership race. We started going about our business ruthlessly and efficiently. We only had 15 games to go. We weren't about to implode.

We snuffed out any hint of danger from Portsmouth by the end of the first half. We were a goal up after 14 minutes. Robbie skipped free from a tackle by Gary O'Neil down the Portsmouth left, took the ball to the byline and threaded his cross through a defender's legs. It reached Didier when he was standing about eight inches from the goal line. He just had to touch it and it was a goal. That took just 14 minutes, although we were indebted to some excellent refereeing by Mike Riley, who ignored his assistant's well-intended flag for a foul on Robbie as he sped past Gary O'Neil. To be fair to Didier, he recognized Robbie's contribution and ran over to where he was celebrating to congratulate him on doing everything but score.

Six minutes later, Robbie put that right. Didier played his part in the build-up this time. He laid a ball off to Lamps and Lamps's short slide-rule pass to Robbie that carved open the Pompey defence was sheer perfection. Robbie ran on to it and managed to drag it round Jamie Ashdown, who had come rushing out of his goal. Ashdown got a touch on it, though, and it cannoned off Robbie's knee and seemed to be heading out for a goal kick.

Like Duffa at Spurs, though, Robbie didn't give up on it and even though he stumbled, he managed to catch up with it as he staggered and steer the ball into the net from the tightest of angles with his right foot, which is supposed to be weaker than his left. That was an astonishing piece of close control. He doesn't use his right foot much but he clearly can when he wants to.

Robben also played a part in the third after 22 minutes. He was tripped on the edge of the box as he ran at the terrified Portsmouth defence. He and Didier stood over the resulting free-kick but Robben stepped over the ball at the end of his run-up and let Didier take it. His shot flew over the wall and down on the other side so that Ashdown could only get a weak left hand on it and palm it into the net.

The rest of the match was a formality. We were 11 points clear when the final whistle went. January had been quite a month. Later that week, I was named the Barclays Player of the Month. The manager was named Manager of the Month and Pete got a special award in recognition of his record for keeping the most consecutive clean sheets. We felt like a very proud trio when we were presented with our trophies together at the training ground.

The month just had one test left: Birmingham in the FA Cup 4th round. I'd missed the third round against Scunthorpe at the beginning of January which we had won 3–1 even though they had put up a terrific struggle. Birmingham was hard, too, but we got off to a great start with a controversial goal from Robert Huth after five minutes.

It was controversial because as a corner from Duffa came over and Huthy made his run to the near post, tracked by Martin Taylor, I stepped into Taylor's way and blocked him, leaving Huthy home free to thump his header into the roof of the net. It's a very common ploy in football and often it gets spotted by the referee. But this time he missed it.

I was asked a lot afterwards if it was something that we practised on the training ground but it wasn't. It was just a spontaneous thing but it was something we did regularly during games. If I made the run, Huthy or Ricky or William would block the runner and if they were making the run, I'd do it for them. We didn't do it every time or it would have become too obvious but now and again it's worth a try. We got asked about it so much after that incident, though, that we didn't think it was worth doing it again for about five or six weeks until people had begun to forget about it.

Duffa could have put us two up after half an hour when a ball from Coley put him clear of the Birmingham defence but he couldn't hit the target. Robbie put one over the bar after an hour but I almost gave Birmingham the chance to equalize when I left a back header towards Carlo Cudicini short. My heart was in my mouth but, to my intense relief, Robbie Blake couldn't finish it off.

I made amends for that 11 minutes from time. Lamps had come on for Kezman for the last half-hour and as he looked for options about 40 yards out, he picked out my run on the left-hand side of their box. His pass was perfectly flighted and I ran on to it, got a great contact, and headed it down and past Maik Taylor. I was well pleased.

We were close now. We could feel it. We felt Arsenal's challenge was over. We were still a little bit worried about United because they were still doggedly plugging away. We looked at the fixtures and we knew that one game held the

RIGHT: Anelka scores the penalty that condemned us to our only league defeat of the season, at the City of Manchester Stadium back in October.

ABOVE: I'm on the score-sheet after only nine minutes against CSKA Moscow at the Bridge in our Champions League Group H match.

BELOW: The boss watches the Porto home game – we were so well prepared against his old team we knew them inside out.

LEFT: The boss parades his new backroom staff at Harlington before the start of the season. From left: Rui Faria, scout Andre Villas, goalkeeping coach Silvino Louro, and assistant managers Steve Clarke and Baltemar Brito.

LEFT: Robbie goes wild. Scoring the brilliant solo goal that won us the game against Everton at the Bridge.

ABOVE: Defending against Blackburn in the league victory at the Bridge, where Eidur got a hat-trick.

BELOW: About to grab William after he scored against West Brom at the Hawthorns.

Talking with Sven at England training, before the game against Wales on 9 October.

At England training with Bridgey before the infamous Spain game in November.

Taking the plunge.

Catching my old pal Jimmy Floyd Hasselbaink by mistake against Middlesbrough at the Riverside. He needed stitches in a head wound.

Strolling in Red Square before the Champions League game against CSKA Moscow.

ABOVE: Tackling Guti in the Spain v England game last November. Unfortunately, it won't be remembered for the football.

BELOW: Scoring my second against Charlton at the Valley – a goal that gave me a whole new set of superstitions.

ABOVE: December 2004 and netting a header against Arsenal after Henry and Sol got in each other's way. It finished 2–2.

LEFT: Hugging Henry after the game – the guy's a class act on and off the pitch.

BELOW: Well done, Duffa! He scored the winner against Villa on Boxing Day.

Coley shows great technique to hit the volley that beat Liverpool
at Anfield on New Year's Day.

key for us. The match at Ewood Park on the second day of February felt like the gateway to the run-in. We had a spell of four straight games against the four lowest teams in the Premiership. If we could win at Blackburn, we knew our minds would start wandering towards the prospect of history being made.

6 The Battle of Blackburn

Some matches tell you everything you need to know about yourself and your team-mates. Some matches tell you whether you've got it or you haven't. Some matches tell you whether you're going to be able to stand the heat or whether you're going to start fading away. Our game at Blackburn at the beginning of February was that kind of game. It was the game that told us we were going to win the title.

It's always tough up there anyway. It's never an easy place to go. They don't get the biggest crowds at Ewood Park but they are always raw and hostile. Whenever I go there, I always look out between the two stands opposite the tunnel and see a group of people standing on the hill overlooking the ground. I always think they must be the same people each year.

The teams up there always seem rather uncompromising, too. That's the best word I can think of for it. They ask no quarter and they give no quarter. It was like that under Graeme Souness and it's like that now under Mark Hughes, a Chelsea old boy. They are an old-fashioned footballing side who try to throw teams off their game with hard tackling and constant pressing.

I've got a lot of respect for the men in charge up there. When I was a young player at Chelsea, Hughes always used to terrorize me. All the other lads called him Sparky or Hughesy but I always called him Mark because he was such a legend. Even though I was a youngster training with the first team, he would bully me and think nothing of it.

It was difficult at the time but it taught me so much and did me so much good. I owe him a debt for that. And what a joy it was to watch him in Chelsea colours. He's one of the best strikers of all time and he scored a volley against Vicenza in the European Cup Winners' Cup semi-final in 1998 that was out of this world.

So I have got a great deal of respect for him and his coaching staff, Kevin Hitchcock and Eddie Niedzwiecki, who were also at Chelsea when I was coming through the ranks. They were both keepers in their playing days and they were both part of the youth set up when I was a youngster. Eddie Neddie was great for me when I was coming through. He was one of those guys who was always enthusiastic and always wanting to stay out and help the trainees do extra work if they wanted to. He was always there to talk to you, always there to listen, to tell you to work hard and reassure you that you would get your chance one day.

He was a lovely bloke, too. And so was Hitchy. A few of the young lads took a few beatings from him but because, like Hitchy, we're from Essex, me and Paul Nicholls got away with it. We used to go out early in the morning before training and

Hitchy was always with us even at the end of his career, trying scissor-kicks, overheads, as many tricks as he could. He was like a big kid. But what a servant to the club he was.

I've got lots of good feelings towards them. Most of them vanished for the 90 minutes at Ewood Park, though, because the Chelsea old boys had prepared a lovely little greeting party for us. And funnily enough, nostalgia and swapping stories about the good old days didn't really seem to be on the agenda. It was clear from the beginning that it was going to be a rough old night but also a crucial night for our championship challenge.

Those of us who had played there before were doing our best to try to prepare the new guys for what lay ahead. We told them that even though Blackburn were in the bottom half of the table, it was still a hell of a place to visit. A couple of weeks earlier, a few of us had been looking through the fixtures and talking about how, if we could go to Blackburn and get a result, then the toughest battles of the season would be behind us. We also knew that in past seasons, Ewood Park was exactly the kind of place where a title challenge we might have been putting together had been thrown away. How many times have we failed at places like Blackburn and Bolton and Newcastle? Too many times for me to count or want to recall.

We got off to an amazing start. Lamps hit a beautiful long ball over the top of their defence, Eidur flicked it on and Robbie turned Andy Todd. Robbie was on fire at that stage of the season and he unleashed a shot from the edge of the box that was so fierce that it went underneath Brad Friedel as he dived to try and smother it. There were only five minutes on the clock.

But Blackburn were still up for it. No team managed by Mark Hughes is going to roll over and die. So it started to get nasty very quickly. They had a midfield guy called Aaron Mokoena who put himself about. In the past, we might have folded in the face of rough-house tactics like that. And I'm sure Hughes, Hitchy and Eddie knew that. I'm sure that their game plan was to try and throw us off our game with some rough stuff. They would have thought they could get amongst the foreign boys and they wouldn't like it. They have been at Chelsea and things were different when they were there. Maybe we were guilty of being soft touches in the past but not any more. Blackburn discovered that that night in Lancashire. I think we gave them quite a shock actually. It is a new side and a new generation and we reacted very differently.

Mokoena was only just getting stuck in when he broke a bone in Robben's foot in the 11th minute. Robben took a high ball cleanly and Makoena came lunging in and stamped a tackle down on the top of Robben's left foot that left him lying on the ground in agony. In his wisdom, Uriah Rennie decided it wasn't a foul even though he was right on top of it. That night at Blackburn wasn't one of his finest hours. Anyway, the tackle put Robben out for more than six weeks. It was just a taste of things to come.

Robbie Savage, recently signed from Birmingham, started getting busy in the way that only he can and the tackles started flying in thick and fast. Nothing wrong with that. In fact, I relish that kind of confrontation. It plays to my strengths.

I can give it out and I like to think that I can take it, too. I was up for the fight and I could see that the rest of the boys were, too.

Big Pete was in fantastic form in goal again. Nothing unusual for him. In fact, at this stage of the season, it felt as if we were playing in front of a keeper who was never going to concede a goal. You can't imagine how much confidence that gives you as a defender to know that there is somebody so commanding and so hard to beat as your last line of defence.

Early in the game, he beat Peter Schmeichel's Premiership record of 694 minutes without conceding a goal. By the end of the match, he had gone 781 minutes without being beaten. Not since Arsenal drew 2–2 with us at Highbury on 12 December had somebody scored against us. It was really something to be proud of.

It looked as though that run was going to end in the first half when Savage went down theatrically under a challenge from Paolo and sprawled at my feet. I looked down at him but there was nothing I could do. Paul Dickov took the penalty and Pete saved it but Dickov kicked him in the chest as he chased forlornly after the rebound. I played peacemaker on that occasion and got Dickov out of the way as the melee began.

But later in the half, Dickov was at it again and this time I lost my temper. Pete made another great save and a couple of seconds after he gathered the loose ball, Dickov came steaming in and launched himself at Pete with a double-footed challenge. Pete sidestepped it and no damage was done but that wasn't the point. Dickov's intent had been clear.

As he got up, I grabbed him by the throat. Or at least by

the lapel of his shirt. There was a ruck around us and various people piled in but nothing else happened. I just thought he had overstepped the mark with that challenge and that he could put someone else out of the game if he carried on like that.

I enjoyed my battle with Dickov, though. The whole game, we kicked lumps out of each other. We were on the floor at one point and I grabbed his nuts and he got up and didn't complain about it. The ball had been in the air and he was backing into me and holding my shirt. We both fell over in a heap and he was trying to give me a bit of a kick while we were down. That's the kind of battle I have had with him in the past, too. He is such a nice bloke off the pitch. I know people must look at him and think he's an arrogant little sod but he's not. I respect him because he's another who gives as good as he gets. He works and works and works, and doesn't really get the credit for it.

Just after Robben was injured, I got done by David Thompson. He caught me on the ankle with a high, late challenge and, as soon as he did it, I thought I'd broken my ankle. I thought that might be me out for the rest of the season. I asked the physio to give me a couple of minutes to try to run it off. Then I asked him for a couple more and gradually the pain began to ease. When the adrenaline of playing wore off at half-time, though, the pain redoubled. I just about managed to get back out there and play in the second half.

But even in the immediate aftermath of that Thompson tackle, Dickov was still flying in at me. He kept saying 'have that' and 'there's more to come', all that sort of stuff. I understand that that is part of the game. But Dickov never stopped.

His two challenges on Pete were just the tip of the iceberg. All game he was backing into me and elbowing me when the ball was up the other end.

At least, there's a bit of camaraderie about a contest with Dickov. Sometimes, if the ball goes down the other end, he'll say, 'Fucking hell, I'm knackered, I'm not chasing the next one.' There's a bit of banter. But when the ball comes back up towards us, he's chasing it again. He never rests. And he never lets me rest either.

He's a decent bloke, too. When I saw him after the match, he congratulated me on our victory and said he hoped we went on to win the title. That's a great thing about football. You've had a great physical contest with somebody and at the end you recognize that that is part of what makes the game so fulfilling. He got booked for a foul on me and, later on in the game, I got booked for one on him. It was even-stevens.

But the game's biggest square-up was nothing to do with either of us. I think it was our friend Mokoena going after Lamps again. He had been niggling away at him right from the first minute. It takes a lot to rile Lamps but Mokoena managed it.

We got fined for our part in that melee which was a joke given that they were the ones trying to kick lumps out of us. Failure to control our players, they called it. What about Blackburn's failure to control theirs?

At that stage of the season, Blackburn were statistically the dirtiest side in the Premiership. They had the most fouls, the most red cards (5) and the most yellow cards (48) of any club in the top flight. Surely it didn't take a rocket scientist to work out who might have been instigating the physical stuff on that night up in Lancashire?

Basically, I like that physical side of the game. It tests you just as much as a skilful winger or a fast, neat centre forward. I knew from the first minute it was going to be a rough game and that they were going to try to bully us. Me and all the other lads were right up for it. When you are getting bullied like that, it takes someone in the Chelsea side to respond with a tackle or a header where you take the man with you just to show them that you are not going to submit to that kind of tactic. When you respond like that, it gives you a real buzz.

And we kept struggling and kept resisting and kept refusing to submit all the way to the final whistle. And when that whistle finally came, it felt like the sweetest, hardest-won victory of the season so far. We all went over to Big Pete to congratulate him on his performance and I looked over to the touchline and saw the manager bending down and pumping his fist in celebration. Mark Hughes got the hump afterwards because Mourinho hadn't shaken his hand.

We realized something significant had just happened. We all felt we had just hurdled a big barrier. And so when we went to salute our fans behind the goal where Robben had scored the winner, the manager told us to throw our shirts to the supporters who had made the long journey up there to give them a memento of the day. After all, they had travelled up and endured 90 minutes in the freezing cold and ensured that we were well supported on a night when we could have felt a long way from home.

One of the pictures of the season was all the lads coming off the pitch at the end after we had saluted our fans. I think Kezman had a T-shirt on but apart from him, we were all bare-chested, even me. I don't usually do that. I've kept all my other shirts from last season. Every single one. Even the ones from the European games. If I ever swap shirts, I go back to the dressing room and get a spare one and use that to swap with. I'm planning to put the rest of them in a giant frame at home as the most treasured souvenir of the season just gone. I'm going to have to overlap them a little bit or the frame would cover an entire wall but I've got somebody working on that.

Anyway, because of that, I'm never normally one for throwing my shirt into the crowd or even changing out of my match shirt to put a T-shirt on. I stick with my own shirt and make sure I keep it safe and get it home to my collection. With all the football memorabilia I've got, it's a good job I've got a big house. Even at Blackburn, even though the rest of the players were chucking their shirts into the crowd, I didn't want to. It was just that circumstances overtook me.

The manager clearly felt that something important had just happened because he came over to the area on the pitch where we were standing and celebrating with the fans after the game. He got us into a little huddle there on the pitch and made it plain how pleased he was with the manner of the victory we had just achieved. He gestured to us that we should all throw our shirts into the crowd.

I tried to avoid eye contact with him. I wanted to keep my shirt like I had kept all the others, particularly as it was beginning to feel as though we were on an unstoppable roll. I kept hold of it but he caught my eye again. I was the only one left by then who still had his shirt so I took it off really reluctantly. I still tried to hang back but the manager said 'throw your shirt to the fans'.

So I chucked it towards the supporters. And now I'm missing one shirt from my collection. I am going to write something in the programme and try and get that shirt back off the fan who has it, maybe in exchange for a pair of boots and a signed England shirt or something like that. I need to make that collection complete.

United had beaten Arsenal at Highbury the night before to move up to second so, as they took points off each other, our victory at Blackburn put us 11 points clear at the top. As we sat on the coach making our way back to Manchester Airport and the flight south, we were beginning to feel as though nothing could stop us any more. We could mix it with the most attractive footballing sides and now we had proved we could mix it with the teams who wanted to kick lumps out of us, too.

None of it had lessened my respect or my admiration for Mark Hughes, Hitchy and Eddie Neddie. They did what they had to do. They did what they thought would give them the best chance of getting a result. They tried to formulate tactics that they thought would play to their strengths and our weaknesses. Nothing wrong with that. It was just that we weren't quite as weak as they had hoped.

I caught a glimpse of the manager being interviewed on the television afterwards. 'It was a big fight and sometimes it was without emotional control,' he said. 'Sometimes it was also without respect for the rules of the game. They felt they could

not beat us by playing football and they had to try to intimidate us with aggression and direct football. They thought we
were not ready for a game like tonight but we were ready.'

He was absolutely right. We were ready. There were no surprises left for us now. The Chelsea of old might have withered
in the face of an assault like that. But on that night more than
any other night of the entire season, I understood that this was
a new Chelsea now. This was a new team, a team that was not
frightened by anything.

7 The Carling Cup

The Carling Cup Final at the end of February came smack bang in the middle of the two legs of our epic Champions League second-round tie against Barcelona. We were already in the final by the time we were paired with Barca in the draw and part of me thought that maybe we would sacrifice the Carling Cup because we had been handed such a difficult Champions League draw. I asked the manager how we were going to approach it in the light of that. He looked at me like I was mad. 'It's going to be our first trophy,' he said. 'We're going to go and win it. We are going to put our full-strength side out.' It was great to hear that. We all loved that.

That had been our attitude right from the start of the competition. We were in it to win it. We didn't want to imitate Arsenal and United and put out shadow sides that were going to get beaten at Burnley or Rotherham.

We were keenly aware that as a group of players we had not won any silverware and we were determined to put that right. I think most of us also believed that fatigue was a state of mind. Most of us wanted to play in every game. I hated it when the manager told me I was being rested for our first game in the competition, the third-round tie at home to West Ham at the end of October. I made it plain to the manager that I wasn't happy and he made it plain to me that he wanted me to have a break.

But I loved the fact that we still put a strong team out. Even if I missed the occasional game or Lamps missed the occasional game, we always had a strong spine. We always had the majority of our first team in the Carling Cup side. We didn't go for the idea that we had to ration ourselves or that by trying to win the Carling Cup, it would cost us later in the season.

We knew that if we did well in the Carling Cup, we would feed off that and it would act as a catalyst. It's been that way for plenty of teams in the past. If a team is having a rough spell in the league, a successful run in the Carling Cup can shake them out of that. And if you are doing well in the league, a good run in the Carling Cup can help you do even better.

I always felt it was a bit humiliating to field hugely under-strength sides in the competition. People seemed to forget that there was a place in a final at the Millennium Stadium at stake at the end of it all. And any day there is an occasion worth fighting for. I was delighted when the manager said we would be approaching the competition aggressively. I thought it sent out a statement that we weren't going to be an easy touch for anybody at any stage of the season in any competition.

The manager had asked us all before the competition how we felt about the Carling Cup and we told him we wanted to go and win it. I said I thought a competition you didn't try and

Alone with my thoughts at Harlington. I've got lots of happy memories of our old training ground.

ABOVE: Lamps buries his penalty against Spurs at White Hart Lane. We never lose against them.

LEFT: The manager and me shaking hands after the Spurs game – we knew it was a big win.

RIGHT: Robbie squeezes the ball home from a tight angle against Portsmouth at the Bridge, our second goal in a 3–0 win.

ABOVE: Tangling with Quinton Fortune during the goalless first leg of the Carling Cup semi against Man U.

BELOW: Trying to shepherd the ball away from Stevie G during the Carling Cup Final in February.

ABOVE: Big Pete saves Dickov's penalty at Ewood Park – he got a boot in the chest from Dickov as a reward.

BELOW: Striding off after beating Blackburn 1–0 at Ewood Park in February. Even I threw my shirt to the crowd after that victory.

LEFT: My first trophy as Chelsea captain – what a feeling.

BELOW: With my girlfriend, Toni, at Wimbledon. This year we watched Andy Murray's great game against David Nalbandian.

BELOW: At the FIFPro World XI Players Awards launch back in March.

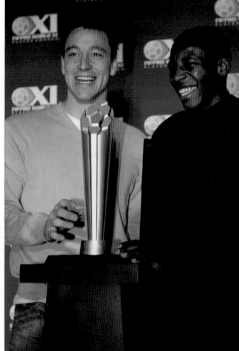

LEFT: We were all proud to lend our support to the 2012 London Olympic bid and even prouder when they won.

RIGHT: Leon McKenzie heads the goal that snapped our run of games (over 1,024 minutes) without conceding a goal. I was gutted.

ABOVE: Big Pete makes another brilliant save against Barcelona in the second leg of the Champions League tie.

RIGHT: Probably the most important goal I've ever scored – the winner against Barcelona in the Champions League tie at Stamford Bridge.

Complaining to the ref after he awarded Ballack a last-minute penalty that allowed Bayern back into the tie.

Rui Faria with the woolly hat that caused all the controversy in the Champions League first leg tie against Bayern.

Tackling Bayern's Paolo Guerrero.

win wasn't worth entering. And the manager wanted to go and win it from the word 'go'. There were a few players in our squad who weren't in the first team and were expecting to get their chance in the Carling Cup. Some of them were frustrated by the fact that they weren't suddenly automatic choices in one competition at least.

I was upset to miss that first game against West Ham because most of my family are from the East End and there were a lot of them there, most of them in the West Ham section. I have to say, though, I didn't envy Lamps that night. He always gets absolute dog's abuse from the West Ham punters because he used to play at Upton Park and they had a field day with him when he came off the bench for the last 20 minutes.

The manager had wanted to rest him for the game, too, but Lamps wanted to prove a point to them because those fans have been giving him stick since well before he even left Upton Park. The manager said he would put him on the bench. He was desperate to play. But when he went out and had a little warm-up, he was getting pelted with stuff.

It seemed perfect for him when he came on and Robben won a penalty in the 77th minute. He was well up for that but they had just signed a new keeper, Jimmy Walker, and he was having an absolute blinder. The West Ham fans were outraged by the decision, too, and Kezman had to go off for treatment to a head wound after he got hit with a missile thrown from the crowd.

Lamps hit the penalty well but the keeper saved it with his legs and their fans went mad with delight. I think that was better than winning for them. Still, if he'd scored, he would have gone mad in front of their fans and that might have got a bit hairy, too. I said to him after I think there would have been a riot. My family were laughing about it with me after-wards.

Kezman had already won the game for us by then. He missed a few chances earlier in the game but then Coley played a sweet ball through for him and he clipped it across Walker and in off the bottom of the left-hand post. It was his first goal for the club since he joined from PSV Eindhoven and he was beside himself with happiness about it.

We got a lucky break at the end when Anton Ferdinand rose above us all at the back and glanced a header over Carlo Cudicini and against the crossbar. But it bounced away to safety and we went into the hat for the fourth round. We drew Newcastle away, not for the last time in a cup competition this season, and braced ourselves for the journey to the north-east.

I always travel up there with a particular sense of antici-pation because a game against Newcastle usually means a game against Alan Shearer. Actually, the Carling Cup tie was the only time I got to play against him during the course of the campaign. He was injured for the league game at the Bridge, I was suspended for the FA Cup fifth-round tie and I was injured for the return league game at St James' Park on the final day of the season.

I had many difficult opponents last season. I respect every-one I play against and I could pick out Andy Johnson, Emile Heskey, Paul Dickov and Kevin Davies as four of the toughest battles I had. But I would still say that Shearer was my most difficult opponent. I still regard him as one of the best strikers around. I admire him a lot, for his durability and his experience and for the problems he poses for me.

Shearer is one of the very best. I think it's a shame he's not playing for England any more. He might have lost some of his pace but he makes up for that with his cleverness. He is so good in the air and there is something about the timing of his headers that he has got down to perfection. When you are defending an opposition goal kick, for instance, he will stand behind you. I wondered what he was doing the first time I played against him.

I thought it was going to be easy if he was going to do something stupid like that. I thought I'd win every ball. Then, when I went to go and win the first one, he manoeuvred himself in front of me at the last minute and rose above me and flicked it on. He did that five or six times and won every one and it took me about 45 minutes to work out what to do and how to stop it. He's full of tricks like that. A lot of it is down to his experience.

His build-up play is still excellent. His finishing is first class. It was a great learning curve for me when I first came up against him. In a funny way, Shearer has taught me an awful lot about defending. Even though I only played against him in the Carling Cup, I was still impressed by his physical presence and the timing of his runs. He knows he is not going to get in behind you any more but he is so good at holding the ball up and shielding it from you that you have to be alive to the threat of Kieron Dyer, Jermaine Jenas and Lee Bowyer running in to feed off his lay-offs.

When the ball goes wide, he does not go bombing straight into the box. He holds back a little bit. My first reaction is always to get back into the box as soon as possible to try and deal with the cross. You look round and he is still on the edge of the box. So do you go out to meet him or do you hold your position? Because if you go out, you might expose the defender behind you to a greater threat from whoever he is marking. He is just very difficult to control.

His favourite thing is getting the ball with his back to goal. I was always coached to keep the man you are marking playing away from goal in that situation. But he might do that five times and you cannot make any contact with the ball and he will be laying off a succession of great balls. After three or four shots have pinged in from his team-mates, you start to think that you're going to have to do something about it because it's getting too dangerous and sooner or later one of the lay-offs he's providing is going to lead to a goal.

So you try and win it, try and get there in front of him, and he wins a foul on the edge of the box which is even worse. Because usually it's him or Laurent Robert taking them and they've both got a shot like a cannonball. But I still like playing against him. I enjoy the contest. He's a fair man to play against. He gives a bit out but he takes it as well. Straight after the game, we always shake hands and look forward to the next battle.

I still feel Scottie won the game at St James' for us with his dressing-room speech before the game, striding around among the players looking like Winston Churchill and sounding like he was going to start saying that we would fight them on the beaches. It's funny to think that he'll be playing all his home games at that ground now. But I think he'll respond to their passion and they'll respond to his.

Everybody seemed pumped up before that match. Perhaps it was Scottie's speech that did it. But before the game, the manager's assistant, Baltemar Brito, offered out of the blue to shave all his hair off if he won. Naturally enough, we took him up on that. Someone had clippers on them – which is a sign of the times, I suppose – so we did it in the dressing room at St James' Park after the match. The batteries ran out halfway through so we had to leave him looking like a half-baked Mohican overnight and finish the job off the next day. That'll teach him to make rash promises.

It was a good game. No holds barred, just like it always is up there. Kezza missed a couple of chances, Olivier Bernard came close for them but Carlo made a terrific save to deny him and then plucked a header from Shearer out of the air. The manager sent Lamps and Robben on midway through the second half and the momentum began to swing towards us even though Carlo had to make a brilliant save from a Robert pile-driver five minutes from the end of normal time.

I always felt we were going to win it in extra-time. Eidur got the first with a fierce drive from the edge of the box that whistled past Shay Given and just inside his right-hand post ten minutes into the first period of extra-time. Eight minutes from the end of the second period, Robben wrapped it up with a stunning individual goal. He took on the entire Newcastle defence as he speared his way in from the left and then waltzed past Titus Bramble so fast he made the Newcastle defender look as if he was standing still. To finish things off, he didn't try and smash the ball into the net. He just stroked it gently across Given and into the far corner. It was like watching somebody roll in a slow pot on a snooker table.

In the next round, we made the short journey to Fulham. We knew they would put it all on the line because this was their best chance of winning a trophy. We'd given them a bit of a spanking in the league a couple of weeks earlier and it was obvious they would still be smarting from that, too. Some people outside the club thought an upset was on the cards.

Didier made his first start back after two months and after Robbie had torn them apart again for most of the first half, we went ahead ten minutes into the second. Robbie did the early damage again, twisting their defence out of shape and then laying the ball square to Duffa 20 yards out. Duffa made a good contact with his strike but Edwin van der Sar seemed to have it covered until it caught a wicked deflection off Ian Pearce and ricocheted into the net.

They got back into the game when their substitute Elvis Hammond got away down the right and crossed for Brian McBride to steer home the equalizer but the manager responded to that by bringing Lamps on and that did the trick. There were three minutes left when Lamps let fly from the edge of the box. His low shot swerved in the air a bit and then bounced awkwardly just in front of van der Sar. Instead of getting his body behind it, the swerve meant he was trying to block the shot with his legs but it flew up off them and into the roof of the net for the winner. We were part delighted and part relieved. The season was starting to heat up back then at the end of

November. We were totally committed to the Carling Cup but we knew that we wanted to avoid replays.

The semis brought us up against United. Funnily enough, when they drew us, they decided they'd better take the Carling Cup seriously as well. So instead of their usual reserve side packed with kids, they fielded a line-up featuring Rooney, Ronaldo, Saha and Heinze. They came for a battle and Ferguson stoked things up before the game by ridiculing the idea that we could win all four of the trophies we were chasing.

We had never boasted we were going to win four trophies. We just felt that we would have a damned good go at them. I don't see any need to apologize for that. I think our fans would be upset if we did anything less. I wanted to win four trophies. I knew it would be hard but I didn't see any harm in being greedy and making up for lost time.

Our side was almost full strength. Big Pete was missing but Carlo is one of the two best goalkeepers in the Premiership in my opinion anyway. Robbie was missing, too, but that was only because he was suspended. We started the better of the two teams and took the game to them.

They had two penalty appeals turned down, the first when Saha tried to run straight through a couple of our defenders and seemed surprised when he bounced off them and the second when Ronaldo took a dive. At the other end, Lamps glanced a header just wide midway through the half after a great cross from Paolo.

Carlo made a good save from Rooney seven minutes before the interval. Darren Fletcher had crossed from the right and even though the ball was a little bit behind Rooney, he managed somehow to get incredible leverage on his header and it was flying into the goal before Carlo flung himself at it and beat it away for a corner. It was the only time Rooney had got away from me.

Coley nearly scored what would have been the goal of the season a minute after half time. Tim Howard fluffed a clearance and it went straight to Coley about 40 yards out. As he controlled it, the ball looped up a few inches off his right foot and as it dropped he tried to volley it back over Howard's head. He made a good contact with it and it was only a couple of yards wide. It was a spectacular effort.

We went close again a minute later. Lamps got the ball on the left side of the United area and took the ball past his marker. On the other side of the box, Heinze saw what was coming and, like the great defender that he is, he ran back to the goal line, ready to make a block if he was needed. Lamps rifled his shot low past Howard but Heinze was there in the nick of time to hack the shot away to safety.

We were growing increasingly frustrated in the second half. I was disappointed with the referee, Neale Barry. He appeared to dismiss anything I put to him about what was going on in the match. The manager also commented on this after the game and I thought he was right.

We had one last chance to break the deadlock when Jiri Jarosik, who had come on for Coley a quarter of an hour from the end, fired in a volley when a corner was only half cleared and then saw it cleared off the line by a combination of Phil Neville and Howard. The game ended goalless and we knew we would still have a good chance of going up to Old Trafford a fortnight later and getting a result but we were all fuming about the referee.

The manager spoke to the press boys about him after the game and told them that his attitude appeared to change in the second half. He was upset because he had seen Alex Ferguson walking down the tunnel with him at half-time, acting in a way that he thought was intimidating to the referee, shouting at him and berating him. He said he wasn't angry with Mr Ferguson, just that he thought that kind of thing was against the rules and that the United boss was using all the experience he had to try and get more favourable decisions for his team in the second half. 'In the second half,' the manager said, 'it was whistle and whistle, fault and fault, cheat and cheat. The referee controlled the game in one way during the first half but in the second, they had dozens of free-kicks.'

The FA threw the book at him for that. He was charged with improper conduct, fined £5,000 and warned as to his future conduct. He appealed against his punishment but the FA rejected the appeal. We felt, just as we were to feel against Barcelona, that we had made a legitimate complaint about a manager trying to influence a game in a way that was outside the rules of the game and that our complaints had been totally ignored.

As the aftermath of the game raged on, Ferguson singled me out for criticism. I'd said that most referees were happy to enter into a dialogue with you about decisions but that Barry had been aloof. 'With most refs, and being captain, you can maybe have a word,' I'd said, 'but he just wasn't willing to listen, which was disappointing.'

Fergie seized on that like it was a gold nugget. He hinted it showed there was some sort of sinister agenda at Chelsea and that my comment had exposed the extent I went to try and influence referees. He said he had never heard anything like it before, which I found very hard to believe.

And anyway, there was nothing sinister about it at all. I know that referees these days are encouraged to try and get on with the players in the same way we try to get on with them. It's a lot easier for everybody if there's a bit of give and take and we can both listen to each other. I'm not talking about trying to change a referee's mind. I would just like to think that now and again, he might listen to a player's opinion and think that once in a while he might have a worthwhile contribution to make.

That was the only point I was trying to get across about Neale Barry. He was not listening to what I thought were fair points. As tempers were flaring I thought this might help him run the game in a smoother way. He disagreed with me.

I was a bit taken aback that Mr Ferguson criticized me for what I said. My dad phoned me up and said, 'You've really done it now.' It's because he's got the same respect for the man as I have. It didn't really concern me too much. It's just part of the game, really, part of the chat that goes back and forth. I'm sure that he would want his captain to be doing exactly the same as me.

I've always got on okay with Mr Ferguson, actually. We always say hello. It's always civil. When I was a kid and not attached to any club, United were down in London preparing for a game against West Ham and they invited me over to their pre-match meal. They were hoping to sign me and they sat me between Mr Ferguson and Paul Ince.

That was a real thrill. A real honour. I was only 14 and that blew me away. It was very special. I have got nothing but respect for the man anyway because of everything he has achieved in the game and the hunger he has created in his players, but that meal talking to him and Incey was something I'll always remember. The move up there never worked out, obviously, but I look at him and know that if you played for him, you would give him unconditional loyalty just like you give to our manager.

As far as me being punished for the comments I made about Neale Barry, by the way, the FA showed mercy. I wasn't charged. The FA said they had 'reviewed the content and context of these comments, [and] decided that it is not appropriate to take formal disciplinary action'.

So the build-up to the second leg was lively to say the least. Going up there at 0–0 felt like an advantage to us because we had kept a clean sheet. Wherever we went, we always fancied nicking a goal from somewhere. We were scoring from so many different positions. For the first time since I had been at Chelsea, we had a whole lot of different players pitching in. In the past, we had been dependent on Jimmy Floyd Hasselbaink in particular, but now the burden was being shared much more equally.

Coley started scoring much more regularly. He got ten over the season. Robbie got some crucial goals and some beauties, too. Didier got his share. Lamps's goal-scoring record was unbelievable. Duffa got a few. Eidur was brilliant and I pitched in, too. It's great to vary the threat because the opposition never know where the danger's coming from. When you're reliant on one goal-scorer, it's a lot easier for your opponents to close you down.

When we got up to Manchester, the boss was at pains to stress there was no problem between him and Ferguson. In fact, he said it was the opposite. Ferguson had told some of the press boys that the red wine the boss had given him in his office after the first leg was like paint-stripper, so the manager had promised he was going to take an expensive bottle of the best Portuguese red up to Manchester with him to share with Ferguson after the match. That day also happened to be the manager's birthday.

The closer it got to kick-off, the more it seemed to me there was another agenda being played out for United in this game. Suddenly, the Carling Cup was important to them, too, because it was giving them an unexpected chance to dent our confidence. If they could put one over on us in this match, then maybe it might just affect us psychologically going into the championship run-in.

I'm sure they thought that if they could beat us, it might have the same effect on us as Arsenal's defeat at Old Trafford had had on them. We had an 11-point lead in the league but if they chipped away at our confidence with a convincing, bruising win, they would have believed that that would sow seeds of doubt in our minds and that maybe we would implode.

And maybe in the past, they might have been right. But this was a different Chelsea now. We were in no mood to lose in the first place anyway. We had our eyes fixed on the prize of the Carling Cup as a symbolic start to our trophy hunt and we knew there was also another kind of reason for winning at Old Trafford. Winning there would underline our superiority to their players and make them understand there was no way they were going to catch us in the league.

The match was played at full tilt but it was hardly full of chances. Lamps missed an early one after Duffa had played him in but apart from that both the defences, the two units that had conceded the fewest goals in the Premiership, were on top. The only alarm we had was when Quinton Fortune fell over Bridgey's outstretched leg in the box but the ref knew it wasn't a pen and waved play on.

Lamps opened the scoring on half an hour after a bit of neat interplay in the United box. A few quick passes stretched their defence out of shape and when Didier knocked a ball into Lamps, he took one touch to control it and then swept it past Tim Howard with his left foot from the edge of the six-yard box.

We should have gone further ahead after that when Didier broke away down the left and rolled a ball across for Tiago. Tiago stepped over the ball to let it run for Robbie but he had to check back slightly to get it and the delay allowed Howard a chance to spread himself and block Robbie's shot with his feet.

But midway through the second half when we were starting to think the game was won, I made a mistake that cost us dearly. United were probing for an opening but we had everything under control and Gary Neville had the ball in the right-back position but midway inside our half. I rate Gary very highly. He's probably also the most professional and dedicated player I have ever come across. He's an inspiration to work with when you're with England. He's a lovely passer of the ball, too, one of the many things about him that is underrated, and he moved the ball on to his left foot and chipped it in my direction.

I was aware of Giggs making a run off me. Gary hit the ball and I thought it wasn't going to get over me. I thought I was going to clear it but it was too high and by the time I realized that, I had lost the runner. Giggs got in front of Big Pete, leapt into the air and flicked the ball over him brilliantly with his left foot for the equalizer. I was gutted. I thought I had blown it for the lads. I felt desperate.

I was praying that I might get a chance to try and make up for it but thankfully someone else did it for me. Heinze was penalized for a foul on the United left and when Duffa swung the free-kick in with his left foot five minutes from the end, one player after another flung themselves at it, but no one connected. Because United had been defending quite deep, Howard didn't really have a chance to come out and claim it and had to let it bounce. Fortunately for us, it bounced right into the top right-hand corner of the United goal.

There were still a few scrapes before the end. Bridgey made a brilliant goal-line clearance to save us when Mikael Silvestre met a corner on the full and Pete tipped away a fierce drive from Ronaldo in the dying seconds. When the referee blew for the end of the 90 minutes, we were in our first final as a group of players and everybody went mad.

But I couldn't quite get into it. I hugged everybody on the pitch and slapped hands and accepted congratulations and applauded the fans but inside I was still annoyed with myself at the way I had been at fault for the Giggs goal. It spoiled things for me. I couldn't get it out of my head. I suppose it's probably similar to the feeling a striker gets if his side has won but he has missed a string of good chances along the way.

The United fans clapped us off the pitch at the end which was a nice touch. That can't have been easy for them. All the rest of the lads were understandably very bubbly but even though we had made it through to Cardiff, I was a bit quiet. I felt like keeping myself to myself because of the mistake I had made. I still felt like I'd let myself and the other lads down.

That's just the way I am. Even if your team wins, if you've made a mistake like that, you're going to have this feeling nagging away at you that you haven't done your job properly. And that's how I felt that night even though the celebrations were raging around me. I felt I hadn't done my job properly and that I couldn't enjoy myself in those circumstances. I didn't want to laugh around other people. I was kicking myself all that night and all the way home.

But everyone else was happy. Roman came in afterwards and he was just delighted to have got to his first final. I was sitting next to Eidur and he could sense that I was struggling. 'Don't worry about it,' he said, 'we've just got to the final.' I knew that and I was happy inside but I didn't want people to see that because I felt I had let them down.

There were other things to think about by the time the final came around. Like the tumultuous game in the Nou Camp that we had played a few days earlier and all the fall-out from the match and the controversy in the tunnel at half-time. We were right in the thick of our season now and we knew that winning the Carling Cup would push us on to another level.

We stayed at the St David's Bay Hotel for the final. It's in a great spot overlooking Cardiff Bay but I didn't really fancy staying there again because it was the same hotel where we stayed before we lost the 2002 FA Cup Final to Arsenal. I had very bad memories of it. I had woken up on the morning of the final with something like vertigo. My balance was shot to pieces. I got out of bed and fell over. I couldn't believe that something that random was happening on one of the biggest days of my career. I got a doctor up there and he gave me an injection and I pleaded with him to keep it all between ourselves. He said he couldn't and I realized that that was the right decision. So I told Claudio about it and I had a late fitness test. I did all right because I was feeling a bit better by then but he decided not to pick me. He thought it wasn't worth the risk. I was absolutely destroyed by that. Just by the coincidence of it. It felt very unfair at the time.

So when the manager said that was where we were staying, I felt nervous about it. I really didn't want to go back there. My superstitious instincts were telling me to stay well clear but the manager's mantra is that history is there to be changed, that bad memories are there to be wiped out. So we stayed there. And when I woke up on the morning of the final feeling fine, I was one relieved player.

Things were relaxed before the game. The manager called us into the team meeting. He touched a button on his laptop and it played for ten or 12 minutes on the screen. It was mostly a DVD of football funnies. There was some footage of an African team who had a goalkeeper with one leg. He was amazing. He could hobble along and then belt the ball up field with his one foot. There was a caption on the screen accompanying the footage of him saying 'be careful of Dudek's long balls'.

There were about ten different funny clips. He realized it was our first final together and that maybe we needed calming down a little bit. It relaxed us all. It took the tension out of us. After that, I knew it was going to be our cup. He is very good at small details like that. He is very good at gauging a mood and tailoring his preparation to that mood.

He asked Carlo to lead the team out, which was typical of him. Carlo had had a good chance of playing in the final but his sending-off at Newcastle in the FA Cup fifth-round defeat had ruined that plan for him. So he put a suit on and walked out in front of us at the Millennium Stadium. I still felt gutted for him that he was missing out. He played a big part in getting us there in the first place.

Before the game, the manager told us to go out and start well and be sharp. But Liverpool were the ones who were up for it. Our passes were slow and we looked laboured in the opening minutes. Even in the warm-up, I could sense that there was an assumption we were going to beat them. We knew we were the favourites and we thought we were going to cruise.

But they scored so early that it gave us the kick-up the backside we needed. It was a dreadful goal to concede, one of the sloppiest we let in all season. It came pretty much right from the kick-off. John Arne Riise was in yards and yards of space on the left of their midfield as they brought the ball forward and we just never picked him up.

Eventually, Fernando Morientes wriggled his way into space on their right and floated a lovely cross to Riise at the back post. He was still standing in glorious isolation but as the ball dropped to him, his left foot exploded into life. He got his head over it and his body behind it and that technique of his did the rest. His left-foot volley hurtled past Pete in an instant. The game was just 45 seconds old.

Coley provided the opening for our first chance to get back in the game. He played a pass for Didier to run on to and Dudek pushed his shot around the post. After the break, they were lucky not to have Sami Hyypia sent off when he chopped down Coley. He had already been booked but Steve Bennett decided not to give him another yellow.

The manager wasn't very happy about that. He came running out into his technical area and started yelling at the ref. Then Jamie Carragher ran over from the other side of the pitch and started yelling at the manager. The manager went ballistic at that point.

Eidur came on at half-time and he started to drag us back into the match. He nearly scored but Dudek pulled off a brilliant save to deny him and then William. It wasn't quite as good as the one he made against AC Milan in Istanbul but it prolonged the agony for us.

We had a couple of nervous moments, mostly when Stevie G came within a couple of inches of diverting a Nunez cross into our net. That would probably have put the game out of reach.

As we started to push forward more, we were getting a bit stretched and I was pleased with an interception I made that took the ball away from Milan Baros.

I was starting to look at the clock ticking down when we finally got the equalizer in the 79th minute. Didi Hamann had brought Lamps down midway inside their half as he burst through. Coley was livid with the referee for giving the foul because the ball ran on to him and Coley felt that, if the ref had played advantage, he would have had a very good chance of scoring. He soon forgave him.

Paolo floated the ball into the Liverpool box and my initial thought was that it wasn't a great free-kick because it drifted towards a clutch of three Liverpool players. But they all seemed to get in each other's way, unaware of the fact that none of our lads were challenging them. Stevie G jumped the highest but the ball flicked off the top of his head and flew past a startled Dudek and in off the inside of the post. A centre-forward could not have directed it better if he had tried.

Some Liverpool fans seemed to view him with a little suspicion after all the rumours of a move to the south started doing the rounds. I still found it amazing that some people were attempting to suggest seriously that he might even have scored that own goal in the Carling Cup Final on purpose.

That was just ridiculous and typical of some of the bizarre accusations people make on talk-radio shows these days. Steve has been the backbone of that side for so long and for people to turn on him like that just seemed strange to me. After the game, that's when I felt for him. He was 12 minutes away from going to lift the cup for the team he has supported all of his life and no one knew then that he was only a couple of months away from finding forgiveness and salvation in Istanbul.

We couldn't get another goal before the end of normal time. Dudek made another brave save from Duffa. He hurt his hip doing it and looked like he was going to have to come off. That would have been interesting because Liverpool had already used up all three substitutions but in the end he managed to soldier on.

A minute into the second period of extra-time, we finally took the lead. Johnno launched a long throw from the right touchline and I went up for it with Hyypia. He was so busy concentrating on me that he lost track of the flight of the ball and it cleared both of us. In the midst of a mass of bodies, Didier managed to control it as it dropped and prodded it underneath Dudek and into the back of the net from close range. Didier whipped his shirt off and set off on a delirious charge of celebration. He was booked, of course.

We put the match out of reach eight minutes from the end when a free-kick reached Eidur on the byline about eight yards away from goal. Eidur drilled a shot back towards Dudek and, probably because he was unsighted and it was hit so hard, he spilled it. As it dropped, Kezza was there to pounce and prod it over the line. Dudek tried desperately to shovel it back out but the linesman had spotted it was definitely a goal.

I was delighted for Kezza. I'd told him that morning that I had a feeling it was going to be his day, that he was going to forget all the troubles he had had this season and that he was going to be a Chelsea hero when he scored in Cardiff. I ran over to him as he celebrated and yelled in his ear to try to make myself heard above the roar of the Chelsea supporters. 'I told you!' I shouted.

When the final whistle went, it was my best feeling in football. My first trophy. My first medal. Our first trophy as a group. What we hoped would be the first of many. The club's first trophy for five years and a trophy that we hoped would usher in a glorious new era of domination for the club. All those thoughts were flooding through my head when that final whistle went.

We sent someone back inside to get the manager and he came out to celebrate with us. After a while, he walked up to the other end of the pitch and made a point of shaking hands with all the Liverpool players. I glanced over at them as he was doing that and they all looked shattered and gutted.

I tried to take my time when I went up to lift the trophy. Some of my friends had told me to try and make sure I savoured it. So I thought about everything it meant to me, all the years of work it had taken to get here, all the good times and the bad times and the promise of a bright future that it seemed to hold. And then I gave it a little kiss and held it up to the fans and just took in the noise that came down from the stands and the sight of all the blue and white confetti exploding into the air.

That was about the last I saw of the trophy, though. Sometimes, when you win a cup for your school football team, there's a squabble because two of the kids want to keep hold of the trophy as you're jogging round the pitch. There's always someone who doesn't want to hand it over and give everybody else a go, and so other players get upset.

Every team has one. Even this Chelsea team. Our guilty men were Coley and Didier. They got hold of the cup and they wouldn't let it go. They ran off with it and they kept it for so long I thought they must have had the handles welded to their hands. The rest of the boys kept asking where the cup had gone and then someone would spot Coley and Didier with it over by the fans lifting it into the air and brandishing it around. For Coley, I suppose holding that cup felt fantastic after all the struggles he had been through. Didier had had his share of stick, too, and the pressure of his price tag. His extra-time goal had been another hefty repayment.

I didn't sleep with the cup that night. But when I finally prised it away from Coley and Didier, I did keep it with me for a while. It was my first trophy in football. It was my best feeling in football. And it was so important for what happened for the rest of the Premiership season.

Somehow, that day in Cardiff cemented all the progress we had made and gave us encouragement and confidence for everything that lay ahead. It felt like it was the gateway to the climax of the season and having won it, we went into that final phase with renewed strength and determination. There was relief for everyone. We had won a trophy. The pressure was off us.

And if anyone had said after that that the Carling Cup did not mean anything, if they had said it was an insignificant bauble that could not possibly have an effect on the pursuit of other trophies that were regarded more highly, I would have laughed in their face and told them to watch us fly.

8 Barcelona and Bayern

Before the draw, the manager said he wanted to be paired with Barcelona in the first knock-out stage of the Champions League. I wasn't so sure. I was all for working our way up to the giants of the competition a little bit more slowly. Leave Barca and AC Milan and Juventus to the semis or the final. That would have been just fine by me. But the manager said he wanted Barcelona and he has got an uncanny habit of getting what he wants.

His attitude was altogether more admirable. He was convinced we were good enough to beat them, so it didn't matter to him what stage of the competition we met them. They were tearing up trees in the Primera Liga under Frank Rijkaard, running away from Real Madrid at the top of the table and playing brilliant, flowing football inspired by Ronaldinho, Deco and Xavi and converted into goals by Samuel Eto'o.

When we played them in the first leg, they were seven points clear of Real. Up until then, because David Beckham and Michael Owen played for Real Madrid and they had their cast of *galacticos* like Ronaldo, Raul and Luis Figo, I think we had always tended to assume that Madrid were the team to beat in Spain, but this Barcelona team was exposing that as an illusion.

There was a feeling that the energy was with them in the Spanish league just like the energy was with us in the Premiership. The torch was passing from Madrid to them, just like we were taking it from Arsenal and United in England. There was a youth and a purpose and a vibrancy about Barcelona that you had to admire and which I saw reflected in us.

They were some team but the manager had a sentimental attachment to them that must have made the prospect of playing against them even more enticing to him. He had worked at the Nou Camp under Bobby Robson and then Louis Van Gaal. He had worked with Ronaldo, Figo and Guardiola, some of the best players in the world. He had learned his trade there. He had effectively completed his managerial apprenticeship there and now he wanted to go back as the boss of one of the best club sides in the world.

Right from the start of the season, I thought Barca would be the team to beat in the Champions League. On the day of the draw, we were all allowed to come into training a little bit later than usual to watch the names being picked out on the television before we went out on to the pitch. We all clustered round the telly. We were one of the last four clubs left in the hat and there was a cheer when we came out with Barcelona.

But it wasn't a totally happy cheer. It was slightly muted. Almost strangled. It was a kind of cheer of recognition that the manager had got what he wanted. But there was a bit of trepidation mixed in there because Barcelona had an awesome reputation. They were kind of regarded as the Brazil of

European club football, I suppose. I looked round the room and I was thinking that I didn't want Barcelona. I didn't want them. Not now. Not yet. The manager, though, had it all mapped out already. He said we would draw with them at the Nou Camp and beat them back at the Bridge.

I am not usually one for watching Spanish football when I am at home because the slow tempo of the games bores me a bit. I'm not a fan. It seems to drag. People like Coley love it. He is always coming in to training and saying, 'Did you see what Ronaldinho did last night?' Primera Liga matches look like training games half the time. I've always got Sky Sports on and I could watch any kind of English football 24 hours a day – Division Three, Conference, anything – but I steer clear of Serie A and Primera Liga. After the draw, though, I changed my habits for a while. Over the next few weeks, I started to watch it to try to study the runs and the movement of Eto'o in particular.

We hardly had the ideal preparation for the first leg in Catalonia. Bridgey got an horrific ankle injury at Newcastle in the FA Cup fifth-round tie up at St James' Park the Sunday before, Duffa got what looked like a nasty knee injury and, just for good measure, Carlo Cudicini got sent off and we lost. Not a very good Sunday afternoon at all. It would have been better to go to Barcelona on the back of a win and with all our players healthy.

There were also suggestions around that time that some of the players were unhappy with Robbie. There was a piece on the back page of the *Evening Standard* that said a contingent of Chelsea players felt he ought to be in contention for a place against Barcelona but that he was somehow dragging his heels as he recovered from the injury he had sustained against Blackburn.

The only problem, really, was a difference in culture. Maybe English players are used to coming back before they are really ready and playing through pain. I've heard that that culture definitely exists in American football, for instance, where being fully fit is considered a luxury and most players are competing with various niggles. It's a bit the same with British footballers.

But not everyone is like that. There are some countries where that would be considered too risky and probably downright foolish. I think Robbie just wanted to make sure he was right so he wouldn't let anyone down. When the story appeared in the *Standard*, he came to me. He asked if the other players had got a problem with him or if they were saying bad things about him.

'Listen,' I said, 'the one thing about the atmosphere we have built at this club is that if anyone has got a problem with you, we will say it to your face.' He accepted that. He got a new injury when he was on international duty with Holland and we were desperate to get him back from that. I was going up to him saying, 'How long?' and 'Do your best' and 'If you possibly can', because I knew how important he was to the side.

And to be fair to him, he worked so hard at trying to recover from that injury that he wasn't leaving the training ground until 7 pm or 8 pm every night. He was doing the best he could but when his foot went a second time later in the season, he really wanted to hold back and make sure it was 100% right before he came back. When you get an injury twice in the same spot, it makes you very wary because you start to worry that some sort of weakness is growing there. He was bound to be more cautious then and so were the people around him. I don't blame him for the way he approached it at all.

I hadn't played at Newcastle because I was serving a one-match suspension but, in the period between the two games, the press played guessing games with the manager about whether Duffa had any chance of making the starting line-up. When we checked in at our hotel in Barcelona two days before the game, we didn't know what his chances were either.

We were staying at the Rey Juan Carlos Hotel right near the ground. A lot of visiting teams stay there. You could even see the tall stands of the Nou Camp rising into the sky from where we were. I found out the next day they put the visiting fans right in the very top tier. The players must look like little specks from up there. It would be enough to give me vertigo. It was the first time I had ever been there, let alone played there. For some reason, when we actually walked up the steps into the stadium from the changing rooms before training the day before the game, I was surprised that it wasn't a lot bigger. I think it was because I've heard so many people talking about what a magnificent stadium it is and how imposing it is, and it didn't quite measure up.

I was probably expecting something a bit more like the Bernabeu in Madrid where the sides are steeper and the crowd seems to be right on top of you, towering over you menacingly. I was reassured that the Nou Camp wasn't like that. I wasn't daunted by it at all. I think a couple of others felt the same.

That put everyone at ease a little bit. Our training was really good. The pitch was spot on. It was like a sponge pitch.

On the day before the game, the manager created a bit of a stir by naming both teams at the end of his official press conference. He got the Barca one right but he named Eidur in ours and not Duffa. Then he made a suitably sharp exit, leaving the room buzzing. That put Rijkaard's nose out of joint straight away. The press lads were still obsessing about Duffa's knee injury but after training we all knew that he would at least give it a go at the start. The physio was telling him the injury could flare up at any time but it was such a big game, Duffa felt it was worth having a go. Once he'd come through training okay, we began to get the vibe that he was going to go for it.

Duffa's a really determined geezer. He gets very frustrated with his injuries. He does so much hard work before matches and after to try to prevent the injuries occurring. Being in the team regularly this season has helped him. He is a quiet guy. He likes to be on his own a little bit. When he first came to Chelsea, he wanted to know where all the lads lived and we told him the names of a few nice streets. But he said he didn't want a big house. He doesn't like showy things.

When he came down, there were all sorts of stories in the press about how he lived like a hermit in a stone cottage up on the moors. They painted this picture of him as a bloke who kept himself to himself, played his football, and that was about it. I was half-expecting a guy who would just grunt at me. The stories were exaggerated but he certainly doesn't mind his own company. He's not a conformist, really.

I think the lads talked him into buying a big old mansion of some sort in the end anyway and he lives there all by himself. He is one of those people who has to be invited round to someone's house. A lot of the boys invite themselves and are more gung-ho about the social side of things but Duffa's a bit more reserved. The lads love him. But he's one of those people who can go to a restaurant on his own and just sit there and read, then go home and have an early night. I think he sleeps most of the day.

He started the game at the Nou Camp and he was flying. A lot of us were quite nervous, though, despite everything I said about not being intimidated by the stadium. There was no getting away from the fact that this was a massive game, a game that might decide whether we won the Champions League or not, and there was a tension in our play at the beginning of the match that sapped our energy and our creativity.

They created their first chance after three minutes. Eto'o nipped in to intercept a pass from Lamps. We were all back-pedalling furiously and Eto'o slipped the ball through to Ronaldinho on the left flank. This was going to be our first taste of what the magician could conjure up and he flashed a shot just wide of Pete's left-hand post.

I rate Eto'o. I think he's one of the best finishers around. He's a modern target man, super-quick and with razor-sharp instincts. He put another shot just wide a couple of minutes later and then, when we struggled to clear a cross from Ludovic Giuly, who had been a thorn in our side when we lost to Monaco the season before, the ball fell to Ronaldinho again. I thought he was going to score this time but his right-foot shot went wide again. I breathed a sigh of relief but at that stage it felt like it was only going to be a matter of time until they scored.

We were really under the cosh. We needed time to draw breath and consolidate. So any time Big Pete got the ball, I was signalling to him to slow it down, to keep it for as long as he could before he kicked it out, just to give us a break and frustrate them out of their rhythm. We just needed to disrupt them a little bit, try and bring them out of this purple patch and make their crowd restless. Quieten it all down a bit. That was the message.

Lamps was saying the same to me. Just kill it for ten minutes. We were telling Pete that if he came to catch a cross to get on the floor, just let the seconds tick away and hope that their hot streak would pass. It was just a case of giving us a breather. They were dominating the game but that was natural in the opening stages and we knew that if we could ride out the storm, we would come into the game more and more.

Makelele was superb in the opening 20 minutes. He worked incredibly hard. He did a lot to shut down Deco and Giuly, and even though Ronaldinho had those couple of early chances, he was still not quite as influential as I had feared he would be. After that initial burst of half-chances for them, things quietened down a little bit and we began to edge our way into the contest.

Then, after 33 minutes, we scored. I have to be honest and say it was against the run of play but it was all the sweeter for that. Sweeter, too, for the fact that the goal was created by a blistering run from our injured hero, Duffa. Lamps floated a magnificent pass over the top for him and he latched on to it just inside their half. I saw him running on to it and I just willed him to open up because once he hits his stride, there is no catching him. He took it on his right foot and hared towards the byline. He put the cross in and Coley tried to get to it to poke it in. He still swears to this day that he would have buried it if it had reached him. He's probably right because he was about two yards out at the time. But Barca's Brazilian full-back Juliano Belletti got to it first and diverted it past Victor Valdes. We were in front.

We could have gone further ahead a couple of minutes later. Makelele made a brilliant interception from Xavi and played a lovely through-ball with the outside of his foot over the top to Drogba, who was one-on-one with the keeper. I don't think he realized quite how much time he had and he blasted his shot wide of Valdes's right-hand post. If we'd scored then, that would have given us a massive advantage. Suddenly they were all over the place.

Coley pinged one just over the bar a few minutes before half-time and when the whistle went for half-time, we strode back to the dressing room in good spirits. We thought we'd weathered the storm and to have hit them on the break so beautifully and got a goal out of it was a real bonus. We didn't realize then that the tie was about to explode into the biggest controversy of the entire season.

We felt in the first half that some of referee Anders Frisk's decisions had gone against us. I have been refereed by him in the past and he's always been absolutely fine, used plenty of common sense, and tried to get on with the players. Ironically,

I had actually been quite pleased when I was told he was the ref for the first leg of the tie against Barcelona.

But in the Nou Camp, he was a different man. He waved away our objections and allowed a lot of bad tackles on Chelsea players to go unpunished, particularly on Didier, who was getting increasingly wound up by the treatment meted out to him by the Barcelona defenders.

We had always got a fair shake out of Frisk in the past, but in the first half I don't think we did. The fact that we were a goal up when the half-time whistle blew stopped us feeling too badly treated, though, when we made our way back to the tunnel.

That half-time turned into the most talked about interval in a football match there has ever been. I didn't pay any attention to Frisk as we headed down the tunnel. As I turned left to go into the Chelsea dressing room, I was vaguely aware of him going in the same direction as the Barcelona players but I've been told that is something to do with the layout of the Nou Camp dressing-room area. There was nothing untoward in that.

That was all I saw. I wanted to get into the dressing room to collect my thoughts and listen to what the manager had to say. I wanted to talk to the rest of the lads and talk about the second half. I wasn't really interested in Frisk at that point. But I didn't realize what Steve Clarke and one of the Chelsea security guys, Les Miles, had seen.

They'd seen Rijkaard walking down the tunnel with Frisk and talking to him all the way to his dressing-room door. Let's get one thing straight here, as well. Steve Clarke is an honest guy. I've known him for a long time. I know that he doesn't tell

Lamps and I elated after Didier scores against Bayern at the Bridge to put us 4–1 up.

Having a laugh at Anfield during training for the Champions League
semi-final second leg. We were relaxed and confident.

ABOVE: The manager lightens things up as we get ready for the Liverpool showdown.

ABOVE: The boss asks a question. When he makes a point, we listen.

LEFT: One of my proudest moments in football was being voted the PFA's 2005 Player of the Year.

Lining up with the lads before the game in Bayern's Olympic Stadium.

Steady. Taking a tumble during the first leg of the Champions League semi-final with Liverpool.

Crunching Ollie Kahn with a challenge in the first leg against Bayern – he wasn't too happy.

The boss thinks things over during training in Bayern's Olympic Stadium.

I'm powerless to stop Luis Garcia's
stabbed effort going past me at Anfield.
William hooked it off the line but the ref
gave it anyway.

You can tell how devastated I was after
the defeat to Liverpool in the Champions
League.

LEFT: Lamps goes wild at the Reebok after he scores the first goal against Bolton in a victory that sealed our first championship trophy in fifty years.

BELOW: The manager hugs Maka after we win the title at Bolton.

BELOW: Lamps takes the ball round Jaaskelainen to score the second goal at the Reebok.

You beauty.
Celebrating
with Lamps
after his goals
clinched the
title.

I brought Roman out on to the pitch to take his share of applause
from the fans after the Bolton game.

lies. He wouldn't just make something up. That is not in his character.

The incident might never have come to light if the second half had passed by without controversy. But Frisk had booked Didier in the first half for an innocuous foul on Rafael Marquez, and ten minutes after the interval he sent him off. We were all unhappy with the decision.

Belletti made another dreadful mistake and chested a cross down for Valdes to collect. But he cushioned it too much and the ball just dropped like a stone. It was there to be won and Didier went for it. It wasn't reckless. He lunged at it, as he had to do, but the only contact between him and the keeper was knee to knee as they both went for the ball and then collapsed in a heap. For some reason, the keeper started clutching his shoulder and Puyol made a big song and dance about it. That's what got him sent off. Frisk bought it and gave Didier a yellow followed by a red. It was a decision that shaped the rest of the game.

Believe me, Drogba had no choice but to go for that ball. If he hadn't, he would have had ten team-mates screaming blue murder at him and asking what the hell was the matter with him that he wasn't trying to win the game for us. I would have been unhappy with him if he had pulled out of that challenge because it would have said something about his commitment to the team. It didn't matter that he was already on a yellow. He did what any striker would have done. It was unfortunate that the keeper was hurt but keepers have to put themselves in that kind of situation, too.

Anyway, Frisk showed Didier the red card. I couldn't

believe it. We all thought it was a poor decision. Just to add to the occasion, the Barcelona fans distinguished themselves by aiming monkey noises at Didier as he headed back towards the dressing rooms. It also meant, of course, that we would have to try and survive for 35 minutes against one of the best attacking teams in the world with only ten men. It was going to be real backs-against-the-wall stuff.

When Drogba went off, we knew it was going to be a long, hard journey to the end of the game. Didier's good at holding the ball up and we lost that with his red card. We had told ourselves not to drop so deep but when we went down to ten men, the back four started dropping off too deep. I remember Mourinho screaming from the sideline to move further up and as a unit we got dug out in a team meeting back at Cobham for failing to do that.

But especially with players like Eto'o up against you, you are always a bit wary of pushing up because of their pace, the intelligence of their runs and the cleverness of their passing. There's a fear in the back of your mind that you might get caught with a perfectly timed run. So we retreated to the edge of the box with two banks of four and challenged them to break us down. And they did break us down.

True to their tradition and their style, Barcelona went for it. After 64 minutes, they brought on a young Argentinian striker they had signed in the January transfer window. His name was Maxi Lopez and he galvanized them. They nearly scored a minute later when their other sub, Andres Iniesta, hit a shot just wide after Ricky Carvalho had blocked an effort from Eto'o.

A minute after that, though, they broke through. They put

together a neat passing movement on the edge of our area. Ronaldinho played a neat pass out to Eto'o and I came out to challenge him. As I stood in front of him, he played the ball square to Maxi Lopez who dropped his shoulder and side-stepped Gallas and pulled his shot across goal and past Pete's right hand.

They were absolutely flying then. The Nou Camp went wild and for the first time I realized what an intimidating place it could be. The momentum was with them, and in the 73rd minute Maxi Lopez, who was unplayable with the crazed energy and verve he had brought to the attack, drove a shot across goal, while Eto'o came in on the blind side of Ricky and buried it in the back of our net with a very smooth left-foot finish. Suddenly, it all seemed to be falling apart.

In the first half, we had been pleased with how we defended. But in the second half, it was just the total opposite. They were getting in, they were creating chances and they were first to headers. The manager brought Eidur on because when we were clearing it, it was just coming straight back at us which didn't give us time to get back.

When the second one went in, we looked at each other and said, 'Now we don't concede any more.' We thought they might settle for 2–1 but they didn't. They carried on. They kept going for it. They wanted more. They wanted to try and kill it. I was a bit shocked by that. I was shocked by how bold they were but I shouldn't have been because they are a great side.

With about ten minutes to go, I started getting cramp. I had to take my shinpads off and I put them by the side of the post. I've had those shinpads since I was about 14. When the final whistle went, I was so distracted that I just headed straight back to the changing rooms. I forgot all about the pads. I only realized before the next game. The kit man said he couldn't find them. I was horrified. Then I suddenly remembered what I had done. I was absolutely gutted. Because I'm so superstitious, it was a real blow to me. We tried phoning Barcelona but they couldn't find them. Lamps gave me a pair of his and I'm sticking with them now.

No wonder I forgot those shinpads. The mayhem of the evening didn't fade away after the game. It seemed to increase. Some wild rumours surfaced in the press the next day that the manager had been kicked up the backside by one of the Barcelona officials after the match. 'Kicked Up the Barce', I think the headline was. It wasn't true. The press boys were just a bit frustrated because none of us had been allowed to talk after the game. They had to come up with something. Actually, even though there was so much bad blood after the game, there were no real afters in the tunnel. There was no commotion with their players.

But the manager was upset about Rijkaard and Frisk, and he didn't want us to make any comment after the game. He didn't attend the usual manager's post-match press conference either, and then when he mentioned in a column in a Portuguese newspaper that Frisk and Rijkaard had wandered up the tunnel together at half-time, UEFA took offence.

It was reported that people started making death threats to Frisk and his family, and he promptly retired. I was surprised. Of course it's not pleasant receiving threats of any kind and it says something about our society that people appear able to make those kind of threats so readily. But I believe most people in public life have to endure that at one time or another and none of them just walk away from what they are doing.

Anyway, Frisk's retirement created a lot of issues for the manager and Chelsea. UEFA charged the club with bringing the game into disrepute and making false declarations. They accused Chelsea of 'deliberately creating a poisoned and negative ambience' after the refusal to attend the post-match news conference and the decision to submit a report detailing their allegations. One of their officials, a bloke called Volker Roth, their head of refereeing, described Mourinho as 'the enemy of football'. I don't understand how he was allowed to get away with that but he did.

In the dressing room at the Nou Camp, straight after the game, the manager guaranteed us we would go back to Stamford Bridge and beat them. He said he was pleased with what we had achieved that night. He said we had sent out a message that we could play one of the best teams in the world and match them.

On the plane back, we believed we could beat them. We felt that having come up against all these players with their great reputations, we had demystified them a bit in our own minds now and there wasn't anything to fear. Some of them hadn't really played that well. Eto'o had been a handful but Ronaldinho had faded out of the game. Paolo Ferreira had done a great job and got really tight on him. We thought we had the measure of him. But he was about to prove us wrong.

We were fired up for the return match. Very fired up. All the criticism of the manager had brought us even closer together. It was the first real wedge of sustained criticism he had received and it made us want to go and stand in his corner. He always stood right behind us and we wanted to return the favour. And even in the midst of all the controversy, he was still willing to listen to our ideas about the second leg.

That's one of the manager's great strengths. He is a decisive man but he is prepared to listen and discuss, and he is happy to take the opinions of others into account. So when we got back from Barcelona, we had a team meeting at the training ground a couple of days later and talked over all the issues arising from the game at the Nou Camp.

We had a discussion about Didier's sending off and the manager invited anyone who wanted to to get up and speak. Eidur stood up and told the manager he thought he should have brought Didier off earlier because there was a good chance that, having been booked early in the game, Didier was going to get into more trouble. He said he realized that he might have been the one to benefit from that because he was sitting on the bench waiting to come on but he felt he had to make his point anyway. He just thought the manager might have got him off earlier.

Even Didier had some sympathy with the argument. Eidur apologized to him and said he hoped he didn't take any offence from it and Didier was adamant it wasn't a problem. In fact, he agreed with him. And the manager just listened to him and took it all in. And I think that says a lot about the kind of spirit Mourinho has built at Chelsea. He encourages us to speak our minds and not to harbour resentments. He wants everything out in the open.

Before that meeting, he said there was no point in us talking about what had happened in the Nou Camp amongst ourselves and moaning about it and he assured us that if we had something to say, he wouldn't get the hump about it or dislike any of us for saying it. Eidur stood up and said what he said and that set the tone and people felt relaxed and a couple of other players got up and made their points, too. From that day on, that relationship grew. If any of us had a problem, we went to see him, and we felt we could confide in him and be open with him.

So we went into the second leg in a confident and secure frame of mind. We had talked through all the issues from the Nou Camp and put them behind us. We were closer together than ever and more convinced than ever that we were good enough to make it through to the quarters. Nothing was going to get in our way.

In the period between the two games, there was a bit of bad-mouthing from the Barcelona players about how we were a boring long-ball team. I was vaguely aware of it but it didn't really register. If it had been another English side saying it, maybe it might have fired us up. Actually, with everything else that was going on, what they saying was the last thing on our mind.

In the dressing room before the game, the manager told us we had to go into the game and start well. There was a slow tempo in Barcelona so this time we wanted to get amongst them straight away, stick a few decent tackles in and shake them up a bit. Let them know right from the start. Whether they were in shock or they didn't expect it, I don't know, but the start of that game was almost surreal.

The atmosphere was amazing inside Stamford Bridge that night. We wanted the fans to be louder and more aggressive than usual. We wanted Barca to feel intimidated in the same way that they think visiting teams are intimidated in the Nou Camp. And it was loud. The European nights are the best for that. I know that happens at other grounds, too, and it was brilliant to walk out at the Bridge and hear the roar and feel the hairs on the back of your neck standing on end.

Didier was suspended so the manager had picked Kezman up front with Eidur just behind him. Kezman was super-confident because he had just scored in the Carling Cup Final and he wanted to seize his chance. He'd struggled for much of the season but he was brilliant against Barcelona.

After eight minutes, he made a great run down the right after Lamps had won the ball in midfield and played the ball through to him. Kezman crossed to Eidur and his first touch took him past Gerard. It looked for an instant as though Victor Valdes might smother the chance but Eidur got there first and lashed the ball past him.

That would have been enough to put us through but we were buzzing and there was no thought in our minds of trying to protect what we had got. It was too early for that anyway. We were on fire, just like Barcelona had been in the closing stages of the match at the Nou Camp, and a few minutes later we went further ahead. Coley was tormenting Giovanni Van Bronckhorst, the former Arsenal player, down their left and he cut inside and shot at goal. His shot was deflected, Victor Valdes was wrong-footed and could only parry it with his left hand, and Lamps was on it in a flash to slam it in. Two–nil up in 17 minutes.

The crowd started singing '*Boring, Boring Chelsea*' to prove a point. But we were doing a pretty good job of that already. In the 19th minute, we went three up. I shadowed Eto'o almost back to the halfway line as he came to receive the ball and he laid it off to no one in particular.

He went down and I half-expected Pierluigi Collina to give a foul but he allowed play to go on. The ball reached Coley who drove a brilliantly weighted ball through to Duffa, who sprinted clear on the left and drilled the ball underneath the keeper's body. I couldn't believe it. I thought I was in dreamland. 'Fucking hell, lads,' I yelled out, 'we're 3–0 up!' Stating the obvious, I know, but it was almost the kind of start where you had to pinch yourself to make sure it was true.

After that third goal, I saw Duffa running back to the halfway line, then I looked across to the other side of the pitch and saw Eto'o and Ronaldinho walking quite close to each other with their shoulders drooping, and their body language said they were beaten. Before the game, they had come bounding off their team coach with their shoulders up, all bright-eyed and bushy-tailed and ready for the match. But now they looked as if they were broken. They were looking daggers at each other, muttering something to each other. Whatever it was, it wasn't positive. They were in bits. And they made me feel even bigger and better than ever and more confident that there was no way back for them.

But after we'd gone three up, instead of pressing the

advantage and taking our opportunity to finish it before half-time, we sat back a little bit. It was almost as if we had stunned ourselves. It was like it had taken it out of us emotionally and we suddenly realized that we were on the verge of making it through into the quarters. The manager said during the interval that he was disappointed with that. We should have kept going. Within eight minutes, they were back in it.

We had a couple of narrow scrapes that were warning signs. Pete made a magnificent diving save to keep out Eto'o and then Ronaldinho put a header inches wide. But the goal came. Belletti swung over a nothing cross from the right and Paolo went up to defend it. He jumped without looking at the ball and it hit him on the hand or low on the arm. I was the other side of him and I didn't see it so I went to protest to the referee. A couple of the players pulled me aside and said they thought it was a fair decision. Ronaldinho took the penalty, converted it and that was like a lifeline for them. Eto'o's shoulders were back up then and their body language changed. They knew they were right back in it.

Seven minutes before half-time, they got another goal back, the Ronaldinho special. I had gone up for a defensive header on the edge of the box and hadn't got as much on it as I would have liked. It fell to Deco who played it short to Ronaldinho. He had it on the edge of the box and Ricky and Eidur were standing in front of him, blocking his path to goal. I looked around. I could see Eto'o. I knew he was covered. He wasn't going anywhere. I didn't think there was any danger from Ronaldinho. He was covered, too. There were no runners coming through late. There was no movement. I thought that defensively we were all right as we were. I was sure he would be forced to play it wide and that we'd be looking at dealing with a cross.

Then he kind of wiggled his hips, one way then the other, like he was preparing to do a samba routine, like he was on Copacabana beach, about to dance. Then he toe-poked it and I looked round expecting that Pete would gather it safely or that it would fly wide. But it bulged the corner of the net. It was an incredible bit of skill. It showed that if you're good enough, you can control a toe-poke.

Suddenly, it was my shoulders that were slumping. Suddenly, it was me that felt as if I'd been hit by a runaway truck. Ten minutes earlier, they looked like they were shell-shocked and that there was no way back for them. Now, they thought they were invincible again. Now they knew that if the scores stayed as they were, they were going through. It was an unbelievable turn-around. Probably the most amazing 45 minutes of football I have ever played.

I couldn't believe that they were in control of the tie again. I'd gone from ecstasy to agony in a few minutes. If any of the Barcelona players were looking at me, they would probably have been just as encouraged by my body language then as I had been encouraged by Eto'o's earlier. But we walked back to the centre circle and we were telling each other we just had to keep it tight until half-time. Maybe play the ball a little bit longer for the next five minutes and turn them round and go in at 3–2.

Even then, there was more incident before half-time. They nearly scored again when Ronaldinho played a sublime through-ball to Eto'o and he skimmed his shot just over the bar. If that had gone in, we would have found it very hard to come back. It would have destroyed our morale. Then, Coley struck a shot against the post and Duffa hit the rebound against the legs of Valdes. In the circumstances, it was amazing any of the players had the energy to make it to the dressing rooms when the half-time whistle blew.

The mood in the dressing room at half-time was okay. The gaffer was quite relaxed. He said we had proved how easily we could score against them already and that we could do it again. He said the first ten or 15 minutes of the second half would be vital. The pitch was watered again at half-time because even though we knew they were a good footballing side, we wanted to get the pitch nice and wet and get a bit of zip on our passing. We came out and the fizz was back on.

There were no clean-cut chances in the early stages but we had it in our minds that we were owed a goal from a set-piece. We had been disappointed we hadn't made more of dead-ball situations at the Nou Camp because the manager had made a point of isolating the fact that they were not a big team. He was frustrated that we hadn't got enough corners in the first leg.

The manager took Paolo off early in the second half and brought Johnno on but it was still hard for us to curb the influence of Ronaldinho. Lamps had a couple of chances and Pete made a remarkable save from Puyol who powered a header at him from about six yards out. Somehow, he got down to it and clutched it right on the line. Next, he tipped a shot from Iniesta on to the post, Johnno let it run over his foot as he tried to clear it and Eto'o blasted the rebound over the bar.

The second half was wearing on. I hadn't got to the stage where I thought it was slipping away from us but I knew it was getting close to the point where the manager would stick Robert Huth on up front to give us an extra aerial presence. With about quarter of an hour to go, we won a corner and as I ran towards their box, I could see Huthy out of the corner of my eye getting ready to come on. I knew then we were about to enter the last phase of the game when we would have to throw everything at them.

Duffa was getting ready to take the corner from the left. Knowing how our manager prepares us for other teams, I try to vary my runs a lot more now so that defenders can't predict with any degree of accuracy how they can counter me. Sometimes it can come down to Didier muttering he wants to go near post as we're running up. It's just a spontaneous thing. For some reason, I fancied the back post that time. I was actually arching away from goal when the corner came over.

It seemed too congested in the middle of the box, I knew Duffa's cross would be swinging out. I gave my marker a little shove and tried to take him into the crowd and he got caught up in it a little bit. I was free of him, and I came back towards the near post and made contact with the ball. It wasn't really a powerful header. Sometimes when you meet a ball with your head, you know it's in straight away, but it wasn't the case with that one.

I didn't think there was enough on it. I thought I hadn't got enough power on it. But I kept watching it and kept watching it and no one got in the way of it. I saw Kezman trying to get a little toe on it so he could claim it. But he couldn't reach it either. And then it was in.

I didn't know at that stage that Ricky had got a bit involved with their keeper so I just wheeled away towards Coley and told the lads just to stay in the celebration for a minute so we had time to regroup. Tiago came on then as well so I didn't actually go that mad. I wish I had run to the fans and gone a little bit more mad. I just screamed 'Whoooooooooooooo!' for about 30 seconds. I was thinking too much about the last ten minutes. After all the switchbacks that game had had, I didn't want any more. I gave a little speech about keeping it tight and the front men holding it up. Huthy came on five minutes from the end so we knew he would come and win everything and we would clean up behind as they poured more men forward.

Certainly, the referee Pierluigi Collina could have disallowed the goal for a foul on their keeper. I've seen challenges like that penalized before. But he didn't. Some you win, some you lose. Maybe we were just owed one from the first leg after what had happened to Didier. I know it's a cliché but these things even themselves up over a season. We found that out again when the referee judged that Luis Garcia's goal had crossed the line in the semi-finals when television replays proved it hadn't.

The manager brought Tiago on for Eidur as soon as my goal went in. And then Huthy replaced Duffa. The final stages were still frantic but we were never going to concede. Not after everything we had been through. We were resolute and they were spent. Deco had a free-kick in a dangerous position but he hit it wide and when the final whistle came there was just this great explosion of joy and emotion.

It's hard to criticize them because they must have been terribly disappointed but Barcelona didn't deal with it very well. They had been the favourites, they had just been knocked out by a team run by a bloke who used to be one of their employees and it was sticking in their throat.

I was still on the pitch celebrating with the lads and the fans but their players got into a ruck with the stewards as they were going back down the tunnel. There were some suggestions that one of the manager's assistants had gone over to taunt Rijkaard at the final whistle and Eto'o claimed afterwards that one of the stewards had racially abused him.

The guy Eto'o accused is a mate of ours called Tootsie. He happens to be one of the biggest black guys you have ever seen and one of the friendliest men I know. The next time we saw him, the lads all gave him stick. 'Oi, Tootsie, you racist!' I shouted at him. UEFA didn't pursue the matter. And just for once, Barcelona kept quiet about it, too.

By the time I got back to the tunnel, everything had died down. The music was turned up loud in our dressing room. The Barcelona players were back in their dressing room. I went in to shake their hands and swap shirts with Eto'o. Lamps swapped with Ronaldinho. They were now all very dignified and gracious. I was impressed with that. I hope I'd be the same. If someone comes in after you've lost, I wouldn't want to sit there and talk to them but I hope I would be polite and shake hands and move on. And after all the bad blood there had been in that tie, they were big enough to do that.

That night against Barcelona was one of the highs of the season. It made it extra-special scoring the winner. I was buzzing about scoring against a team like them. After the game, we went out as a team into the West End and had a little drink together. We had a day off the next day so the manager told us to go out and have a few beers together.

Everyone was euphoric. In a way, it felt like we had just won the Champions League that night. Because it had been such an epic, because there had been so much bitterness and so many recriminations surrounding the whole tie, it felt like a massively significant win. It felt as though it would unlock the rest of the season. It felt as though, after that, nothing could be as difficult or as testing again. More than ever, we felt our name was on the trophy.

There was so much euphoria after that victory that we forgot for a little while that UEFA seemed determined to punish the manager and the club for what happened in Barcelona. The various pronouncements from UEFA officials made it plain that the whole thing had turned into a personalized vendetta against the manager and that he had very little chance of a fair hearing.

But still UEFA pressed on. The hearing at UEFA headquarters in Nyon, in Switzerland, took place after the second leg. The manager didn't attend and neither did the chief executive, Peter Kenyon. They both knew what was coming. The upshot was that the manager was banned from the touchline for the next two Champions League matches and the club was fined. We all felt for the manager and thought the punishment was very harsh.

It was strange that after all of this a senior UEFA official admitted that Rijkaard and Frisk had been talking in the tunnel and just outside the ref's dressing room door. It was obvious immediately that the conversation consisted of a lot more than just the 'Hello, Anders, how are you?' that other UEFA officials had sworn was the extent of their exchange.

'The referee told us he had contact with Rijkaard from the pitch to the front of his dressing-room door,' UEFA's venue director Pascal Fratellia said. 'Rijkaard wished to say hello at the beginning of the tunnel and then tried to talk to him climbing the stairs. Frisk told him it was not the place or the moment to speak about the match.'

In other words, what Clarkey had been saying was true. But there was no apology to Mourinho and no lifting of his touchline ban. And there was no suggestion that Rijkaard should have been the one punished. The whole thing seemed very unjust.

We were reasonably pleased when we drew Bayern Munich in the quarter-finals. They had just beaten Arsenal fairly comfortably, they were top of the Bundesliga and they were clearly a very good side. But I was relieved we had avoided AC Milan with their galaxy of stars like Andrei Shevchenko, Paolo Maldini and Cafu. I wanted to save them for the final. We knew we would be playing Juventus or Liverpool in the semis if we beat Bayern. We all thought it would be Juventus.

In the same way, everyone seemed to assume we would beat Bayern. Probably because we had just beaten Barcelona. But the lads knew it was going to be tough. Bayern hadn't just beaten Arsenal, they had battered them. And when we faced up to each other at Stamford Bridge, there was a definite edge to the clash.

Part of that was because Mourinho was banned from the touchline. The build-up to the game was totally overshadowed by that issue and by the crazy soap opera the press created about where the gaffer would actually watch the match from. Some rumours said he would be watching at home in central London. Some said he would watch from his office at Stamford Bridge. Some said he would be in the Chelsea TV studios. There were cameramen on motorbikes outside his home, waiting to shadow him wherever he went on that day. The obsession with the manager was reaching unprecedented levels for English football.

We all felt it was very unjust. We felt the manager was being punished for expressing an opinion and that we were being deprived of our biggest influence in the immediate run-up to the game. Of course, we knew there was a great support team there who would not let anybody down but it was still going to feel strange looking over to the bench and not seeing the manager there in his coat.

The manager tried to limit the differences to the build-up as much as he could. He tried to compensate in advance for his absence. He held the team meeting the night before the game instead of an hour before it. He conducted it as if the match was only an hour away. There was still the same kind of urgency about it that there always is. He said that we had nothing to be worried about because we were the people who had been getting the job done on the pitch every week anyway. He said we didn't need him once we got out on to the pitch. He said his assistants would do everything that needed to be done. He was calm about it all.

It felt weird not having him in the changing room before the game, too. Usually, he would have come in an hour or so before the game and chilled out a bit with the lads, read the programme, that kind of thing. Then there would have been the team meeting. He plays such a big part before the game because he is such an inspiring speaker. No matter how good the other guys were, and even though it did not show in the two games, it felt like a piece was missing from the jigsaw.

He's a good speaker but I think he knows that before the game he doesn't need to be giving speeches like Winston Churchill. He realizes that his players don't need too much motivation before a game like the tie against Bayern. The motivation comes from within and if you haven't got that, you shouldn't be in the team anyway.

Normally, he'll do something like stick a couple of quotes up on the board. He will spread a few reminders about the dressing room on pieces of paper. Towards the end of the season, there were bullet points about how we only needed four more wins and then Arsenal wouldn't be able to catch us. That kind of thing. Morale-boosting things. They seem basic but they're the kind of things that start to make you feel so confident you think you're invincible.

He puts tactics up on the wall and diagrams of set-pieces. He is fairly relaxed before a game. You can have your phone on. The television is usually on. Then we go to a separate room and the phone goes off, the telly goes off, the music comes on and it's like 'bang, we're in game mode now'.

Clarkey took charge in his absence. Baltemar Brito came round saying a few things in his pidgin English. Rui Faria, the fitness coach, made a few points. Everyone chipped in. It wasn't just one person deputizing for the manager. It was a collective effort. His entire support team rallied around to deputize for him. He has chosen them all carefully but he would have been proud of the cool way they handled it all.

They must have done something right because we went one up after four minutes. Robert Kovac failed to clear the ball properly on the edge of their area and Duffa laid it off to Coley. Coley had a ping but it was going wide of Oliver Kahn's right-hand post until it struck Lucio on the leg. It changed direction dramatically and rolled into the unguarded goal with Kahn stranded.

But even though we had other chances in the first half, we couldn't capitalize on them. Their top two strikers, Claudio Pizarro and Roy Makaay were both out with injuries, but Bayern still posed a threat coming forward. I had my hands full with Paolo Guerrero, who was playing on his own up front, and Hasan Salihamidzic, a clever, energetic player, who was playing off him. If people had thought they were going to be an easy touch, they soon realized Bayern were a formidable force. They caused us problems.

There was a bad-tempered edge to the game, too. Perhaps it was the old rivalry between England and Germany stirring. I suppose I contributed to that with a challenge on Oliver Kahn that they all seemed to get a bit upset about. There was a high ball. He went for it and I went for it. I had my eye on the ball and I smashed into him by accident and bundled him into the net. It was just a case of my momentum taking me into him. I didn't think anything more of it but he did. He sought me out before the return leg at the Olympic Stadium and made that clear.

They equalized six minutes into the second half. Michael Ballack's free-kick cannoned into the wall and when Ze Roberto lashed it back towards goal, Pete parried it but their young superstar Sebastian Schweinsteiger blasted it back past him from close range.

They were nervous moments because Bayern now had a crucial away goal and they were suddenly full of confidence. It was crucial that we re-established our lead before they had had a chance to settle properly and consolidate. Lamps didn't let us down. Six minutes after they had equalized, we were back in front.

William pumped a long ball forward from right back and Didier won it with a fantastic header on the edge of the box and nodded it down for Lamps. He took one touch to control it and then dug it out from underneath his feet and drove in his shot from about 20 yards. He hit it well but not as fiercely as some of his specials. There was still enough on it to beat Kahn, though. He looked a bit flat-footed as it squeezed past him into the bottom left-hand corner. I'm not surprised there's a bitter rivalry between him and Jens Lehmann for the German goalie's jersey.

There was nothing he could have done about Lamps's next goal, though. There was nothing anyone could have done about it. Makelele floated a lovely ball over the Bayern defence towards Lamps who was about 12 yards out. He took it on his chest but, because it was a little bit high, it fell over his head rather than dropping at his feet. But Lamps just swivelled on it as it dropped and hit it on the half-volley past Kahn. It was an instinctive goal. Any striker would have been proud of it and it put us firmly back in charge of the tie.

We thought we were as good as through when Didier scored our fourth ten minutes from the end. Huthy flicked on a Lamps corner at the near post and when Kahn blocked Eidur's stabbed shot, the ball broke free. I was right in there, too, and I thought for a moment it was coming to me but Didier reacted quickest and rammed it into the net.

That should have been the end of it. That should have turned the second leg in Munich into a formality. But deep into injury-time, Ballack took a dive in the area on the vague pretext that he had been held back by Ricky, and the referee bought it. I remember staring up at the ref, who was the tallest ref I have ever seen, and just asking him, 'Why?' I felt like Roman after our defeat at Man City.

The ref wouldn't tell me why. Ballack stepped up to take the penalty himself and buried it. I lost a bit of respect for him that night, though. He's a terrific player and he was mag-nificent at the 2002 World Cup. I thought he showed a lot of guts when he got a booking in the semi-final that was going to rule him out of the final and he still turned in a man-of-the-match performance to get Germany through. He was too good a player to be diving like that.

If there was going to be controversy after the game, I thought it would be about that. When he got up from his dive, a lot of us got right in his face. After he had scored the penalty,

Huthy gave him a little barge that he reacted to. I told the press boys that a player like Ballack should be above pulling cheap tricks like that because he was such a special talent. I said I thought it was a shame that he had stooped to that level. I think what I said got back to them in Germany because both Ballack and Kahn tried to intimidate me before the second leg.

But actually, the controversy wasn't about Ballack's dive at all. It was only after the game when we saw television pictures of Rui Faria fiddling with his woolly hat and the commentators suggesting that he had been relaying messages from the manager to us that we realized there was more trouble brewing.

The theory, apparently, was that the manager was calling Rui and giving him instructions and then Rui was telling Clarkey, who was passing the message on to us. Some of the television stations were going into it all in obsessive detail, training the camera on Rui and claiming that every time he touched his hat and then said something to Clarkey, Clarkey got up and yelled something out at the players on the pitch. There were even stories that some of the television stations had employed lip readers to try and decipher what Rui was saying to Clarkey.

It was all a bit like a Bond movie. Football espionage at work. It was a nice idea but total garbage. I didn't even know where the manager was. I read later that he had watched the game in the health club attached to the ground. But at the time, I didn't know where he was and, anyway, it didn't really matter. All we knew was that he wasn't with us. As far as we were concerned, we had absolutely no contact with the manager.

We gave Rui a bit of stick after that. We said to him that before the return leg in Munich, he ought to walk out to the dug-out with a massive model mobile phone like Dom Joly's in *Trigger Happy TV*. He could have started shouting, 'Yeah, Jose, I'm in the Olympic Stadium, what do you want me to tell the boys?' That would have been brilliant but I don't think it would have gone down well with UEFA.

We were urging him to do it if things had been going well late in the second leg but I suppose it wouldn't have been fair to Bayern. It might just have lightened the mood a little bit though. As it was, some UEFA officials searched him at half-time in Munich and made him take his hat off in case he was wired. There was nothing there, of course. Except his hair.

We felt confident when we travelled out there, even if Ballack's penalty had left some room for doubt. When we were 4–1 up, everyone was thinking we were through. After the penalty, we were so deflated it was almost as if we had lost the game. We didn't even go and acknowledge the fans. We got sucked down into the tunnel and into the dressing room. Everyone was sitting there quietly. The music wasn't on. The manager came in after the time limit set by UEFA for his ban had lapsed, freed from his day's exile at last, and asked what the matter was. He said: 'We've just won 4–2.'

The run-up to the return leg with Bayern went fairly smoothly. There wasn't quite the pressure there had been before the second Barcelona game because this time we felt pretty confident that we would get through. We certainly knew we were favoured and that we would have to have a very bad night at the back to lose it from the position we were in.

But they were still bristling from the first leg. When I walked out into the tunnel to line up before the game with the rest of the lads, Kahn and Ballack both started coming towards me and gave me big shoulder barges before we got to the area where the television cameras would have picked that kind of thing up.

As we got out, Lamps shouted to ask what had happened. He wanted to know if I wanted him to come and step in. Kahn and Ballack were still staring at me. Kahn kept saying 'after, after' as though he wanted to have a big scrap after the game. I said. 'OK, I'll see you in here after.' They were obviously upset about what I'd said after the first game. I looked to my right again and they looked like they wanted to start it there and then. In the end, some of the Chelsea lads got between us. And then we walked out.

I've never had that kind of thing before a match. Plenty of times, it has happened during a game and sometimes after one, too. That's just part of the back and forth banter that you get in football. But this was all a little bit strange. It took me by surprise, really, because we had just been thinking about the football but they had clearly been building themselves up to a pitch of hatred about what had happened at Stamford Bridge. That made me think we had the advantage before we even walked out. But I thought the game might get a little bit tasty, too. The reality was that it never hit those heights of animosity again.

The manager was back in his hotel room by that stage. He had come to the stadium with the idea of watching from the stands.

Within a couple of minutes, there was a German television crew right in his face, apparently, and all sorts of people pestering him. Before long, it became clear there was no way he was going to be able to watch the match in a situation like that so he walked outside, jumped in a cab and went back to the hotel. The next we heard from him was when he called us on our mobiles after the game to congratulate us.

We knew we had to try to keep it tight at the back in the early stages but we were grateful to Pete yet again for a brilliant save from Pizarro. He was fit again for the second leg and so was Makaay, and they threw everything at us in those opening exchanges.

But we did not buckle. We were helped by the fact that they seemed to keep wasting their crosses from the flanks and things got even better when Lamps put us ahead after half an hour. He got the ball 25 yards out and his shot cannoned off Lucio, the same player who had deflected Coley's effort in the first leg. Kahn had already dived to his right. He tried to keep the ball out with his legs but it bounced through them and into the net. Kahn looked as though he couldn't believe his bad luck. Funnily enough, I didn't feel sorry for him.

Ballack wasted a chance to give Bayern a foothold in the tie when Huthy misdirected a header straight to him five minutes before half-time. But he blazed it high over the crossbar. I didn't feel sorry for him, either.

Kahn made a great save from Duffa after an hour to stop us putting the game utterly out of reach and they equalized four minutes later when Makaay's glancing header came back off the post and Pizarro tapped it in.

They needed two more goals to go through and they went for it. They nearly scored a freak goal in the 68th minute when Bixente Lizarazu's cross flicked off Huthy's head out near our right touchline. The spin on the ball sent it fizzing over Pete and left him helpless but it crashed off the face of the crossbar and bounced away to safety. A few seconds later, Ballack powered a great header past Pete from a corner but Eidur volleyed it off the line with his left foot from his position on the post.

It was seat-of-the-pants stuff for a while but then the pressure lifted. Coley chased a ball into the corner flag and the Bayern defence seemed to think there was no danger. We hardly had anyone in support and they had several defenders back. Coley looked up and swung a cross into the box, then suddenly Didier exploded away from his marker, leapt high in the air and glanced the ball down and past Kahn. It was the killer blow. They needed three goals now to take the game into extra-time and there were only ten minutes left.

Credit to them, they didn't give up. Guerrero turned in a Schweinsteiger cross-shot from close range and Mehmet Scholl, who was a late substitute, clipped in a shot that won the game for them on the night but could not salvage the tie. We kicked off at the restart and the referee blew the final whistle.

Khan and Ballack never followed through on their promise of having a fight after the match. I saw Kahn a good hour after the game and he came up to me and shook my hand and wished me good luck. I didn't really know how to take that. I thought he might try and smack me. But I think these days, altercations like the one we had before the match are forgotten the moment you walk off. I don't think Kahn's a fighter, really.

He's got that mad stare and he was flaring his nostrils before the game like a raging bull but he was Mr Nice Guy afterwards.

A bit later, the whole team went to a restaurant in Munich to wind down. Boris Becker was in there. He's something to do with the Bayern board, I think. He got up and left after about five minutes. I'm not sure if he got the hump with something we did or whether he just didn't fancy being in the same restaurant as the team that had beaten his beloved Bayern. Everyone was buzzing. The semi-finals of the Champions League were beckoning us again and the heartbreak of losing to Monaco at the same stage the previous season suddenly seemed a long way away.

9 The Home Straight

After the Battle of Blackburn, we felt we could see the finishing line. We were on the home straight in the race for our first league title for 50 years and we knew that unless we lost our nerve and collapsed totally, no one was going to catch us. The romantics were hoping that we would clinch the title against Fulham on 23 April, fifty years to the day since we sealed our last championship victory.

We didn't really care about when we did it. The sooner the better was our view. We knew that at the beginning of March we had four successive games against the four bottom teams in the Premiership. We heard all the warnings about those clubs fighting for their lives and being difficult to beat because of it. But the truth was that when we saw matches against Norwich, West Brom, Palace and Southampton, we hoped that might be 12 points.

I never got nervous really. Never got twitchy. Never got caught up in what Sir Alex Ferguson once referred to as 'squeaky bum time'. That was probably because even by the beginning of February, we had a comfortable points cushion and we had a reasonably easy run-in. United had put us under a bit of pressure with a decent run but we had withstood that and, even without Robbie, we were confident we could extend our lead rather than see it whittled away.

There was no hint of complacency about that attitude. It was the opposite. We were getting hungrier and hungrier the closer we got to the title. We wanted to be even more ruthless than before so we could reach our goal as quickly as we could. We were conscious of the fact that we had big tests coming up in the Champions League and that the sooner we won the title, the earlier we could rest key players if they needed it. Winning the Premiership early might give us an advantage if we got to the European Cup Final. That was how we were thinking.

We didn't quite put that into practice when Man City came to Stamford Bridge the Saturday after our victory at Ewood Park. We were jinxed against City. They'd dealt us our only defeat at the City of Manchester Stadium in October and now we just couldn't find a way past them at home.

I made a couple of blocks early on, charging down a shot from Antoine Sibierski and then cutting out a driven cross from Shaun Wright-Phillips, who was causing us plenty of problems on the City right.

After that, we took control. David James spilled a shot from Duffa after half an hour but somehow Kezman stabbed the follow-up wide from a couple of yards out. William nearly put us ahead seven minutes before the interval but Paul Bosvelt cleared his header off the line.

And City should have scored on the stroke of half-time when I slipped as I was trying to cut out a cross from Wright-Phillips.

I realized that the ball was going to go just behind me, tried to change direction and ended up on my backside. The ball ran to Robbie Fowler and I thought he couldn't miss but he stooped low down to try and steer it in and sent his header wide. It would have been his 150th Premiership goal. It was a real let-off.

I got a cut on the lip after a collision with Joey Barton and everything got bad-tempered when Bosvelt pulled Duffa back on the edge of their box. Danny Mills was at the heart of all the bother but it was just handbags.

Just when I thought City had frustrated us again, there was a pinball scramble in their box and the ball broke to Lamps about ten yards out. He made a great connection with it and I thought it was a certain goal. I even flung my arms up above my head to celebrate. But Jamo pulled off one of the saves of the season, flinging himself to his right and palming the ball away. It was one of the best reaction saves I have ever seen.

United closed the gap to nine points after that draw and I'm sure their spirits were raised by the fact that our next game was away at Everton who were still confounding expectations by hanging on to their fourth place in the table ahead of Liverpool and Bolton.

But not long into the game at Goodison, everyone who was still hoping that we might slip up, and saw the Everton game as the last chance to make up ground on us, was cursing the name of James Beattie. Only eight minutes had gone when he chased a loose ball down towards the corner flag. William Gallas was in front of him and I was a bit further towards the byline, ready to shepherd the ball out of play.

I missed it at the time because I was concentrating on the ball, so when Willo went down and ref Mike Riley produced the red card a few seconds later, I had no idea what Beattie had done. It was only when I watched the highlights on television later that I saw what had happened.

What Beattie did was silly. Out of character, too, I thought. He had only just arrived from Southampton for £6 million so he was probably keen to impress his new boss and team-mates and just got a bit too fired up. Their manager David Moyes criticized William for overreacting at first but then when he saw the pictures, he took the criticism back and admitted Beattie was to blame.

I thought it was going to be easy after that but it seemed to get harder. They knew they were up against it and they raised their game. I realized then what a good side they actually were. I'd said earlier in the season how surprised I was that they were doing so well and that there wasn't any way they would stay the course but they proved me wrong. I thought Marcus Bent had a terrific season and Tim Cahill scored a lot of goals from midfield. He was a real handful.

They fought for everything after Beattie was sent off. It all got a bit wild midway through the first half when Cahill and Kevin Kilbane got stuck in with some tasty challenges. It was turning into a good physical battle without ever approaching the level of the Blackburn game although one scything tackle from Cahill on Macca got him a yellow card and a ban from Everton's FA Cup tie with United the following weekend.

Nigel Martyn was on brilliant form. He was so good that day I voted for him in my PFA team of the year. He made one

One of the new generation of Chelsea fans turns out for our parade.

MAIN: Maka stabs in the penalty rebound against Charlton – it was his first goal for about 30 years and it won us the game.

The boss celebrates Maka's late penalty.

With chief executive Peter Kenyon as the celebrations kick off after the Charlton game.

ABOVE: Ricky makes a great tackle on Van Nistelrooy during the win over United in May. It was the first league game I'd missed all season.

LEFT: Clutching the Premiership trophy in the changing room. I didn't want to let it go.

ABOVE: Eidur catches up on a bit of shaving before we show off the Premiership trophy to the fans.

BELOW: It's champagne all round after the Charlton game. I hate the stuff. Spraying it is the best thing for it.

The end of a great day of celebration with the Premiership trophy. It was finally starting to sink in that we'd won it.

The boss and Mr Kenyon at the Samsung factory on the post-season trip to Korea – I didn't go because of my foot operation.

Roman and I, with his son Arkady, on the top deck with the Premiership trophy.

ABOVE: A sea of Chelsea fans celebrating the club's first league title for half a century.

RIGHT: The boss holds aloft the Premiership trophy. He made the difference for us.

BELOW: Robbie grabs the trophy as the parade gets into full swing.

RIGHT: With Lamps and the lads on the top deck. We were amazed at how many people came out to greet us.

OVERLEAF: A moment that will live with me forever – lifting the Premiership trophy after the Charlton game in May.

excellent save from a shot from Duffa that was deflected and pushed away a stinging drive from Lamps. I thought maybe we were going to have another David James situation on our hands but 20 minutes from time we finally got the break-through.

Paolo fired in a great cross from the right and William flung himself at it as it got past their last defender. William's header came down off the bar and landed at Eidur's feet and he tapped it into the net. I got myself booked for dissent near the end and watched with relief when Pete saved Lee Carsley's header from the resulting free-kick. By the end, we were under siege at the back and they even sent Martyn up for dead-balls. But we hung on. It was our ninth 1–0 victory of the season and it moved us back 12 points clear at the top of the table. I got the feeling that day that we had just extinguished the last little bit of hope that our nearest challengers may have been cherishing.

Our hopes of a clean sweep of all four trophies ended the following weekend at St James' Park when we lost to a fourth-minute headed goal from Patrick Kluivert and had Bridgey carried off on a stretcher with his shattered ankle. Winning four trophies was always going to be a close to impossible task but we wanted to win everything we entered and we didn't go down at Newcastle without a fight.

I was suspended for that game and six other players were rested so Carlo Cudicini was captain in my absence. It wasn't the happiest day for him, either. It finished with a sending-off in injury-time after he brought down Shola Ameobi on the edge of the box.

When we lost to Barcelona, too, it was the only time all

season we lost two matches in consecutive games. We put that right when we won the Carling Cup on our return from Barcelona and then at the beginning of March we started our series of games against the bottom four clubs in the Premiership.

Norwich were first up at Carrow Road. They had lost at home to Manchester City the previous Monday, the game that will be remembered for Delia Smith's plea of 'Come on, let's be having you!' at half-time. Fair play to her for that. At least she's passionate about her club.

It was a tough game for us. Norwich were showing the first signs of the comeback that nearly dragged them clear of relegation. It wasn't nearly such a comfortable match as when we had trounced them at the Bridge the weekend before Christmas.

We got a boost before our game kicked off at tea-time when we heard that United had been held to a goalless draw by Palace at Selhurst Park. That would have brought them to within three points of us even though we had two games in hand but they couldn't manage it. That was another chance gone for them to get even remotely close to us. It gave us more of an incentive to beat Norwich and put yet more distance between us and United.

We went close to opening the scoring after eight minutes. Lamps played a clever ball through to Duffa and he lifted his shot over Robert Green as he rushed out to meet him. The ball was on target but a lad called Jason Shackell, who was starting only his second league game for Norwich that day, made a bit of a name for himself with a spectacular diving header clearance off the goal line. I stood back and applauded that one.

But midway through the half, Coley produced a shot that ten men standing on the line couldn't have stopped. He was really coming into his own by this stage of the season and the way he took his goal showed me how much he had matured as a player. He got the ball with his back to goal and got hacked down from behind by Shackell. But he realized the ball was still there so he leapt up and took it on. Marc Edworthy flew in and tackled him next but Coley rode that one, too, and the way to goal opened up for him. He nudged the ball on to his left foot and unleashed a shot from 15 yards that flew into the top corner of the net. He was always a strong character but suddenly there was a real steel about him that was inspiring to see.

The Chelsea fans started taunting Delia then. '*Going down with a soufflé*,' they sang at her. But Norwich got their revenge midway through the second half when Leon McKenzie finally ended our run of not conceding a goal. We had gone 1,025 minutes in the league without our opponents scoring when McKenzie got between me and Paolo and nodded his header past Pete.

I was absolutely gutted. Not just because they were back in the game but because we had lost our record of consecutive clean sheets in the Premiership. Walking back to the centre-circle knowing that we had conceded felt really strange and unfamiliar. I didn't like getting to know that feeling again.

We knew we had a fight on our hands now. Norwich began to think they could win it but the manager brought Kezman on and, two minutes after he got up off the bench, he scored. Norwich only half-cleared one of our attacks, Eidur lobbed a clever pass back into the box, Lamps stretched for it and tried to prod it in but it ran square to Kezman who just had to clip it over the line.

Ten minutes from time, Ricky got his first and only goal of the season to wrap things up. Lamps swung a corner over from the left with pace and power and Ricky rose head and shoulders above everyone else to thump his header over the line.

West Brom were next. The night before we played them, 14 March, Chelsea Football Club celebrated its 100th birthday at a pub opposite the ground called The Butcher's Hook. It used to be called The Rising Sun when the first Chelsea board meeting took place there on 14 March 1905.

Wisey was there and Ruud Gullit, Terry Venables and Claudia Schiffer. There was even a geezer who played in the reserves in the 1930s. His name was Willie Brown and you can see him in team photos with legends like Hughie Gallacher. Willie cut the centenary cake. Mourinho was there, too, a new hero chewing the fat with old ones like Ron Harris and Bobby Tambling. It looked like a great night. The players weren't there, though. We had a new piece of history to create.

West Brom were vastly improved from when we last played them at the end of October. I wanted Southampton to stay up out of the bottom four but I couldn't help but be pleased for Bryan Robson when he worked the miracle and got West Brom safe on the last day of the season.

We played them on a Tuesday night because they represented our game in hand on the rest. We dominated the game from start to finish but they refused to give in and we were sweating on the victory a little bit. But it opened up our lead at the top of the Premiership to 11 points again.

I almost put us ahead in the first minute when I headed Duffa's corner towards goal but Eidur tried to make sure it was going in and managed to put it wide. Nice one, pal. Didier had a series of chances, Coley went close and Lamps whistled a shot wide before we got the goal we needed.

Lamps yet again supplied the killer pass, threading the ball through to Duffa. He crossed and Didier was left with the simple job of turning it in from six yards. They didn't really threaten us at all and Didier should have doubled our lead and his own tally when Lamps played a slide-rule pass down the middle for him. Didier turned Thomas Gaardsoe and tried to curl his shot past Russell Hoult like he had done against Middlesbrough at the Bridge earlier in the season. This time, though, he misjudged his shot a fraction and the ball went inches wide.

I was grateful to Huthy late in the game when he blocked an absolute piledriver from Kanu – with his head! I think he put it there on purpose, too. If he hadn't got in the way, Kanu's shot was coming straight for me. I was standing on the goal line but it was travelling so fast it would have knocked me through the back of the net.

Didier should have had about four goals that night. He missed two more chances in the last 12 minutes. Coley found him in the box with a great cross but he headed it wide and then he lifted a pass from Duffa high over the bar when it looked like it was easier to score. He was getting incredibly frustrated with himself by the end. Still, the one goal he did score was the only one that mattered.

The matches were coming thick and fast now. Four days later, Palace came to the Bridge. I thought they might be the toughest of the sides haunted by relegation to beat because I admire the team spirit Iain Dowie has built at Selhurst Park. He's done a great job at Palace and I'm sure they'll come straight back up next season.

Our manager and him provided quite a contrast on the touchline. Dowie wore a T-shirt and shorts, Mourinho wore a suit and a woollen scarf. If some people thought that was a symbol of the difference in quality between the two teams, the first-half action didn't quite reflect that.

We went ahead after 28 minutes when Lamps scored one of his best goals of the season. He picked the ball up in space about 25 yards out and lashed it into the bottom right-hand corner. He seems to have perfected a shot that he hits with the outside of his right boot that swerves away at the last minute. The keeper never even bothers to dive for them. The Lamps special always leaves them flat-footed.

You could count Lamps's errors this season on the fingers of one hand but when Wayne Routledge mishit a corner to the near post, Lamps tried to sweep it clear but somehow the ball squeezed underneath his foot. It squirted across the box and Aki Riihilahti turned it in from close range despite Ricky's best efforts to block it.

I felt for Lamps. You want the ground to swallow you up when something like that happens. It's bad enough when you make a mistake and get away with it. But when you get punished for it, like I did in the Carling Cup semi-final second leg against United, it's a hundred times worse. All you can do is try and make up for it in the rest of the match but it stays with you.

Palace could have taken the lead just before the break. Pete came to punch a cross and got a reasonable fist on it but it went straight to Gonzalo Sorondo. He knocked it back into the box where Andy Johnson was waiting. Pete was still on the deck and I was on the goal line by myself. Johnson controlled it and then tried to volley it in but he mishit it badly and it went well wide. I breathed a sigh of relief.

We punished them for that miss, too, thanks to a wonderful piece of creativity from Eidur. He got the ball in midfield as we tried to counter-attack. Michael Hughes was marking him tightly but Eidur turned him so comprehensively with a drag-back turn that Hughes fell over on his backside. Eidur was free then. He took the ball and then played it into the path of Coley who took one touch and then creamed it across Gabor Kiraly and into the bottom corner.

Coley had really seized his chance since Robben's injury at Blackburn in February and when Robbie returned in this match after six and a half weeks out, it seemed right that it wasn't Coley who should give way. People had been saying he would automatically be dropped once Robbie came back but the manager kept him on when Robbie got up off the bench with 17 minutes left. I think he wanted to show him he appreciated the efforts he had put in for the team over the past six weeks. He wanted to show him that he accepted he had become a team player.

Kezman got a third goal 12 minutes from time when his tame shot from out wide squirmed through the grasp of Kiraly as he dived forward to catch it and rolled slowly between his legs and over the line. Kezza got a second a minute from the end when he stretched to poke a loose ball over the line after a scramble in the six-yard box.

The international break that followed the Palace game was costly for us. I believe the injuries we sustained in those couple of days shaped our Champions League destiny. We lost Robbie again, this time with a sprained ankle he got playing for Holland. And just as important, we lost Paolo Ferreira who broke a bone in his foot while he was on duty with Portugal. That was the end of his season.

We sent Southampton a step closer to the drop at the beginning of April and when United drew at home on the same day, leaving Arsenal in second place, we were 13 points clear at the top, our biggest advantage of the whole season.

We took the lead at St Mary's after 20 minutes when Lamps's free-kick took a heavy deflection off Rory Delap on the end of the Southampton wall. Antti Niemi had already dived in the other direction and could only watch the ball bounce into the net. It was Lamps' 11th goal of the season and even though Eidur got the next two, Lamps stayed just ahead of him as the club's top scorer in the league when he scored on the last day at Newcastle and finished with 13.

Eidur got his first in the 39th minute after a brilliant run by Johnno. Johnno got the ball about 40 yards out, skipped past a tackle from Graeme Le Saux and then dribbled past two more challenges into the box. He said afterwards that he was on the verge of shooting when he saw Eidur unmarked in the box and squared it to him instead. Eidur took one touch and then lashed it past Niemi.

They got one back midway through the second half when Eidur allowed Rory Delap to cross from the right and Kevin Phillips tucked the ball away from close range. But we saved the best for last. Eidur started a move on the edge of the box that involved Lamps and Didier and Tiago. It was one-touch stuff, complemented by blurs of movement, and when Eidur got the ball back on the right-hand side of the area, he guided his shot across Niemi and into the corner of the net. It was bewitching stuff.

We stumbled the next weekend at home to Birmingham. We were in the middle of our second European epic, against Bayern Munich, when we played Steve Bruce's side. It looked for a while against Birmingham as though we were going to surrender our season-long unbeaten home record. We were proud of that record and proud that we had made the Bridge a fortress. And in the end we managed to preserve it.

They had taken the lead in the 64th minute after the referee gave a free-kick against Coley even though he seemed to have won the ball with a fair tackle. Coley was so disgusted he kicked the ball away which earned him a booking and cost us another ten yards as the ref marched forward with the ball.

It looked like Jermaine Pennant had over-hit the kick when it sailed over Pete's head but Matthew Upson stopped it going into touch and nodded it across goal. Walter Pandiani leathered it towards the net where I was standing in my usual place on the line. I flung myself at it but it bounced up off my chest and arms and into the net. In a way, I was lucky. If I'd kept it out, I might have been sent off for handball. But I didn't feel lucky at the time.

We had gone 22 games without losing a match at the Bridge so we poured forward looking for the equalizer. We got it eight minutes from the end when Lamps crossed for Didier to slot the ball home. We were more relieved about the unbeaten record than anything else.

The midweek game against Arsenal on 20 April felt like a passing of the torch to us. The old champions handing over to the new ones. They had been worthy winners the year before when they had conquered everybody with that remarkable unbeaten season. It felt right that they had re-emerged as our closest challengers after all their mid-season problems. And now we were to be their worthy successors.

Ashley Cole got plenty of stick that night at the Bridge. Most of it was good natured. From the Chelsea fans anyway. They cheered him when he touched the ball and sang his name just to wind the Arsenal supporters up. He had a good game, actually, which was a credit to him in the circumstances.

The closest the game got to a goal was in the second minute when Robert Pires struck a beautiful left-foot volley crashing against the underside of the bar. It was a lovely strike, technically perfect. If it wasn't Arsenal, I might have said it deserved a goal. But then we haven't beaten Arsenal in the league since 1995 when Mark Hughes scored the winner and I was a 14-year-old ball-boy, so we need all the luck against them we can get.

I had a marginally quieter night than I usually get against

THE HOME STRAIGHT 211

Arsenal because Thierry Henry was absent with the injury that was set to keep him out of the FA Cup Final. But I still had a dodgy moment when I made a mess of a hasty clearance and kicked it straight against the legs of Philippe Senderos. The ball bounced into space and Pires pounced on it eight yards out. He looked a certainty to score but he snatched at the shot and dragged it well wide of the far post.

We didn't threaten them much. The game was a bit of stalemate apart from the two Pires chances. Lehmann made one good save with his legs from Didier's shot, Lamps shot just wide of the post in the second half when I would have backed him to score, and Didier spun cleverly on a cutback from Duffa and hooked his shot inches wide of the far post with Lehmann nowhere near it.

I looked across to the bench at the final whistle and saw the manager hugging his staff and shaking hands and I knew we were almost there. We were still 11 points clear at the top and even if we couldn't win the title at home to Fulham now, 50 years to the day after Roy Bentley's side had clinched the title at the Bridge by beating Sheffield Wednesday, it was only a matter of time.

We weren't at our best against Fulham. The first leg of the Champions League semi-final against Liverpool was only a few days away and perhaps our minds were wandering. We had managed to get off to a decent start when Coley put us ahead after 17 minutes, curling a shot past Edwin van der Sar but John Collins equalized when he muscled Ricky out of the way and slipped his shot past Pete a few minutes before half-time.

Robbie came on for Coley at the interval and set up our

second goal for Lamps. It was an almost identical shot to the one he had put just wide of the post against Arsenal. Lamps said later that that miss had been playing on his mind. The goal against Fulham got rid of that bad memory for him.

Four minutes from the end, Eidur put the game out of Fulham's reach when he ran on to a raking through-ball from Tiago just inside their half. He took the ball on until he was one on one with van der Sar and then slid the ball expertly past him. We were within touching distance of the title now.

In fact, if Arsenal had failed to beat Tottenham at Highbury the following Monday, we would have been champions without kicking another ball. Some of the boys would have been quite happy for that to happen but I didn't really want the chase to end like that. I wanted to win it on the pitch and celebrate on the pitch. Not in a hotel room somewhere. I wanted to win it at Bolton the following Saturday. So I was pleased when Arsenal beat Spurs.

Before we played Liverpool on the Wednesday, I had one more important engagement to fulfil. I had been nominated for the PFA Player of the Year Award. The awards dinner was at Grosvenor House Hotel in Park Lane the night after the Fulham game and I felt immensely proud as I walked into the huge downstairs dining room.

Lamps and Big Pete had been shortlisted for the award, too. Thierry Henry, Stevie G and Andy Johnson, my own choice, had also been in the last six. So I was in good company. The best company, actually.

I felt like I was ten-feet tall when they announced my name and I went up to get the trophy. To be voted the best player of the season by the men you play against every week was a sign that they respected me and that was incredibly important to me. I'm not being falsely modest, but it also exceeded my wildest dreams. Before the shortlists were made public, I had been hoping that I was still eligible for the Young Player of the Year award because I thought I might have a chance of winning that.

You look at players like Henry and Stevie G and Lamps and they are going to be up there in the running for this award year after year. To be in the top six once was really the most I thought I could hope for. But when I was on England duty, Stevie and Jamie Carragher said all the Liverpool players had voted for me and that made me feel as honoured as if they had told me that I'd won there and then. I also know I got all of Yeovil's votes. My brother, Paul, plays there. He turned the screw. Suddenly, I thought, 'Fucking hell, I might have a chance.'

Look, I hope I go on to have better seasons than this season just gone. I hope I grow and learn and get wiser and more mature as a player and keep my hunger to improve. But I'm not sure how many more shots I'll get at winning this award and that makes me treasure it even more. A defender hasn't won it for a long time. Not since Paul McGrath won it when he was at Aston Villa in 1993. What a player he was, by the way. No Chelsea player had ever won it before me.

In the future, it might be hard for me to get to this position again and that's why I value winning it this year so highly. I was very nervous when I made my speech but I just wanted to express my gratitude to my fellow professionals and to thank the rest of the lads at Chelsea. People always say this when they win awards but it was theirs as much as mine because without them, none of it would have happened.

I had one glass of wine to try and take the edge off my nerves before I made the speech but that was it. We had Liverpool on Wednesday. A couple of the other lads had come down to support me and the manager had told us all to enjoy ourselves but to make sure that when the dinner ended we got ourselves home to our beds. So I said my goodbyes, wandered back upstairs and out on to Park Lane clutching the trophy in my hands. I felt on top of the world. All my dreams seemed to be coming true at once. Now only Liverpool stood in the way of an appearance in the Champions League Final, the greatest club competition of them all.

10 Walking Alone – Losing to Liverpool

Everybody assumed we would beat Liverpool in the Champions League semi-finals. They were supposed to be just another stepping stone on our route to Istanbul. Okay, so everybody had assumed Juventus would beat them in the quarters, too, but Juventus hadn't turned up in the second leg at the Stadio Delle Alpi and, even without Stevie G in their midfield, Liverpool's defence had managed to keep them at bay.

No one was really talking about the Champions League being Liverpool's destiny yet. There was an email doing the rounds about various coincidences linking 1978 and 1981, years when Liverpool won the trophy, and 2005. It was all to do with mumbo-jumbo like Ken and Deirdre from *Coronation Street* marrying in 1981, when Liverpool beat Real Madrid in the final, and then again in 2005. Prince Charles also got married in 1981 and 2005.

Liverpool beat FC Bruges in the final in 1978, a year when the Pope died and Wales won the Grand Slam in rugby union. Liverpool also lost to that year's league champions in the League Cup Final. All those events were repeated in 2005. It was that kind of stuff. Just stuff to let Liverpool fans cling on to their dream for a bit longer.

If anything, most people thought it was our year. They dismissed those Liverpool coincidences as sentimental garbage. We were the ones who had beaten Barcelona and Bayern Munich. We had knocked out the favourites. We were steaming along. We felt unstoppable. We had momentum. We had the best players. We had the best manager. It felt like it was our year to me. Not someone else's.

I wasn't complacent going into the tie. But I was confident. Maybe that sounds arrogant knowing what we know now but I'm just being honest. Chelsea were 31 points clear of Liverpool in the Premiership at that time and we knew we were the better team. We had beaten them home and away in the league and we had beaten them again in the Carling Cup Final, coming from behind in Cardiff to win 3–2. We thought we had the measure of them.

They weren't a bad side but they were in transition. It was the first season for their new coach, Rafa Benitez, and he had made a lot of changes and brought in a lot of new players. He is clearly a good manager and I am sure Liverpool will improve in the league in the years to come but they were so inconsistent in his first eight months in charge that it had begun to become obvious that they weren't even going to qualify for the Champions League next season by finishing in the Premiership's top four. Everton were in fourth place and Liverpool never caught them. Their only shot at next season's Champions League was to win this season's and then hope

UEFA caved in and changed their rules to let them in. No one really thought it would come to that.

A couple of days before the first leg, they played Crystal Palace at Selhurst Park. Palace were desperately trying to scramble away from relegation and gave it everything. You expect that. But Liverpool were dire. They never looked like getting anything out of it and Andy Johnson won the game for Palace with a clever header. I watched the game with a couple of the lads and when the final whistle went and Liverpool had lost, I turned to someone and said: 'We've got a great chance here.'

Of course, they had a few brilliant players. Any team with Steven Gerrard at its heart has always got a chance, Jamie Carragher is a magnificent central defender, John Arne Riise has got a sweet left foot and Xabi Alonso is a clever foil for Stevie G. But I just didn't feel that they would pose a real goalscoring threat to us. I certainly felt we had more goals in us than them and that we were tighter at the back.

I know it sounds as if we were complacent. We weren't. We knew it would be hard to break them down and we knew that there would be a tremendous atmosphere at Anfield for the second leg. But we thought we were capable of taking a lead north with us and then riding out the storm in Liverpool. We didn't think Liverpool were capable of bridging the gap that the league table proved existed between the two teams.

We knew what the big danger was. The big danger was familiarity. The danger was that it would feel like just two more league games against Liverpool and that we might be too relaxed. A group of us had got together to watch the second leg of their quarter-final with Juve and we were cheering for the Italians. We watched it in a restaurant on the King's Road somewhere, me, Scottie Parker, Bridgey, Duffer, Lamps and Eidur, and we knew what result we wanted.

We knew that if Liverpool won, the semi-final would turn into a kind of up and at 'em English derby. And we didn't want that. The football would be lost in the hype and the hoopla of an all-English clash. But if it was Juve, we thought we would be able to get amongst them and bully them a little bit, perhaps. And most of all, we were confident that we would be able to play better football than them and that our superiority wouldn't be negated by the feverish atmosphere we knew we would face up at Anfield.

The build-up to the first game at the Bridge was fairly relaxed. The mood in the dressing room was focused. We were missing Duffer, who was injured, and Robben still wasn't quite fit enough to make the starting eleven but he was on the bench. As we expected, they started with Milan Baros on his own up front and they sat and defended for all they were worth. They didn't offer a lot coming forward, although Pete did have to make one magnificent save from a looping Baros header after Stevie G had curled in a great cross from the right just before half-time. Pictures of that save were on all the back pages the next morning.

The game was a bit of an anti-climax, really. It seems crazy to say that for such a big game but it never really sparked into life. We both played cagey football. Neither wanted to give away the advantage. Chances were few and far between. The best, by far, fell to Lamps in the first half. Willie got free down the left and put a deep cross to the back post. Coley headed it back across goal and Lamps made a great contact with a right-foot volley. If it had been a couple of inches lower, it would have gone through the roof of the net, he hit it that hard. But somehow, it cleared the bar and Liverpool made the most of their reprieve.

It was just a case of our forwards trying to break them down. They were cautious and I think we were too. We had Didier on his own up front. We didn't even create that many chances. I had a half-chance and I know I should have done better. We just weren't as sharp as usual. Our passes didn't quite have their usual zing and Liverpool were sitting deep and stifling midfield.

Even though Baros was lively and tested Pete with that header, we always thought that, with just him up front, we could deal with their threat. The plan was for Ricky and I to keep tight on him and allow the full-backs to push on more. Makelele was controlling Luis Garcia fairly comfortably, too, but we seemed to tire a little bit and we could not break them down.

We never got another chance as good as Lamps's in the first half. The manager brought Robben on with half an hour to go but he couldn't make any headway either. Kezman came on later but he didn't get any joy. Credit to Jamie Carragher and Sami Hyypia that night. They were absolutely superb. Steve Finnan, too. They did not make any mistakes and we couldn't find a way through.

There was lukewarm applause at the end. No one quite

knew what to make of it. If felt as if the tie still hadn't really started properly. It was almost as if the first half of the tie had been 90 minutes of shadow boxing and the real fight with the bloodied lips and the black eyes was going to take place up at Anfield.

But it wasn't all doom and gloom when we got back into the changing room. The manager came in and said it was a great result for us and that we would go up to Anfield and win. Xabi Alonso had been booked in the closing seconds of the game for a tackle from behind on Eidur so he would be missing from the second leg. Liverpool said afterwards that Eidur had got Alonso booked deliberately but that was the closest the game came to provoking any kind of controversy.

We also had the decent consolation of having kept a clean sheet and, even given the atmosphere we knew we would be facing, we were confident of going there and scoring goals. Then the pressure would be back on them. We were hoping we could soak the pressure up in the first five or ten minutes of frenzy and then get at them and score and be home free.

The following Saturday, we went to Bolton and won the title. That was a wonderful day but by the time we got back to the team hotel in Preston, the celebrations were almost over. The lads were a little bit distracted, and I could tell that even though we had just won Chelsea's first championship for 50 years, the boys had just one thing on their mind: Liverpool.

The big talking point, more than anything to do with team selection, had been around what the atmosphere was going to be like at Anfield. Juventus had been unsettled by it and were 2–0 down inside 25 minutes when they went there at the beginning of April. Roared on by a capacity crowd, Liverpool had run Juventus ragged in that first half. And since then, all the old legends about how the Kop were Liverpool's 12th man and how they could suck a ball over the line had been wheeled out again.

There's no point denying there's a special atmosphere there. A lot of other grounds seem to have lost it, particularly with the growth of the corporate sector at stadiums these days. But there's still an intensity about Anfield that they are proud of. Somehow, they seem to have kept hold of more of their traditional fan base than other clubs.

There's a kind of furious pride about Liverpool fans as if they're always striving to recapture something that they've lost and that they won't rest until they've done it. European matches mean something extra to them because so much of their heritage is caught up in the four European Cups they had won before this year. You could feel that all around you when our coach drove slowly through the Shankly Gates an hour and a half before the kick-off and pulled up outside the main entrance.

There's a great feel about the place. You can sense the old glories. There's an honours board upstairs with all the famous names on it and the number of caps they won for their countries while they were at Anfield. Dalglish, Rush, Lawrenson, Souness, Hansen, Thompson, Hughes, Keegan. The history comes at you from everywhere.

I've been there a few times now. This time, I didn't even notice the famous old 'This Is Anfield' sign on a wall above your head when I wandered out to have a little walk on the pitch an hour or so before the game. There was a time when the very sight of that sign was supposed to strike fear into Liverpool's opponents but their invincibility has disappeared since then. By the time of the second leg, they were 33 points behind us in the league. While we were winning at Bolton, they were scraping a draw at home to Middlesbrough.

I think their league form lulled us a little bit. It conned us. I said to Lamps when we were in the dressing room about an hour before the game that it felt too relaxed in there. It wasn't that people weren't pumped up. But we were all so confident, because we go to Anfield every season and because the Premiership table told us we were so much better than them. It didn't feel like the build-up to a Champions League semi-final. That's why we'd all wanted Juventus instead. We wouldn't have been relaxed if we'd been about to play them.

The manager put the points difference between the two teams up on the board in the dressing room. It screamed out to us how much better we were than them. It was there in big red ink, the first thing we saw as we walked in. I looked at it. 'No way will we lose this game tonight,' I thought.

We could hear little bits of the atmosphere before the game. We have our music quite loud, though, so it wasn't overwhelming. We tried to block it out with a bit of Luther, a bit of Usher, a bit of R & B. And when you walk out on to a pitch, it's as though you seal yourself into a suit that blocks out sound and makes you oblivious to everything except the other 21 players and the task that lies ahead of you.

Even in that context, though, I have to say that the Liverpool fans that night at Anfield were amazing. When the two teams walked up the steps and out on to the pitch to line up for the Champions League anthem, I have never heard anything like it before and I don't think I ever will again. It is the best atmosphere I have ever played in.

The gaffer just told us to forget the atmosphere and we knew he was right. He told us there were a lot of players who would give everything to be in the position we were in, so close to the Champions League Final. He told us the crowd wasn't playing. We were. I did the speech in the huddle in the dressing room that night. 'It's not about the fucking crowd,' I said. 'It's about us, eleven players in a team.' Then I walked out into that cauldron and heard that singing and saw that passion.

Going out there was an amazing walk. The hairs on my arms were standing up. It must have given the Liverpool players a tremendous lift. But it lifts you even though you are the away team. To see a spectacle like that is inspiring to anyone. If you love football, you've got to love a night like that. I just kept looking around, trying to take it all in. I wasn't daunted by it but it was amazing. I wish there were more crowds like that.

On the Kop, they were singing 'You'll Never Walk Alone'. They were all holding their scarves up. So there was a wall of scarves to go with the wall of noise. Apart from the volume, it looked spectacular, too. And then in the seconds before the referee blew his whistle for the start of the match, the whole stadium let out this great long roar as if they were going to power Liverpool to victory by a triumph of the will.

They came at us like a blitzkrieg in those early minutes. Before we had had time to settle, Stevie G flicked the ball over our defence and Baros lifted it over Pete. Geremi came in from one side and the ball spun back a bit, then Willie cleared it off the line. It's all a blur to me and I haven't been able to bring myself to watch any of the game again. I know simulations suggest it wasn't a goal. I wish now that we had kicked up more of fuss about it because there wasn't the kind of furious reaction you might have expected in that situation when there was a real doubt about whether the ball had crossed the line.

It wouldn't have changed the decision but it might have encouraged the ref to right the wrong later in the game and give us the benefit of the doubt over another important decision. Perhaps it was because it was so early, but it all seemed a bit surreal. The noise was still deafening. The crowd was still going bananas. Our supporters, tucked away at the opposite end to the Kop were singing as best they could.

Because only four minutes had gone when Garcia scored, I don't think we were too distraught about going behind. There was still no doubt in our minds that we were going to beat them. The manager had instilled in us the belief that we were better than them and that it didn't matter if we went a goal behind because we would come back and prove our superiority.

Predictably, they were a different proposition to the rather lacklustre team we had met at Stamford Bridge. The spirit was in them. Baros was chasing everything and not giving us any time. Stevie G was there as well. He's the last man you want running at you and closing you down and getting amongst you. He was even putting pressure on our wide men when they were carrying the ball and we had been expecting to make quite a lot of inroads from our full-backs making forays down the flanks. Stevie helped to cut off that source of supply.

I'm a massive fan of Stevie's. I think he and Lamps are the

best two midfield players in the world. They can change a game and they can win a game. Somebody like Stevie believes and he gets everyone else believing. They were clinging to their lead but someone like him draws a team closer together in a situation like that and breeds a determination in them. If you've got a player like him at a club, you fight tooth and nail to keep him.

If there was one player I had to pick out as my favourite player in world football outside Chelsea, it would be Gerrard. Not only because of what he was to go on to achieve in Istanbul, but because of the influence he wields over his team. I know him from meeting up with England and he's a great lad. I like everything about him. His character. His spirit. His passing. His tackling. His shooting from range. He's a class act. I watched some of the highlights of the Champions League Final and I loved the way that after he scored the header that pulled the score back to 3–1, he ran back to the centre-circle windmilling his arms around to gee up the crowd and tell the rest of the players that Liverpool weren't dead yet.

He played in a few different positions this season and he took plenty of stick in Liverpool when people questioned his loyalty to the team at various times. But he showed real strength of character by refusing to be affected by those ups and downs. He kept his eyes on the prize and he was rewarded with the greatest night he will probably ever have as a footballer. Short of winning the World Cup with England anyway.

People talk about the wages footballers earn these days but you can't buy that kind of inspiration and that kind of leadership and that kind of refusal to accept that a task is beyond you. Maybe earlier in the season, he had thought Liverpool did not have the players to mount a realistic tilt at the Champions League but Benitez had a word with him about that and he did more than anybody to get them to the stage where he was walking up to that dais in Istanbul and planting a kiss on that trophy.

His presence in the Liverpool team and the heroic way Jamie Carragher had been defending were the only things that made me uneasy about the away leg. But as the night wore on and we still couldn't claw that goal back, my unease started to grow. Liverpool had tightened up in midfield. It was harder for Lamps and Makelele to get free so we were forced to go a little bit longer and Hyypia and Carragher were winning everything in the air and it was coming straight back. We had also thought that Stevie might sit back a bit more and we were a bit surprised he was pushed so far forward. We had to adjust to that.

Rather than playing the ball through midfield, we started to get Pete going longer with his goal kicks with the intention of winning the second ball. But that didn't work either. Carragher was dominant that night. He still doesn't get the credit he deserves. He was another who was superb in the final. The way he kept flinging himself into intercepting crosses even though he was crippled by cramp in extra-time made me wince because it was clear he was in a lot of pain. But the interceptions he made were absolutely vital. If he hadn't made them, AC Milan would have won the Champions League and the Liverpool fairy tale would have been over. Stevie G was named the man of the match that night in Turkey but Carra was not far behind.

So suddenly, it seemed like these players whose perform-
ances had only got them to fifth place in the Premiership had
suddenly been transformed into epic heroes in front of us at
Anfield. It was all about 'they shall not pass' for them and if
they could not make a tackle, they flung themselves at the pass
or the shot to try and block it. They didn't outplay us but they
played well enough so that we couldn't outplay them.

It worked in their favour, too, that Didi Hamann was playing instead of Xabi Alonso. Hamann was playing a blinder.
You only needed to see the difference he made when he came
on in the second half of the final in Istanbul to realize what a
class act he is. On a night like this, when Liverpool were
defending for their lives, he was the best midfielder they had
to do a job shielding their back four and stifling the best
intentions of Lamps and Eidur.

We had flashes of hope. Didier burst on to a through-ball
from Coley but couldn't get past Jamie Carragher, who was
immense again for Liverpool. In the second half, we won a
couple of free-kicks in promising positions but Didier couldn't
get either of them on target. We got another and Lamps took
it this time. He hit it sweet and true and I thought it was
arrowing straight into the bottom corner but suddenly Dudek
flung himself to his right and palmed it away. Lamps held his
head in his hands. I was aware time was starting to run out.
I couldn't quite believe it.

Robbie came on with just over 20 minutes to go and even
though he wasn't fully fit, he gave them something else to think
about. He got a shot off pretty soon but Carragher flung
himself at it and blocked it. A few minutes later, Robbie looked

as if he might be about to squirm free and into a position of real danger but Stevie G stopped him with a shuddering tackle.

I looked up and there were 80 minutes on the clock. The gaffer had just brought Robert Huth on. I looked over at the manager and gestured that I was going to move up front, too. He told me to wait five minutes. I started to panic a little bit. For the first time, I started to see that it was all slipping away. Arsenal and Manchester United have got the experience to keep the ball and believe that they will make things happen anyway. But with ten minutes to go, I wanted to go up and make something happen.

When I saw the clock going to 88 minutes, my eyes started filling up with tears. I thought 'Fucking hell, we've blown the chance again.' There was still one opportunity to come. I went up and won a header back across goal. I fell over and got myself back up, then saw the shock of blonde hair. I thought, 'Eidur, it's gone to Eidur, that's a fucking goal!' If it was going to fall to anyone, you would want him or Lamps on the end of it, especially that late on.

I saw him strike it cleanly and I saw Didier just miss it on the far post and it went out into touch. I can't explain quite how I felt. I felt a kind of sinking feeling. It was like everything went from my body. We had had one more chance. This was it. And then it was all gone in a split second. Eidur said it touched Carragher's leg and who knows what would have happened if we had been awarded a corner. But not for the first time in the competition, and not for the last, there was something about the game that felt that, for Liverpool, it was just meant to be.

I was distraught after the game. I didn't know what to do

with myself. What I couldn't quite comprehend was that for the second year in succession, we had lost a Champions League semi-final we were supposed to win. For the second year in succession we had got so close to the final, the match that is the Holy Grail for every professional footballer, and then we had blown it.

We should have beaten Monaco in the semis the year before. We all knew that. It had been ours for the taking. We were level at 1–1 early in the second half and they got a man sent off. We could have killed that tie there and then. But Claudio Ranieri made a couple of substitutions he later admitted were mistakes, Fernando Morientes got a second goal for them with 12 minutes left and Nonda got a third a few minutes later.

Then, in the second leg at the Bridge, we were 2–0 up and going through before they pulled it back to 2–2. That felt desolate. To know we had lost a game we should have won: A game that would have given us our shot at immortality against Porto and the man who was to become our coach. But this night at Anfield, this was worse.

Because after the desperation of losing to Monaco, we had climbed back up the mountain, hauled ourselves back into position, gone through those emotionally draining matches against Barcelona and Bayern and put ourselves in pole position again. And then, when we were exactly where we wanted to be, when everything was in place, it fell around our ears just as it had a year earlier. How many chances do you get at something like that?

I wanted to run straight back down the tunnel when the final whistle went. But I went up to Stevie and Jamie. I said to Stevie:

'Go and lift it now geezer. Go and lift it for yourself and for your club.' I said the same to Carra as well. They have been absolutely brilliant this season. I would go and watch Liverpool just for Carra. People talk about me pressuring Sol Campbell and Rio Ferdinand for the centre-half position with England but I always interrupt them and tell them not to forget about Jamie. He and I are quite similar characters and players. Sometimes we might have a bad game but you know we are still giving it absolutely everything. I walked over to him. 'Make sure you go and fucking win it now,' I said. 'This is your year.'

It was hard to go over to them because a big part of me just wanted to get back to the dressing room away from the cameras and the eyes of the crowd and just wallow in my despair. When you have got grown men on the pitch crying because they have just lost something they have worked so hard for, well, the rawness of that can be quite shocking. William Gallas was beside himself with despair. A few of us were, to be fair. A few of the lads went straight in but I just felt, as captain of the side, it was my duty to go and wish Stevie and Jamie good luck. Even though it was killing me, I knew I had to do it.

Before the game, the manager had said, 'Whatever happens tonight, no tears, put on a brave face.' But when I heard the final whistle, I broke down. I was crying. People were saying to me that it wasn't our year and that our chance would come again. But I was in bits. Willie was the same. And Eidur. The manager came over and said 'no tears' again. 'We will have our time,' he said.

When I got back to the dressing room, that was the lowest I have ever felt in football. I know when I walk in there next year, whenever we play Liverpool in the league, it's all going to come flooding back and I'm already dreading that. I can tell you one thing for sure: I won't be sitting in the same spot in the dressing room. I'll be in a different spot, doing everything I can to break the spell of that semi-final.

I sat there in the dressing room that night with a towel over my head, just crying. Roman was there. He was gutted. He was really disappointed. He couldn't get his head round how Liverpool could have beaten us. Straight away, he said: 'How can we improve?' That's the way he thinks. Always moving forwards. Always moving upwards.

Nobody wanted to move from their seat. We sat there for an age. No one wanted to look up. No one wanted to speak. No one wanted to move. No one wanted to get up to get showered. No one wanted to get changed. Nobody wanted to answer questions from the press. No one wanted to run the gauntlet of the Liverpool supporters going to the bus. It was an hour and a half before the lads were out of the dressing room.

The manager said his bit. He tried to pick us up because he knew we were all on the floor. But he kept it brief. He had been desperate to keep hold of the trophy he had won with Porto the year before and that dream had died for him, too. It was a night where we all had to struggle with our thoughts and I had to fight myself to make sure mine didn't get too dark.

I kept thinking about something Marcel Desailly once said to me. He had done everything it was possible to do in his career. He'd won the World Cup, the European Championships, the

Champions League, Serie A. He was a top man and a big influence on me when he was Chelsea captain. He said to me once that in the Champions League, you get one chance at it and if you don't take it, it doesn't happen.

That haunted me that night on Merseyside as we drove away from Anfield past Stanley Park on our left and the streets of tightly packed terraced houses on our right. We were big favourites to beat Monaco the season before and we blew it. This year, once we had beaten Barcelona we thought our name was on the trophy. That whole tie was such an epic, such an upheaval, such an achievement, that we felt nothing could be harder than that. We felt once we had overcome that, we could overcome anything. Getting past Bayern was tough, too. We thought we had done the hard work but then we blew it against another side we should have beaten. To blow two great opportunities feels very cruel but I have to keep believing we will put it right soon.

The team coach was a strange and quiet place. You have to remember we had lost only one league game and one cup tie all season so after the vast majority of our away trips, we get back on the coach and there is food and there is banter flying about and there are people joking and laughing and talking about the victory that we have just achieved. And then you have a night when you lose and there was nothing.

There was silence. We couldn't even look at each other. It was 40 minutes of nothing all the way to Manchester Airport. It was like a ghost bus. Mobile phones were ringing but nobody was answering them. We were like the men who weren't there. Nobody could bear to speak to the people who were calling to try to commiserate with them. There was nothing anybody could say. We just had to learn to try to live with it.

We had a restaurant planned for that weekend. We cancelled it. I don't think anyone ventured out for three or four days. Everyone just trained and went home to lick their wounds. It was a hard blow but I'm doing my best now to try to find a positive in it.

If we had won the lot this season, perhaps the incentive to chase everything again next year might have been diminished. As it is, we won't just be hungry for the Champions League this season. We will be ravenous. The Chelsea team will be clawing their way towards that trophy because it has dashed our hopes in successive seasons and I can't bear the idea of having to suffer that pain a third season in a row. It would be too much. We are desperate for the Champions League now.

This season, we said the Premiership was our goal. It was the one. And it feels magnificent to have won a championship medal. But missing out in the Champions League is like an itch I can't scratch. Not until next year anyway. Next year, we're going to give everything to win that trophy. We know what it takes to get close. But that isn't good enough. We have to take the extra step now. We have to go one better next time. Other teams will be stronger but we will be stronger, too.

I was in Dubai with my dad and my girlfriend when Liverpool played AC Milan in Istanbul. I was recovering from an operation to my toe which was taking a while to heal. I was generally feeling a bit sorry for myself and trying not to think too much about the fact that I should have been in Turkey, not Dubai.

I said to my dad and my girlfriend that I didn't want to watch the game. I told them they could watch it if they wanted to but I wouldn't be joining them. So for much of the evening, I was in a restaurant and on the phone to my agent Aaron. Then I started getting texts from Lamps. It was 1–0 Milan, then 2–0 Milan, then 3–0 Milan. It sounded like it was a rout. I didn't really have any stomach for watching that. I went back to my hotel and went to bed.

Then Aaron phoned me again and said, 'Oh my God, Stevie just scored!' A couple of minutes later, he was back on. 'Oh my God, it's 3–2!' It was just before 2 am Dubai time but I got out of bed, put some flip-flops on, some shorts and a T-shirt and went downstairs to the bar. They were showing it on a big screen and there were loads of Liverpool supporters in there. But I had to watch it. I'd been gripped by the drama of it by then. And as I walked into the bar, there was this massive roar because Xabi Alonso had just smacked his penalty rebound into the roof of the net. It was 3–3.

Loads of the Liverpool supporters grabbed me and started going on about how gutted I must be not to be playing. Give them a badge for stating the bleeding obvious. That didn't improve my mood a lot but I sat there and found myself willing Liverpool to win it. When you see lads you count as your friends playing the game of their lives, you want them to win and you want the English team to win. When Dudek made the double save from Shevchenko, I texted a few of the lads. 'It's their year,' I said.

But when I saw Stevie lift that Champions League trophy with its big jug ears and all the names of the famous clubs inscribed on its side, I thought, 'I want that.' I phoned Lamps that night and I said to him that that has to be our trophy next year. It's not an empty boast. I want it. I want it badly.

11 The End of 50 Years of Hurt

Every player dreams of winning the league title. If you do that, it sets you apart. It gives you something to show for your career. It gives it meaning and respectability. It's something no one can ever take away from you. It establishes you as part of an elite. Since I broke into the Chelsea team, a league title had always been my goal. I had always hoped the day would come when I was able to hold a Premiership medal in my hand but there have been occasions when I wondered if it was all going to go wrong.

Football is so unpredictable. Your own fortunes can wax and wane. You can be on top of the world and an injury can ruin you. You can be valued by one manager and discarded by another. Your club can be in rude health and then, for any number of reasons, it can slide into a decline. And so, yes, there have been occasions when I worried the opportunity might be about to slip away.

The one that sticks out in my mind was the last day of the 2002–03 season. We were playing Liverpool to decide who got the last Champions League place. It was when Ken Bates was still the chairman and it was an uncertain time for everyone at Chelsea. The players had heard consistent rumours that we were going into administration if we lost that game.

It was a mad day. There was so much riding on it, it hardly bears thinking about. If we had lost, we might have been heading for obscurity. The club might have been in a lot of trouble. But we won. We were in the Champions League for the first time since 1999 and, a few weeks later, Roman bought the club.

That seemed an awful long time ago when we began the journey north for the game at Bolton on the last day of April. Thankfully, that kind of uncertainty has been banished at the new Chelsea. As we flew up to Manchester Airport, we weren't struggling for our very survival any more. We were travelling there knowing that if we beat Sam Allardyce's side, Chelsea would be champions for the first time since Roy Bentley's team won the title back in 1955.

Sir Alex Ferguson had warned us we would find it tough up north. Earlier in the season, when United were still pressing us, he had told anyone who had wanted to listen that we still might come unstuck when we played in some of the Lancashire strongholds where we have struggled in previous years.

I think he genuinely thought there was a chance that because none of us were really accustomed to the sometimes intolerable pressure that can come with the title run-in, that some of us in the Chelsea side might freeze in the glare of the limelight. But he was also hinting that we were still soft touches and that he thought we might fold when it came to the crunch. Effectively, he was saying of Chelsea, 'They don't like it up 'em.' He was playing his mind games again but this time we were beyond him.

There was something particularly sweet about the idea of winning the Premiership at Bolton. We had had so many problems there in the past that to win the title there would be a symbol of quite how much we had improved. I remember coming back from White Hart Lane in mid-January after we had won there 2–0 and hearing on the radio that Stelios Giannakopoulos had won the game for Bolton against Arsenal at the Reebok. I felt a slight sense of foreboding about the fact that we still had to go there, too, because since I had been at the club we had never done well there.

It had become a bit of a joke. We had a team packed with amazing talents like Marcel Desailly and Gianluca Vialli and Gianfranco Zola, and yet we could never win at Bolton Wanderers. We had been bullied by them in the past. But we had shown at Blackburn that we weren't a team who could be bullied any more. We had shown that our foreign boys were up for the fight, too. After Blackburn, we had felt that whatever anybody wanted to throw at us, we could deal with it and we were going to go all the way.

Some people had pointed out that, back in 1983, Chelsea had scraped a 1–0 win at Bolton's old ground, Burnden Park, that had saved the club from relegation to the old Division Three. That seemed like a good omen. And Mourinho had predicted even before the season had begun that this would be the match when we sealed the title. Sometimes, there is something spooky about the way he predicts what is going to happen. He did it when he said he wanted Barcelona in the second round of the Champions League. Sure enough, we got Barcelona. He said we would win the title at Bolton. Right again.

We respected Bolton and we all knew that Sam Allardyce had put together a great side up there, a side that deserved all the success they were getting. I have never been one for patronizing them. I admire their style of play. They are hard but they are honest. They had some terrific players and we knew it would be tough. But we didn't fear them any more. There was no apprehension as we flew up there the day before the game.

We weren't thinking about Liverpool any more by then. We had closed that off in our minds. All we were thinking about was the chance of winning the club's first championship for 50 years. For the first time, we were going there and knowing that it was in our own hands. It didn't matter what Arsenal did any more. If we won, there was nothing they could do about it. If we won, the title that was theirs would now be ours. We felt it was going to happen. Usually, the lads are a bit cautious about predicting what's going to happen. You don't want to tempt fate. But on that trip, we all brought our camcorders and I asked the kit man Stuart Bannister if he would video a few bits from the game. I asked him to video the manager getting up to shout instructions, that sort of thing. I knew it was going to be a special day. The manager had said it was going to happen and he was so confident, it spread to the rest of us.

We stayed at the Preston Marriott, on the edge of the town, and on the way in to the Reebok Stadium we were talking about how important it was to get the job done against Bolton so we could concentrate fully on the second leg of the Champions

League semi-final against Liverpool, which we still expected to win. The plan after that was to rest a few of us during the last few games of the league season and get Paolo Ferreira back from injury before we got to the Champions League Final in Istanbul. We would have a full-strength squad and we would be raring to go. We were expecting that we would be playing against AC Milan. As it was, they nearly blew it against PSV Eindhoven in the semis as well. It might easily have been a Liverpool–PSV final.

But we weren't thinking about those kinds of permutations when we went out on to the pitch at the Reebok before the start of the game. There was an air of expectancy among our fans that sent a new buzz through us all. There were more of them there than usual at Bolton. You can hardly blame them for not fancying that particular trip much over recent years, given the way we often perform there. But this time they were ranged over two tiers behind the goal to our right as we wandered out of the tunnel. There was a party atmosphere out there and maybe that lulled us because we didn't start very brightly.

We were missing Duffa and Robbie and the manager left Coley on the bench. He knew that it wasn't going to be pretty. He knew Bolton would throw everything at us. So he started with Geremi at right-back and Jiri Jarosik in midfield to give us a bit more height and muscle to cope with their tactics and bolster us at set-pieces. He'd seen the way Bolton had played in the draw at the Bridge earlier in the season, he knew they would fight right until the bitter end and he wanted to pit our steel against theirs.

Big Pete was busy in the first half. He had to make a smart save from Stelios and another from a Gary Speed header. Fernando Hierro pinged a shot in and we were having a bit of trouble with El-Hadji Diouf on our left flank. Diouf's a good player. I know he's had his problems after the way he spat in the face of Arjan de Zeeuw in the match against Portsmouth and I agree that that is one of the worst things you can do to another player. But I have never had a problem with him. I have never had that much to do with him, to be honest. I've certainly never had a confrontation with him. And in a way, I like him. I hope he's learned from his mistakes because I think the fans appreciate that he has got a bit of fire in his belly. He's got a talent, too, which is probably why they just gave him a new long-term contract.

He caused us problems throughout the match with his dribbling and his crosses from the right. We also got a piece of luck when Kevin Davies directed a free header straight at Petr when he was unmarked. I was impressed with the way Davies played. He was strong and he was awkward and he worked very hard. He had a rough time for a while when he was at Blackburn but I think he's a class act. He's underrated.

He caught me with an elbow just before half-time. I don't know whether it was intentional but it went right in my eye. I've had plenty of elbows before but this one put me down for about five minutes. The physio was worried it might have cracked my socket. After he had treated it for a while, I felt just about able to carry on. I couldn't see properly but it was so close to the break, I thought I might as well carry on and see if it improved during the interval. I got back inside the changing rooms and walked straight into a bollocking from the manager.

I don't think he had been that angry before in his time at Chelsea. Perhaps he sensed that we were starting to think the title was a formality. Perhaps he thought our minds were wandering forward to the second leg of the Champions League semi-final against Liverpool. Anyway, he was livid. He was asking us whether we wanted to win the Premiership or not. He said that he could put a Chelsea shirt on his back or Steve Clarke's back and both of them would play with more determination and passion than us. He tore us apart, which had only happened once or twice through the rest of the season.

It worked. We were much better second half. We were up for it now. We got wound up with Diouf when he pulled Geremi down. He got booked and we got a free-kick in a useful position midway inside their half out towards the right touchline. The free-kick was knocked in high and long and when Didier knocked it down, Lamps picked it up inside the box. Bolton were already complaining about some kind of infringement on the edge of the area but Lamps cut back inside Vincent Candela and slotted the ball past Jussi Jaaskelainen.

I nearly put us further ahead a couple of minutes later when I launched myself at a low cross from Lamps but it was just too far ahead of me. The manager brought Huthy on for Drogba to make sure we kept it tight but Bolton started to bombard us. They poured so many men forward that we knew we had a chance of catching them on the break and 14 minutes from the end, we wrapped it up.

Big Pete had just made an amazing reaction save from an inadvertent Geremi back-header that was going in at the near post. A few minutes later, they got another corner and it ran long and wide. Eidur retrieved it and played it down the line to Makelele who played it first time to Lamps, who was hurtling down the middle and clear through on goal. As I watched him, he seemed to be running for ever. I know it was only a couple of seconds but it felt like it took him about five minutes to get from the halfway line to the point where he was confronting their keeper. But it was a classic Chelsea counter-attack. Ricky was right there with him as he bore down on Jaaskelainen but Lamps used him as a decoy, dropped his shoulder, took the ball round the keeper's flailing right hand and slid the ball into the net.

What a feeling that was. I knew it was ours in that moment. I knew that that was the Premiership. Before I realized it, I was leaping all over Lamps. We were all engulfed in a great big pile of bodies, everybody lost in celebration. We were there dancing in front of our own fans. It was perfect. For a minute, I forgot there was still a game to finish. Nothing seemed to matter. It was pure joy and I looked into the faces of the fans who were going mad with the emotion of it all and felt so happy for them. Fifty years is a long time to go without winning the league and I'm sure there were some supporters who thought it would never happen. It must have been one of the longest goal celebrations in the history of the Premiership and even when play restarted, I was running around, with my vision blurred again, this time because my eyes were filling up with tears on account of what we were about to achieve.

I felt especially for some of the older fans who had waited all their lives to see this moment. And I was so happy for Lamps, in particular. Scoring those goals on that day will be with him for the rest of his days. What an achievement. What a thing to be able to tell your kids and your grandchildren about. The night before the game, Lamps, Eidur and I had followed our usual routine. We all get a massage one after the other and have a couple of coffees. We were sitting there trying to imagine what the feeling would be like of scoring the goal that won Chelsea the Premiership. We were all in our own little worlds thinking about it. I said to Lamps when the game finished that we had all been talking about it but he was the one that actually did it.

He still seemed to have the freshest legs of all of us. The way he kept kicking on and scoring so many important goals was amazing. His second goal at the Reebok was his 18th of the season. He was our top scorer. Which is quite an achievement for a midfield player who does his fair share of defensive duties as well. He deserved his Footballer of the Year award he won from the football journalists.

When the final whistle went, I wanted to celebrate with Lamps first. He and I have been through a lot together as young professionals, good and bad. I was just breaking through at Chelsea when he got his big move from West Ham and there were people trying to put question marks against him and the £11 million fee the club paid for him. I have seen him work so hard and improve so much that I knew what this day at the Reebok meant to him just as surely as he knew what it meant to me.

Out there on the pitch, in the melee of triumph, we ran over to our supporters and stayed there celebrating with them. 'Let's

not go back in,' I said to him. 'Let's just stay out here as long as
we can and remember this.' I lost track of time then. I heard the
Bolton fans applauding us, which was a classy touch. When I
finally looked round, everyone else was making their way back
to the tunnel. But Lamps and I were still singing and dancing
and kissing our shirts. We were almost delirious with the
excitement of what we had done. It was the biggest day of our
footballing lives. I got him in a headlock. We were like little
kids again.

It meant even more because we were both ever-present in
the league up until then. Even when there was an opportunity
to have a rest, we both wanted to keep playing. My target was
to play every game of the season and Lamps was the same. I
wasn't quite able to do it because I had to have an operation on
my toe that kept me out of the last two league games. But for
him to play in every single match the year we won the title is an
amazing achievement. I would have loved to have done that.

Roman was already in the dressing room when we got back
in. Everybody was spraying each other with champagne.
I don't know where the bottles were coming from. I sprayed
Roman with champagne, too. He looked like he didn't have
a care in the world. He was loving it. He was drenched, too.
He always comes in after the games and asks how we are
feeling. He wants to know what's going on. He'll talk about
the opposition sometimes. He wants to learn. Sometimes, he
will come into team meetings and sit at the back. Then he
will come out and watch us train. He wants that involvement
and that communication with the lads. I have spoken to other
lads at other clubs and none of them have that. We're very

lucky to have an owner who takes such a pride in the club.

It was great to have him in that changing room. All the lads were dancing and drinking together. I could see the manager was starting to get a little bit uneasy. He was already thinking about Liverpool. He said we should just have one glass of champagne and then go back to the hotel and all have a nice meal together and a beer. It was so raucous in there that even the physios were getting nervous.

I got Roman and took him out to the fans. After an eternity of celebrating, I went up to the top floor of the stadium to do an interview with the press boys. I was clutching my shirt in a little plastic bag. I didn't want to let that shirt of all shirts out of my sight. When I got back downstairs, I walked out of the front entrance and there were thousands of Chelsea fans singing and cheering all around the team coach. The police and some stewards had formed two lines so there was a narrow corridor for us to walk down to get on the coach. When I climbed aboard, I could hear some thuds coming from the roof. Didier and Coley had climbed up through the skylight. They were dancing on top of the bus.

I wanted to get up there, too. But Coley said he had tried a little dance move and he had nearly fallen off. That would have looked good. It would have been Steve Morrow breaking his arm when Tony Adams dropped him after the 1993 League Cup Final, and then some. So I contented myself with poking my head out through the skylight, getting my camcorder out and recording the sight of all those happy faces yelling out their congratulations and their joy. Out there, in the middle of a new industrial estate with its fast-food restaurants and its Ibis

Hotel, a few hundred yards from the M61, a new Chelsea team was celebrating putting the past behind it.

By then, the gaffer had disappeared. No one quite seemed to know where he was. There was a rumour that he was on the bus. We got on the bus and he wasn't there. Then a few of us tried to text him but he was calling his family in Portugal. It turned out he was already on his way back to the hotel in a club minibus. I think Frank Steer had been detailed to drive him back. He had said he wanted this to be our day and for all the attention to be focussed on us. I guessed he was already back at the Preston Marriott looking through his notes on the Liverpool game, already starting to plot the fine details of what we hoped was going to be another night of glory for the club. That's the kind of bloke he is.

On the journey back, we sang a song to Bridgey and Scottie and Paolo on their mobile phones because they weren't there with us. Cars were honking their horns at us and we were singing and cheering. A lot of Chelsea fans followed us in their cars so it was like a cavalcade. We got back to the hotel and there was a wedding on. The bride and groom were just coming out of the front door when our coach pulled up so the bride got a few good-natured wolf whistles.

We had dinner and I went to my room and played computer with Johnno, Coley and Lenny Pidgeley. After the lads had gone, I just sat on my bed with my window open and my phone off and just tried to take it all in. Just tried to take in what had happened. And tried to burn it all into my memory so I'd never forget it. I stared at the video the kit man had done for me. I just kept thinking that this was something I had dreamt of for so long and now it was here. Now it was real. I went to bed about 4 am.

The defeat at Liverpool the following Tuesday shattered us but we worked hard in training in the days leading up to the Charlton game, and when it came to the day of the match, the atmosphere was incredibly relaxed. There was still some regret in the air about what had happened against Liverpool. I think there will always be regret about that. But the day of the Charlton game was not a time for regrets. It was a time for celebrating the piece of history we had achieved that season and for looking forward to what the future might hold for us.

It was a day for celebrating everything about Chelsea, too. Our heritage and our past is often overshadowed by the legends of the Busby Babes at Manchester United and Herbert Chapman and Bertie Mee at Arsenal but we have our legends, too. And we were determined that they should be there that Saturday against Charlton to share in our triumph. It was going to be their day as well as ours.

It was a great day from start to finish. In the morning, the Sky reporter Geoff Shreeves was doing a piece to camera for *Soccer AM* by the side of the pitch at the Bridge. There was a discussion going on between him and the studio about who had soaked him when he had come into the dressing room at the Reebok and Shreevesy was saying he still hadn't found out. So Coley and I dashed out with a couple of bottles of water and soaked him again.

None of the players did the pre-match huddle that day. The manager decided that the masseur, Billy, could do it instead. But instead of doing it live, he had to prepare a video. So he went into Chelsea TV and laid out each player's shirt on a table. And he went through the whole team. He started off by putting Big Pete's goalkeeper's jersey on and giving him a bit of banter about the clothes he wore and he ended with the manager.

He walked over to a chair and picked up a grey coat off it and it was the manager's overcoat. So he put it on and then pretended he was dishing out orders to the players. And that was our huddle.

The game wasn't the best. There was too much of a party atmosphere for that. It was too much like an end-of-term event. I thought we were still the better side. We made more chances. Lamps put a free header over the bar in the first half and their keeper, Stephan Andersen, produced a brilliant save to tip a drive from Coley on to the bar.

In the second half, I hit the bar with a back-post header from Johnno's cross that I looped back across goal. It beat the keeper but hit the face of the bar and bounced away to safety. I thought then it was going to end in a stalemate which was not really the way we wanted the afternoon to end.

The manager made a nod to sentiment when he brought Lenny Pidgeley on for his Premiership debut eight minutes from the end. Lenny deserved that because he's a great lad and he had been great back-up for Pete and Carlo all season, always enthusiastic and always willing. He's a good keeper, too. Within a couple of minutes of him coming on, he made a great block that kept us in the game.

Then, we took the ball up the other end, Talal el Karkouri brought Lamps down on the edge of the box and the referee decided the foul had happened inside the area. And guess who stepped up to take it? The man who never scores, Claude Makelele. When the manager had told him he was putting him on penalties before the game, he was very cocky about it but when I leapt on his back as soon as Lamps won the penalty, he didn't seem quite so sure. 'No, no, no,' he was saying again and again.

I don't think he'll be taking another one. He mishit it and it bobbled straight to their keeper. He was so surprised at what a bad penalty it was that he spooned it out and somehow Maka mishit it into the ground with his left foot and it bounced over the keeper and into the net. It was quite possibly the spawniest goal I have ever seen but we all swamped him in a celebration and the game was won. It was his first goal in 94 appearances for the club. I think it was probably his last, too. I'd put money on it.

With the game over, the proper business of the day began. And first of all, we were determined that we would honour the men who won the league title in 1955. Fifty years ago, that Chelsea side captained by Roy Bentley didn't actually get their trophy. It was never presented to them. It seems unbelievable in these days when such a fuss is made of the winners and there is so much pomp and ceremony surrounding the presentation. It would be pretty hard to miss the handing over of the trophy these days, what with the fireworks and the announcements and the rock music and the applause. But back in 1955, they just went back to the changing rooms, had a shower or a bath, then hopped on the train home.

So we had made plans to put that right after the Charlton

game. All but one of that 1955 team came to Stamford Bridge and when the 90 minutes were done they did a lap of honour with the old trophy they had won. Lamps, Coley and I stayed out on the pitch to have pictures taken with them, which was an honour and a privilege and something else that made the day even more special.

You hear so many stories these days about football clubs failing to respect the achievements of their past players, ignoring them or disrespecting them. Sometimes, it seems people in football have short memories so it made me really proud that Chelsea behaved in such a classy way with the boys of '55. I thought it reflected very well on everybody at the club.

Perhaps in 20 or 30 years, they will be calling me and Lamps out on to the pitch when a Chelsea side managed by one of the young apprentices at the club now wins the double or something. I'd look forward to that. And for 15 or 20 minutes of that Saturday afternoon, the day belonged to Roy Bentley and his team. And it was right and proper that it should.

I was proud of the club that they gave due attention to the backroom staff that day, too. I think the manager had a lot to do with that. Instead of programme notes that day, he just wrote a long list of names under the headline 'These are my Champions'. The players were there but not just the players. Far from it. There were 100 people or more listed there, all of whom had made a major contribution to what we had achieved. That was typical of the team spirit the manager has helped to build. We are a real team now. A team from top to bottom.

A lot of the people who worked so hard behind the scenes

and away from the limelight walked out on to the pitch before the players came out and their names were announced so they all got their rounds of applause. The club even went to the trouble of putting chairs out on the pitch for the wives, girl-friends and children of the players so that they would have the best view of the trophy being lifted and the medals being presented.

There was an honour guard of Chelsea pensioners there and their red coats looked even more bright and splendid than ever. We were called out in the order of our squad numbers so I came out near the end and made the short walk to the dais where all the lads were waiting. It felt great to have done it. It felt great to be able to relax and enjoy the moment.

And that was my last game. I have had a problem for about seven years now that has recently been diagnosed as a bone spur growing from the inside of the little toe on my left foot. Every time I put a boot or a trainer on, that bone spur would bang against the bone on the next toe along. It got to the point a couple of years ago, when Claudio was in charge, that I would have to go to him and tell him that I was just in too much pain to train on a given day. It was difficult getting it across why I couldn't train but I would know that there was just no way.

I had the same problem this season, right from the opening friendly games on the pre-season tour of America. A doctor finally diagnosed the problem early in the season and the plan was to try to last until this summer and then get the operation done straight away to correct it. But halfway through the season, the pain had got so excruciating again that I had to

have two injections. Not just before matches. But before training, too. One at the bottom of my toe to numb it and another
one halfway up to complete the job. It wasn't cortisone. It was
just a local anaesthetic. But it wasn't ideal. Wasn't particularly
pleasant, either. Not on such a regular basis.

But it was the only viable solution. At first, the pain had
been there for a week and then it had gone away for two
weeks. But soon, it was staying for two weeks and hardly going
away at all. It just got worse and worse. I have got Athlete's
Foot in there as well and the bone spur actually caused a hole
where the bone pierced the skin.

When the surgeon finally did the operation after the
Charlton game, he said the nerve in the toe had been exposed
and was constantly being jolted and banged. That was why the
pain had been so exquisite. It's pretty gruesome when you
think about that nerve just dangling there. Bit like being in the
dentist's chair in *Marathon Man*.

It got to the point where the manager was telling me not
to train from Monday to Wednesday. He wanted me just to
come in Thursday and Friday and play Saturday. But I am one
of those players who feels he needs to train every day to stay
sharp. And so towards the end of the season when the pain was
at its worst, I was having those two injections every single day.

After we played Charlton, the pain went to a new level. I
was in the pub with a few of the lads, then all of a sudden
I could feel my toe throbbing. The anaesthetic was wearing off.
So I had to call the club doctor, Bryan English, and get him to
bring some needles down with him and inject me. I knew I had
a long night of celebration ahead of me and that I wouldn't be

able to deal with the pain if it wasn't numbed. He had been brilliant with me while we trying to find a solution to the problem earlier in the season. He had come round to my house and we had tried slipping different gadgets and gizmos into my boot to ease the pain. But none of them worked. Anyway, that night he came round to the pub and gave me a jab that lasted for 12 hours.

It was getting to the stage that if I got a bang on it early in a game, which seemed to happen fairly often, I would be in agony. I couldn't feel the pain in the little toe because it was anaesthetized but I would get it in the next toe along which has taken its own share of wear and tear over the years because it has been damaged by the friction from the bone spur.

After the Charlton game, I went out to train as usual the following Monday. The surgeon had advised me that I should get the operation done straight away but I was desperate to play in every game. It was a goal I had set myself and part of me couldn't bear to fail, especially now that I was so close and especially now that it had become a historic season. There was only Man United away and Newcastle away remaining and I thought I would be able to hold out.

But when I went out to train that Monday, the pain was unbearable. And that was with the two injections. So I went back inside to see the manager and told him that I just couldn't carry on any more. I think he was probably relieved. I had the operation the night after we won at Old Trafford. I went round to Aaron's to watch the United game with him and Bridgey. He had just had the screws taken out of his ankle. I was part of the injury world now.

It was a horrible feeling watching the lads and not being there. Not being part of it. I felt as if I was letting them down. It was the same when they played Newcastle. I saw Lamps leading the team out and I was wishing it was me. I was kicking myself really. I was beating myself up for not just having had a few more injections. I started to think I could have missed training and just got through those last two games.

But people around me told me I was being foolish. And now it's done, I can see the logic in what they said. I gained two weeks of recovery time by having the operation when I did. And more importantly, I suppose every game I played with my toes in that state risked me doing long-term damage. It wasn't great, playing with those injections. It was just that I hated to miss those final two games.

At least I didn't miss the parade the weekend after the Premiership season finished. There was an FA Cup Final in Cardiff the previous day but that wasn't the big event of the weekend in west London. People talk about Liverpool's parade after they won the Champions League and I'm sure it was tremendous but it couldn't have been any more special than ours. There were so many people there. And as we stood on the top of the double-decker bus, more and more kept flocking towards us. It was an incredible sight and an incredible feeling to be at the heart of something like that.

The police said there were 200,000 people there but it felt like even more. We left Stamford Bridge just after midday and crawled down the King's Road. I spent a lot of time at the front of the bus with Lamps, Eidur, Roman and his little boy just trying to drink it all in. The surgeon had told me not to go on the bus but I couldn't miss it. It finished up at Parson's Green, three miles away, but it felt like a journey into heaven. The manager sang the first verse of 'One man went to mow a meadow' and we all lost ourselves in the happiness of the occasion. That was another day that will live with me for ever.

That was the end, really. Or at least the end of the beginning. I went on holiday to Arizona for a week, played some golf and sat by a pool. I went over to Prague to spend a weekend with Big Pete when he won a special honour in the Czech Republic. By the time I got back, Scottie had been sold to Newcastle and I realized that, in football, things never stay still for very long, even when you think you've found a winning formula.

I couldn't help feeling sad Scottie had gone. He and I have become close mates and I know we'll stay that way. He lived very close to me, and his partner and my girlfriend got on well, too. I thought he was going to be a key player for the club in years to come and I know he didn't want to leave. But when the club made it clear they were willing to sell him, he didn't have much choice. I'm sure he'll be a great success in the north-east. Newcastle have signed a great lad and a brilliant footballer. He will be missed.

But he's locked in my memories of the season like all the other lads. Nothing can ever change that. What a season it was. It had its low points. I don't want to experience the feeling of losing to Liverpool in the Champions League semi-final ever again. But that pales into insignificance compared to the joy and the satisfaction of everything that we achieved, most of all winning the league title for the first time.

The league was about the best team over 38 games. That's the ultimate test. And we only lost once in those 38 games. The Champions League, despite its name, is more of a cup competition. For now, I feel utterly content with my Premiership medal. I want more in the season ahead but I know the future's bright with Chelsea. There's time to win more trophies.

It's going to be very tough to win it again next season. That's going to be our aim and midway through the summer, when I was still soaking up the sun in Arizona, I got a text from the manager saying, 'We have to come back better and stronger next season.' He's right. Other clubs will be after our scalp next season. They will want to beat us and humiliate us if they can. They will want to make a name for themselves by beating the champions. They will be raising their game against us.

Individually, they will have a point to prove as well. Think of all the praise Lamps got this season and how opposing midfielders will consider it a badge of honour if they outplay him. It will be the same for me. But all that's nothing new. The players from every other team that has won the title have had that to deal with in the past. It's just that it's the first time for us.

I'm not kidding myself either when I say I know a lot of people will be willing us to fail. I don't think it's anything particularly they've got against Chelsea. It's just the way it always is with successful teams. It's human nature to want change and to want success to be spread around. It's boring if the same team is winning things all the time. Unless you're the team that's doing it.

I think what we need to guard against most of all is our

reaction when we lose a game next season. I'm saying 'when' because I still consider it virtually impossible in the modern era to go an entire season unbeaten. I know Arsenal did it and they deserve immense credit for that. And I know that we only lost once ourselves. But Arsenal's example shows us that we have to be careful that we do not allow one bad result to ruin our season.

That's what happened with them. They lost their long unbeaten record at Old Trafford at the end of October and then everything crumbled to dust. They didn't deal with it. We have to make sure we are not affected in a similar way if we lose a match. I know that when I saw Arsenal lose, it gave me a lot of encouragement. 'So they *can* be beaten,' I thought.

And the same will happen with us. If we lose a match, the aura of invincibility that we have built up in the Premiership will be dented a little. And it will be up to us to swat away the next few opponents who think they sense that they can get us while we are vulnerable. We have to make sure that we are not vulnerable and that as soon as one unbeaten run ends, another even longer one begins.

I think United will be our most dangerous rivals. Last season certainly wasn't one of their best and we beat them home and away and in the Carling Cup for good measure. But I think they're still very much in the mix. Even when they didn't start too well, I always knew they'd go on a long unbeaten run and have a spell when they looked invincible. There was one stage where we were winning and they were winning but for some reason it felt as though they were catching us. It felt like they were closing the gap and breathing down our necks but

I suppose that is just the pressure of being at the front that everyone talks about.

I think that over the next few years they are going to get better and better and leapfrog Arsenal. Look at the youth of Ronaldo, Rooney and Rio. Gary Neville is still a great defender. I really like him. Gabriel Heinze has been a great signing. You look at the two teams and Arsenal have got the older players, so maybe in a couple of years they will have to change a few things.

Whereas with United, the side they have got now could be the same for the next four or five years and they are going to be the major threat. The hardest thing for them, the biggest question mark, is how long Roy Keane can keep playing and how they replace him. You still look at him and he is one of those players who can set the tone of the game straight away. He can win one tackle and that will dictate the whole game. He does not let anyone slacken off. He will continue for a little while yet.

Their problem is that we are going to go from strength to strength, too. Some of our critics seem to be clinging to the idea that Roman might get bored with Chelsea and pull all his money out and the club's going to collapse. In their dreams, maybe. Roman is going to be at Chelsea for a long time to come. He has promised me that. He's not just there for a bit of early success. He loves football and his little boy loves football and they have become fanatical supporters. It means too much to him for him to want to turn his back on everything he has built.

He doesn't just pour money into the first team. He's put a lot of money and effort into the youth system. He wants to see kids coming through from the academy to the first team. He cares about that sort of thing, too. And anyway, he's got people in place below him, like Peter Kenyon and now Frank Arnesen, who are the top men in bringing more money into the club. I hope that the longer Roman stays involved at Chelsea, the more he can keep his money in his pocket and watch the product of everything he has created.

We've had a taste of what it means to win a major honour now and we all want more. We are more hungry than ever. To have won the league means the world to me. Manchester United and Arsenal had dominated it for so long but I always believed our time would come. As a player, winning it has fulfilled me. It is the best league in the world and I am part of the team that has just won it. I can look people like Ashley Cole and Gary Neville in the eye and know that I have got one of those precious medals, too, now.

Most of all, I've got the memories. The memories of the smiling, happy faces and the celebrations at Bolton. The images on my camcorder from that day at the Reebok, all the lads singing and cheering together. And I've got my medal. Sometimes I open my safe, look into it and take a peek at that medal. I just stare at it for awhile to remind me of what it represents, and I think back to a season of dreams.

STATISTICS OF THE SEASON
Courtesy of Mark Baber, Association of Football Statisticians

CHELSEA'S MATCH RESULTS 2004/05

15 August 2004   Chelsea 1   Manchester United 0
Premiership Attendance: 41,813; Stamford Bridge; Referee: Graham Poll
Chelsea: Cech; Ferreira; Terry; Gallas; Bridge; Geremi (Carvalho 89); Makelele; Lampard; Smertin; Drogba (Kezman 70); Gudjohnsen (Parker 82).
Scorer: Gudjohnsen 15
Manchester United: Howard; Neville; O'Shea; Silvestre; Djemba-Djemba (Forlán 73); Fortune (Bellion 84); Giggs; Keane; Miller (Richardson 84); Scholes; Smith

21 August 2004   Birmingham City 0   Chelsea 1
Premiership Attendance: 28,559; St Andrews; Referee: Barry Knight
Birmingham City: Taylor; Melchiot; Upson; Taylor; Savage; Lazaridis; Johnson; Izzet; Gray; Grønkjaer (John 76); Heskey
Chelsea: Cech; Carvalho; Ferreira; Terry; Bridge; Geremi (Cole 63); Makelele; Lampard; Smertin (Tiago 46); Drogba; Gudjohnsen (Kezman 46).
Scorer: Cole 68

24 August 2004   Crystal Palace 0   Chelsea 2
Premiership Attendance: 24,953; Selhurst Park; Referee: Chris Foy
Crystal Palace: Speroni; Hudson; Popovic; Hall; Boyce; Granville; Routledge; Riihilahti; Kolkka; Kaviedes (Hughes 67); Johnson. **Yellow cards:** Hudson 74

Chelsea: Cech; Ferreira; Terry; Gallas; Babayaro; Tiago; Makelele; Lampard; Cole (Geremi 76); Kezman (Mutu 70); Drogba (Gudjohnsen 75). **Scorers:** Drogba 28; Tiago 72. **Yellow cards:** Babayaro 62

28 August 2004   Chelsea 2 Southampton 1

Premiership Attendance: 40,864; Stamford Bridge; Referee: Steve Bennett
Chelsea: Cech; Ferreira; Carvalho; Terry; Bridge; Tiago; Makelele (Geremi 90); Lampard; Cole (Duff 57); Gudjohnsen (Kezman 60); Drogba. **Scorers:** Beattie og 34; Lampard pen 41
Southampton: Niemi; Higginbotham; Lundekvam; Le Saux; Telfer; Svensson (Van Damme 83); Prutton; Fernandes (Folly 23 (Crouch 70)); Delap; Phillips; Beattie. **Scorer:** Beattie 1. **Yellow cards:** Delap 40; Phillips 40; Prutton 63; Le Saux 81

11 September 2004   Aston Villa 0 Chelsea 0

Premiership Attendance: 36,691; Villa Park; Referee: Rob Styles
Aston Villa: Sørensen; Delaney; Mellberg; Samuel; De la Cruz; Barry; Solano (Hendrie 57); McCann; Hitzlsperger; Vassell (Whittingham 90); Angel (Moore 67)
Chelsea: Cech; Carvalho; Ferreira; Terry; Babayaro; Tiago (Smertin 66); Cole (Mutu 61); Lampard; Makelele; Drogba; Kezman (Gudjohnsen 61)

14 September 2004   Paris St Germain 0 Chelsea 3

Champions League Group H Attendance: 40,000; Parc des Princes;
Referee: Enrique Mejuto González
Paris St Germain: Letizi; Armand; Mendy; Pierre-Fanfan; Helder; Cana; Coridon (Ljuboja 66); Mbami; Rothen (Ateba Bilayi 84); Ogbeche (Pancrate 72); Pauleta. **Yellow cards:** Helder 63
Chelsea: Cech; Ferreira; Terry; Gallas; Bridge; Tiago; Makelele; Lampard; Cole (Geremi 70); Gudjohnsen (Kezman 11); Drogba (Duff 81). **Scorers:** Terry 29; Drogba 45, 75. **Yellow cards:** Lampard 64

19 September 2004   Chelsea 0 Tottenham Hotspur 0

Premiership Attendance: 42,246; Stamford Bridge; Referee: Mike Riley
Chelsea: Cech; Ferreira; Carvalho; Terry; Bridge (Smertin 85); Tiago

(Duff 66); Makelele; Lampard; Cole (Kezman 66); Gudjohnsen; Drogba.
Yellow cards: Smertin 90
Tottenham Hotspur: Robinson; Pamarot; Naybet; King; Atouba (Brown 74); Edman; Redknapp; Mendes; Davies; Keane; Defoe (Kanoute 86).
Yellow cards: King 50; Redknapp 73

25 September 2004   Middlesbrough 0 Chelsea 1

Premiership Attendance: 32,341; Riverside Stadium; Referee: Mark Halsey
Middlesbrough: Schwarzer; Cooper; Southgate; Parnaby; Queudrue; Zenden; Boateng; Doriva; Parlour (Job 36 (Downing 66)); Viduka (Morrison 76); Hasselbaink
Chelsea: Cech; Ferreira; Carvalho; Terry; Gallas; Smertin (Tiago 65); Makelele; Lampard; Duff (Huth 88); Gudjohnsen (Kezman 65); Drogba.
Scorer: Drogba 81. **Yellow cards:** Smertin 61

29 September 2004   Chelsea 3 FC Porto 1

Champions League Group H Attendance: 39,237; Stamford Bridge;
Referee: Herbert Fandel
Chelsea: Cech; Ferreira; Carvalho; Terry; Gallas; Smertin; Makelele; Lampard; Duff (Tiago 66); Gudjohnsen (Kezman 80); Drogba. **Scorers:** Smertin 7; Drogba 50; Terry 70. **Yellow cards:** Gallas 41; Carvalho 53; Smertin 60
FC Porto: Vitor Baia; Jorge Costa; Pepe; Ricardo Costa; Bosingwa; Costinha; Diego; Maniche; Ricardo Quaresma (Alberto 58); Derlei (Postiga 80); Fabiano (McCarthy 57). **Scorer:** McCarthy 68. **Yellow cards:** Fabiano 35; Derlei 72; Pepe 78.

03 October 2004   Chelsea 1 Liverpool 0

Premiership Attendance: 42,028; Stamford Bridge; Referee: Phil Dowd
Chelsea: Cech; Carvalho; Ferreira; Terry; Gallas; Lampard; Makelele; Smertin (Tiago 86); Duff (Geremi 83); Drogba (Cole 38); Gudjohnsen.
Scorer: Cole 64
Liverpool: Kirkland; Josemi (Baro? 72); Riise; Traore; Hyypia; Carragher; Alonso; Diao (Hamann 78); Kewell; Cisse; Garcia (Finnan 78). **Yellow cards:** Carragher 90

16 October 2004   **Manchester City 1 Chelsea 0**

Premiership Attendance: 45,047; City of Manchester Stadium; Referee:
Howard Webb
Manchester City: James; Mills; Jihai (McManaman 43); Distin; Dunne;
Thatcher; Sibierski; Bosvelt; Wright-Phillips; Macken; Anelka. **Scorer:**
Anelka pen 11. **Yellow cards:** Mills 64
Chelsea: Cech; Ferreira; Carvalho (Geremi 78); Terry; Gallas (Bridge 46);
Tiago (Cole 64); Makelele; Lampard; Duff; Kezman; Gudjohnsen. **Yellow**
cards: Ferreira 11; Lampard 54

20 October 2004   **Chelsea 2 CSKA Moscow 0**

Champions League Group H Attendance: 33,945; Stamford Bridge;
Referee: Lubos Michel
Chelsea: Cech; Ferreira; Terry; Gallas; Bridge; Smertin (Parker 84);
Makelele; Lampard; Duff (Cole 76); Kezman (Tiago 62); Gudjohnsen.
Scorers: Terry 9; Gudjohnsen 45. **Yellow cards:** Kezman 56
CSKA Moscow: Vagner Love (Dadu 60); Akinfeev; Berezoutski;
Ignashevich; Semberas; Carvalho (Laizans 24); Aldonin; Odiah; Rahimic;
Semak (Krasic 71); Zhirkov

23 October 2004   **Chelsea 4 Blackburn Rovers 0**

Premiership Attendance: 41,546; Stamford Bridge; Referee: Graham Poll
Chelsea: Cech; Johnson; Carvalho; Terry; Bridge; Smertin (Tiago 65);
Parker; Lampard; Cole (Robben 63); Duff; Gudjohnsen (Kezman 72).
Scorers: Gudjohnsen 37, 38, pen 51; Duff 74. **Yellow cards:** Parker 41
Blackburn Rovers: Friedel; Emerton; Short; Neill; Matteo; Gray
(Johansson 84); Reid; Flitcroft; Ferguson; Djorkaeff (Stead 53); Dickov
(Bothroyd 53). **Yellow cards:** Flitcroft 19; Neill 76

27 October 2004   **Chelsea 1 West Ham United 0**

Carling Cup 3rd Round Attendance: 41,774; Stamford Bridge;
Referee: Andy D' Urso
Chelsea: Cudicini; Ferreira; Carvalho; Gallas; Babayaro; Tiago; Robben
(Gudjohnsen 82); Parker (Lampard 68); Geremi; Cole (Duff 64); Kezman.
Scorer: Kezman 57

West Ham United: Walker; Repka; Ferdinand; Brevett; Reo-Coker; Mullins; Lomas; Etherington (Rebrov 85); Nowland (Noble 65); Zamora (Hutchison 83); Harewood. **Yellow cards:** Repka 78

30 October 2004   West Bromwich Albion 1   Chelsea 4
Premiership Attendance: 27,399; The Hawthorns; Referee: Barry Knight
West Bromwich Albion: Hoult; Moore; Scimeca; Clement (Koumas 64); Gaardsoe; Robinson; Gera; Greening (Dyer 80); Johnson; Earnshaw (Dobie 56); Kanu. **Scorer:** Gera 56. **Yellow cards:** Robinson 54
Chelsea: Cech; Ferreira; Gallas; Terry; Bridge (Carvalho 46); Cole (Robben 46); Lampard (Tiago 83); Smertin; Makelele; Duff; Gudjohnsen. **Scorers:** Gallas 45; Gudjohnsen 51; Duff 59; Lampard 81

02 November 2004   CSKA Moscow 0   Chelsea 1
Champions League Group H Attendance: 20,000; Lokomotiv Stadium (Moscow); Referee: Massimo De Santis
CSKA Moskva: Vagner Love (Kirichenko 82); Akinfeev; Berezoutski; Ignashevich; Semberas; Zhirkov; Gusev; Jarošík; Krasic (Aldonin 46); Rahimic; Semak (Olic 70). **Yellow cards:** Olic 79; Semberas 90
Chelsea: Cech; Johnson; Carvalho; Gallas (Ferreira 54); Terry; Lampard; Makelele; Parker (Tiago 65); Robben; Duff; Gudjohnsen (Kezman 68). **Scorer:** Robben 24. **Yellow cards:** Johnson 61; Kezman 75

06 November 2004   Chelsea 1   Everton 0
Premiership Attendance: 41,965; Stamford Bridge; Referee: Mike Riley
Chelsea: Cech; Ferreira; Carvalho; Terry; Babayaro; Tiago (Kezman 58); Robben; Makelele; Lampard; Duff (Huth 82); Gudjohnsen (Geremi 78). **Scorer:** Robben 72. **Yellow cards:** Robben 90
Everton: Martyn; Watson (Campbell 80); Pistone (McFadden 84); Weir; Stubbs; Osman (Chadwick 90); Kilbane; Hibbert; Gravesen; Cahill; Bent. **Yellow cards:** Kilbane 52; Gravesen 80; Bent 90

10 November 2004   Newcastle United 0   Chelsea 2 (aet)
Carling Cup 4th Round Attendance: 38,055; St James' Park; Referee: Steve Bennett
Newcastle United: Given; O'Brien; Johnsen; Bramble; Bernard (Hughes

118); Robert; Jenas; Butt (Dyer 46); Shearer; Kluivert (Ameobi 105);
Bellamy. **Yellow cards:** Butt 23
Chelsea: Cudicini; Johnson; Ferreira; Terry; Gallas; Bridge; Tiago; Parker
(Gudjohnsen 96); Cole (Lampard 66); Duff (Robben 63); Kezman. **Scorers:**
Gudjohnsen 100; Robben 112. **Yellow cards:** Tiago 19; Johnson 31; Cole 40

13 November 2004   Fulham 1   Chelsea 4

Premiership Attendance: 21,877; Craven Cottage; Referee: Uriah Rennie
Fulham: Crossley; Volz; Rehman; Bocanegra; Knight; Pembridge (McBride
72); Malbranque; Diop; Radzinski; Cole; Boa Morte. **Scorer:** Diop 57
Chelsea: Cech; Ferreira; Carvalho; Terry; Gallas; Smertin (Tiago 63);
Robben; Makelele; Lampard; Duff (Kezman 76); Gudjohnsen (Huth 83).
Scorers: Lampard 33; Robben 59; Gallas 73; Tiago 81. **Yellow cards:**
Makelele 23; Lampard 45

20 November 2004   Chelsea 2   Bolton Wanderers 2

Premiership Attendance: 42,203; Stamford Bridge; Referee: Dermot Gallagher
Chelsea: Cech; Carvalho; Ferreira; Gallas; Terry; Tiago; Lampard; Makelele;
Robben; Duff (Kezman 80); Gudjohnsen (Johnson 81). **Scorers:** Duff 1;
Tiago 48. **Yellow cards:** Kezman 85
Bolton Wanderers: Jaaskelainen; Hunt; Jaidi; N'Gotty; Speed; Gardner;
Nolan (Campo 59); Okocha (Hierro 75); Davies; Diouf (Giannakopoulos
54); Pedersen. **Scorers:** Davies 52; Jaidi 87

24 November 2004   Chelsea 0   Paris St Germain 0

Champions League Group H Attendance: 39,626; Stamford Bridge;
Referee: Rene Temmink
Chelsea: Cudicini; Johnson; Carvalho; Gallas; Bridge; Cole; Lampard
(Gudjohnsen 63); Smertin; Robben (Duff 46); Parker; Kezman (Drogba 62)
Paris St Germain: Letizi; Armand; Mendy; Pichot; Yepes; Pierre-Fanfan;
Cana; Cisse (Boskovic 83); Mbami; Pauleta (Pancrate 89); Reinaldo
(Coridon 76). **Yellow cards:** Pichot 59

27 November 2004   Charlton Athletic 0   Chelsea 4

Premiership Attendance: 26,355; The Valley; Referee: Mark Clattenburg
Charlton Athletic: Kiely; Young; Fortune; El Karkouri; Konchesky;

Kishishev (Rommedahl 64); Thomas (Hreidarsson 63); Murphy (Euell 64); Holland; Johansson; Bartlett
Chelsea: Cech; Ferreira; Carvalho; Terry; Gallas; Tiago; Lampard; Makelele; Robben (Babayaro 79); Duff (Geremi 71); Gudjohnsen (Drogba 61).
Scorers: Duff 4; Terry 47, 50; Gudjohnsen 59. **Yellow cards:** Terry 42

30 November 2004   Fulham 1   Chelsea 2

Carling Cup Quarter-Final Attendance: 14,531; Craven Cottage;
Referee: Steve Dunn
Fulham: Van Der Sar; Volz; Rehman; Pearce; Bocanegra; Pembridge; Malbranque; Legwinski; Diop; McBride; Cole (Hammond 73). **Scorer:** McBride 74
Chelsea: Cudicini; Johnson; Carvalho; Terry; Bridge; Smertin; Robben (Cole 62); Parker; Makelele; Duff (Lampard 76); Drogba (Gudjohnsen 58).
Scorers: Duff 55; Lampard 88

04 December 2004   Chelsea 4   Newcastle United 0

Premiership Attendance: 42,328; Stamford Bridge; Referee: Rob Styles
Chelsea: Cech; Ferreira; Carvalho; Terry; Gallas (Bridge 61); Tiago (Kezman 61); Robben; Makelele; Lampard; Duff; Gudjohnsen (Drogba 46).
Scorers: Lampard 63; Drogba 69; Robben 89; Kezman pen 90. **Yellow cards:** Carvalho 16
Newcastle United: Given; Taylor; Hughes; Johnsen; Bramble; Robert (Ameobi 77); Jenas; Dyer; Bowyer; Kluivert; Bellamy. **Yellow cards:** Taylor 37; Jenas 65

07 December 2004   FC Porto 2   Chelsea 1

Champions League Group H Attendance: 42,409; Estádio do Dragão;
Referee: Massimo Busacca
FC Porto: Nuno; Areias; Jorge Costa; Pedro Emanuel; Seitaridis; Costinha; Diego (César Peixoto 77); Maniche; Derlei (Ricardo Quaresma 59); Fabiano (Postiga 75); McCarthy. **Scorers:** Diego 60; McCarthy 85. **Yellow cards:** Diego 62
Chelsea: Cech; Carvalho; Ferreira; Terry; Gallas; Bridge; Lampard; Parker; Smertin (Tiago 65); Duff (Robben 54); Drogba (Kezman 77). **Scorer:** Duff 33. **Yellow cards:** Smertin 38; Tiago 74

12 December 2004   Arsenal 2 Chelsea 2

Premiership Attendance: 38,153; Highbury; Referee: Graham Poll

Arsenal: Almunia; Toure; Campbell; Lauren; Cole; Pires; Fabregas; Flamini; Reyes (Clichy 82); Bergkamp (Van Persie 82); Henry. **Scorers:** Henry 2, 29. **Yellow cards:** Cole 79

Chelsea: Cech; Ferreira; Carvalho (Drogba 46); Terry; Gallas; Tiago (Bridge 46); Robben; Makelele; Lampard; Duff; Gudjohnsen (Parker 77). **Scorers:** Terry 17; Gudjohnsen 46. **Yellow cards:** Robben 30; Drogba 67; Lampard 73

18 December 2004   Chelsea 4 Norwich City 0

Premiership Attendance: 42,071; Stamford Bridge; Referee: Mike Dean

Chelsea: Cech; Ferreira; Terry; Gallas; Bridge; Tiago (Parker 76); Robben (Kezman 78); Makelele; Lampard; Duff; Gudjohnsen (Drogba 60). **Scorers:** Duff 10; Lampard 34; Robben 44; Drogba 83

Norwich City: Green; Edworthy; Fleming; Doherty; Safri (McVeigh 70); Helveg; Charlton; Jonson; Svensson (McKenzie 8); Huckerby; Bentley

26 December 2004   Chelsea 1 Aston Villa 0

Premiership Attendance: 41,950; Stamford Bridge; Referee: Peter Walton

Chelsea: Cech; Ferreira; Terry; Gallas; Bridge; Tiago; Lampard; Makelele; Robben (Johnson 90); Duff (Smertin 80); Gudjohnsen (Drogba 66). **Scorer:** Duff 30. **Yellow cards:** Robben 45; Tiago 69; Terry 86

Aston Villa: Sørensen; Delaney (Solano 46); Mellberg; Barry; De la Cruz; Berson; Davis; Hendrie (Moore 80); Ridgewell; Whittingham; Angel. **Yellow cards:** Solano 59; Ridgewell 60; Mellberg 82

28 December 2004   Portsmouth 0 Chelsea 2

Premiership Attendance: 20,210; Fratton Park; Referee: Alan Wiley

Portsmouth: Hislop; Griffin; De Zeeuw; Primus; Taylor; Faye; O'Neil; Quashie (Berkovic 83); Stone (Cisse 76); Yakubu; Kamara (Fuller 65). **Yellow cards:** Kamara 32

Chelsea: Cech; Johnson; Ferreira; Terry; Gallas; Lampard; Makelele; Robben (Geremi 81); Smertin (Cole 73); Duff; Drogba (Gudjohnsen 58). **Scorers:** Robben 79; Cole 90. **Yellow cards:** Ferreira 75; Robben 80; Lampard 84

01 January 2005   Liverpool 0   Chelsea 1

Premiership Attendance: 43,886; Anfield; Referee: Mike Riley
Liverpool: Dudek; Finnan; Traore; Riise (Mellor 86); Hyypia; Carragher; Hamann; Gerrard; Alonso (Nuñez 27); Sinama-Pongolle; Garcia. **Yellow cards:** Garcia 47; Hamann 90
Chelsea: Cech; Johnson; Ferreira; Gallas; Terry; Tiago; Lampard; Makelele; Robben (Kezman 83); Duff (Cole 76); Gudjohnsen (Drogba 61). **Scorer:** Cole 80. **Yellow cards:** Lampard 21; Johnson 84

04 January 2005   Chelsea 2   Middlesbrough 0

Premiership Attendance: 40,982; Stamford Bridge; Referee: Steve Bennett
Chelsea: Cech; Ferreira; Gallas; Terry; Cole (Tiago 62); Lampard; Makelele; Robben; Smertin (Johnson 50); Duff; Drogba (Kezman 79). **Scorers:** Drogba 15, 17. **Yellow cards:** Cole 25; Robben 32
Middlesbrough: Schwarzer; Reiziger; Cooper; Southgate; Queudrue; Zenden; Doriva (Morrison 72); Downing; Parlour; Hasselbaink; Nemeth (Job 60). **Yellow cards:** Parlour 82

08 January 2005   Chelsea 3   Scunthorpe United 1

FA Cup 3rd Round Attendance: 40,019; Stamford Bridge; Referee: Dermot Gallagher
Chelsea: Cudicini; Johnson; Watt; Morais; Tiago; Smertin; Geremi (Ferreira 69); Cole; Kezman (Robben 81); Gudjohnsen; Drogba (Jarošík 68). **Scorers:** Kezman 26; Crosby og 58; Gudjohnsen 86. **Yellow cards:** Geremi 40
Scunthorpe United: Musselwhite; Byrne; Ridley; Butler; Crosby; Baraclough; Beagrie (Williams 90); Kell; Sparrow; Hayes; Rankine (Taylor 68). **Scorer:** Hayes 8

12 January 2005   Chelsea 0   Manchester United 0

Carling Cup Semi-Final 1st Leg Attendance: 41,492; Stamford Bridge; Referee: Neale Barry
Chelsea: Cudicini; Ferreira; Terry; Gallas; Bridge; Tiago (Kezman 66); Makelele; Lampard; Cole (Jarošík 75); Duff; Gudjohnsen (Drogba 46). **Yellow cards**: Drogba 89
Manchester United: Howard; Silvestre; O'Shea; Heinze; Neville; Fortune;

Fletcher; Djemba-Djemba (Scholes 61); Ronaldo (Smith 90); Saha; Rooney.
Yellow cards: Heinze 52; Ronaldo 90

15 January 2005   **Tottenham Hotspur 0   Chelsea 2**
Premiership Attendance: 36,105; White Hart Lane; Referee: Graham Poll
Tottenham Hotspur: Robinson; Pamarot (Marney 71); Naybet; Ziegler
(Gardner 67); King; Edman; Carrick; Brown; Mendes (Yeates 78); Defoe;
Keane. **Yellow cards:** Brown 86; Yeates 90
Chelsea: Cech; Johnson; Ferreira; Terry; Gallas; Smertin (Jarošík 70);
Robben; Makelele; Lampard; Duff (Cole 80); Drogba (Gudjohnsen 76).
Scorers: Lampard pen 39, 90. **Yellow cards:** Duff 35; Johnson 42; Terry 85;
Makelele 86

22 January 2005   **Chelsea 3   Portsmouth 0**
Premiership Attendance: 42,267; Stamford Bridge; Referee: Mike Riley
Chelsea: Cech; Ferreira; Terry; Gallas; Bridge; Cole; Robben (Kezman 75);
Makelele; Lampard; Duff (Tiago 67); Drogba (Gudjohnsen 65). **Scorers:**
Drogba 15, 39; Robben 21
Portsmouth: Ashdown; Cisse; Stefanovic; Unsworth (Mezague 54); Primus;
Taylor; Berger; Hughes; O'Neil; Yakubu (Fuller 65); Kamara

26 January 2005   **Manchester United 1   Chelsea 2**
Carling Cup Semi-Final 2nd Leg Attendance: 67,000; Old Trafford; Referee:
Rob Styles   .
Manchester United: Howard; Silvestre; Neville; Heinze; Ferdinand;
Scholes; Keane; Giggs; Fortune (Rooney 59); Ronaldo; Saha. **Scorer:** Giggs
67. **Yellow cards:** Keane 57
Chelsea: Cech; Ferreira; Terry; Gallas; Bridge; Tiago; Robben (Cole 90);
Makelele; Lampard; Duff (Jarošík 87); Drogba (Gudjohnsen 68). **Scorers:**
Lampard 29; Duff 85. **Yellow cards:** Makelele 57

30 January 2005   **Chelsea 2   Birmingham City 0**
FA Cup 4th Round Attendance: 40,379; Stamford Bridge; Referee: Mike Dean
Chelsea: Cudicini; Johnson; Terry; Huth; Bridge; Smertin; Jarošík; Cole;
Duff (Robben 46); Kezman (Lampard 60); Gudjohnsen (Drogba 85).
Scorers: Huth 6; Terry 80

Birmingham City: Taylor (Tebily 25); Melchiot; Upson; Taylor (Tebily 25); Clapham; Gray; Clemence; Carter; Anderton (Yorke 76); Heskey (Morrison 73); Blake. **Yellow cards:** Upson 79

02 February 2005　**Blackburn Rovers 0　Chelsea 1**

Premiership Attendance: 23,414; Ewood Park; Referee: Uriah Rennie
Blackburn Rovers: Friedel; Nelsen; Emerton; Mokoena; Todd; Neill; Matteo; Thompson (Reid 81); Savage; Pedersen; Dickov. **Yellow cards:** Matteo 38; Dickov 62
Chelsea: Cech; Ferreira; Gallas; Terry; Bridge; Tiago; Lampard; Makelele; Robben (Cole 11 (Jarošík 79)); Duff; Gudjohnsen (Kezman 82). **Scorer:** Robben 5. **Yellow cards:** Terry 57; Kezman 90

06 February 2005　**Chelsea 0　Manchester City 0**

Premiership Attendance: 42,093; Stamford Bridge; Referee: Howard Webb
Chelsea: Cech; Ferreira; Terry; Gallas; Bridge; Makelele; Lampard; Jarošík (Tiago 56); Duff; Kezman (Cole 63); Gudjohnsen. **Yellow cards:** Makelele 41; Gudjohnsen 64
Manchester City: James; Mills; Distin; Dunne; Thatcher; Sibierski (McManaman 85); Musampa; Bosvelt; Barton; Wright-Phillips; Fowler. **Yellow cards:** Bosvelt 72

12 February 2005　**Everton 0　Chelsea 1**

Premiership Attendance: 40,270; Goodison Park; Referee: Mike Riley
Everton: Martyn; Pistone; Weir; Stubbs; Yobo; Naysmith (Ferguson 73); Kilbane; Carsley (Arteta 85); Cahill; Bent; Beattie. **Yellow cards:** Cahill 33. **Red cards:** Beattie 8
Chelsea: Cech; Ferreira; Terry; Gallas; Bridge; Tiago (Johnson 90); Makelele; Lampard; Cole (Jarošík 72); Duff (Carvalho 90); Gudjohnsen. **Scorer:** Gudjohnsen 69. **Yellow cards:** Terry 80; Jarošík 89

20 February 2005　**Newcastle United 1　Chelsea 0**

FA Cup 5th Round Attendance: 45,740; St James' Park; Referee: Mark Halsey
Newcastle United: Given; Carr; Boumsong; Bramble; Babayaro; Butt; Dyer (Milner 68); Jenas; Robert; Shearer (Ameobi 64); Kluivert. **Scorer**: Kluivert 4

Chelsea: Cudicini; Johnson; Carvalho; Gallas; Bridge; Tiago (Gudjohnsen 46); Smertin; Jarošík; Geremi (Lampard 46); Cole (Duff 46); Kezman. **Yellow cards:** Tiago 38; Carvalho 90. **Red cards:** Cudicini 90

23 February 2005   Barcelona 2 Chelsea 1

Champions League Last 16 1st Leg Attendance: 89,000; Nou Camp; Referee: Anders Frisk

Barcelona: Valdés; Belletti (Gérard 85); Márquez; Puyol; Xavi; Giuly (Lopez 64); Albertini (Iniesta 57); Deco; Ronaldinho; Van Bronckhorst; Eto'. **Scorers:** Lopez 66; Eto'o 73

Chelsea: Cech; Ferreira; Carvalho; Terry; Gallas; Tiago (Smertin 90); Makelele; Lampard; Cole (Johnson 70); Duff (Gudjohnsen 76); Drogba. **Scorer:** Belletti og 33. **Yellow cards:** Drogba 15, 56. **Red cards:** Drogba 56

27 February 2005   Chelsea 3 Liverpool 2 (aet)

Carling Cup Final Attendance: 71,622; Millennium Stadium, Cardiff; Referee: Steve Bennett

Chelsea: Cech; Ferreira; Carvalho; Terry; Gallas (Kezman 74); Makelele; Lampard; Jarošík (Gudjohnsen 46); Cole (Johnson 81); Duff; Drogba. **Scorers:** Gerrard og 79; Drogba 107; Kezman 112. **Yellow cards:** Lampard 27; Kezman 81; Drogba 108; Duff 114

Liverpool: Dudek; Finnan; Traore (Biscan 67); Riise; Hyypia; Carragher; Hamann; Gerrard; Kewell (Nuñez 56); Morientes (Baro? 74); Garcia. **Scorers:** Riise 1; Nuñez 113. **Yellow cards:** Hyypia 13; Traore 35; Hamann 79; Carragher 117

05 March 2005   Norwich City 1 Chelsea 3

Premiership Attendance: 24,506; Carrow Road; Referee: Mark Halsey

Norwich City: Green; Shackell; Edworthy; Fleming; Drury; Stuart (McVeigh 75); Holt; Francis; McKenzie (Henderson 90); Huckerby; Ashton. **Scorer:** McKenzie 64. **Yellow cards:** Drury 19

Chelsea: Cech; Johnson; Ferreira; Carvalho; Terry; Tiago (Kezman 67); Makelele; Lampard; Cole; Duff (Jarošík 73); Drogba (Gudjohnsen 67). **Scorers:** Cole 22; Kezman 71; Carvalho 79. **Yellow cards:** Cole 39; Makelele 58

08 March 2005   **Chelsea 4 Barcelona 2**

Champions League Last 16 2nd Leg Attendance: 41,515; Stamford Bridge;
Referee: Pierluigi Collina

Chelsea: Cech; Ferreira (Johnson 51); Carvalho; Terry; Gallas; Makelele;
Lampard; Cole; Duff (Huth 85); Kezman; Gudjohnsen (Tiago 78). **Scorers:**
Lampard 17; Duff 19; Gudjohnsen 26; Terry 76. **Yellow cards:** Ferreira 26;
Kezman 83; Johnson 84

Barcelona: Valdés; Belletti (Giuly 84); Oleguer; Puyol; Xavi; Van Bronckhorst
(Silvinho 46); Ronaldinho; Iniesta (Lopez 85); Gérard; Deco; Eto'o. **Scorers:**
Ronaldinho pen 27; 38. **Yellow cards:** Van Bronckhorst 29; Xavi 68

15 March 2005   **Chelsea 1 West Bromwich Albion 0**

Premiership Attendance: 41,713; Stamford Bridge; Referee: Neale Barry

Chelsea: Cech; Ferreira; Terry; Huth; Gallas; Makelele; Lampard; Cole
(Kezman 86); Duff (Smertin 90); Gudjohnsen (Jarošík 74); Drogba. **Scorer:**
Drogba 26

West Bromwich Albion: Hoult; Albrechtsen; Gaardsoe; Clement;
Robinson; Wallwork; Richardson (Greening 86); Gera; Kanu; Horsfield
(Earnshaw 83); Campbell. **Yellow cards:** Clement 16

19 March 2005   **Chelsea 4 Crystal Palace 1**

Premiership Attendance: 41,667; Stamford Bridge; Referee: Phil Dowd

Chelsea: Cech; Johnson; Ferreira; Carvalho; Terry; Makelele; Lampard;
Cole; Duff (Robben 74); Gudjohnsen (Kezman 77); Drogba (Tiago 63).
Scorers: Lampard 29; Cole 54; Kezman 78; Kezman 90. **Yellow cards:**
Terry 80

Crystal Palace: Kiràly; Leigertwood; Sorondo (Freedman 74); Hall; Boyce;
Granville; Soares; Routledge (Torghelle 73); Riihilahti (Watson 88); Hughes;
Johnson. **Scorer:** Riihilahti 42

02 April 2005   **Southampton 1 Chelsea 3**

Premiership Attendance: 31,949; St Mary's Stadium; Referee: Mark Halsey

Southampton: Niemi; Lundekvam; Jakobsson; Le Saux (Svensson 63);
Bernard; Telfer; Redknapp; Quashie; Delap; Camara (Phillips 63); Crouch.
Scorer: Phillips 69

Chelsea: Cech; Johnson; Terry; Gallas; Huth; Cole (Tiago 46); Lampard; Makelele; Duff (Jarošík 80); Gudjohnsen; Kezman (Drogba 65). **Scorers:** Lampard 22; Gudjohnsen 39, 83. **Yellow cards:** Kezman 62; Tiago 89

06 April 2005　**Chelsea 4　Bayern Munich 2**

Champions League Quarter-Final 1st Leg Attendance: 40,253; Stamford Bridge; Referee: Rene Temmink
Chelsea: Cech; Johnson (Huth 65); Carvalho; Terry; Gallas; Makelele; Lampard; Cole (Tiago 82); Duff; Gudjohnsen; Drogba (Forssell 89). **Scorers:** Cole 5; Lampard 60, 70; Drogba 82. **Yellow cards:** Drogba 11; Carvalho 32; Gallas 51; Makelele 54
Bayern Munich: Kahn; Sagnol; Kovac; Lucio; Lizarazu; Zé Roberto (Scholl 73); Salihamidzic (Schweinsteiger 46); Hargreaves; Frings; Ballack; Guerrero. **Scorers:** Schweinsteiger 53; Ballack pen 90. **Yellow cards:** Frings 38; Schweinsteiger 63

09 April 2005　**Chelsea 1　Birmingham City 1**

Premiership Attendance: 42,031; Stamford Bridge; Referee: Chris Foy
Chelsea: Cech; Johnson (Jarošík 69); Gallas; Huth; Terry; Tiago; Cole; Lampard; Smertin (Gudjohnsen 46); Duff; Kezman (Drogba 46). **Scorer:** Drogba 82. **Yellow cards:** Cole 65; Tiago 66
Birmingham City: Melchiot; Cunningham; Nafti; Taylor; Upson; Clapham; Carter (Lazaridis 60); Johnson; Pennant (Gray 80); Heskey; Pandiani (Morrison 87). **Scorer:** Pandiani 65. **Yellow cards:** Cunningham 21; Nafti 50

12 April 2005　**Bayern Munich 3　Chelsea 2**

Champions League Quarter-Final 2nd Leg Attendance: 59,000; Olympiastadion; Referee: Manuel Mejuto González
Bayern Munich: Kahn; Sagnol; Kovac; Demichelis (Scholl 52); Lucio; Lizarazu (Salihamidzic 78); Zé Roberto; Schweinsteiger; Ballack; Pizarro; Makaay (Guerrero 73. **Scorers:** Pizarro 65; Guerrero 90; Scholl 90. **Yellow cards:** Kovac 27
Chelsea: Cech; Carvalho; Terry; Huth; Gallas; Makelele; Lampard; Cole (Morais 90); Duff (Tiago 77); Gudjohnsen (Geremi 88); Drogba. **Scorers:** Lampard 30; Drogba 81. **Yellow cards:** Gudjohnsen 50

20 April 2005   Chelsea 0 Arsenal 0

Premiership Attendance: 41,621; Stamford Bridge; Referee: Steve Bennett
Chelsea: Cech; Johnson; Carvalho; Terry; Gallas; Makelele; Lampard; Cole
(Tiago 79); Duff (Kezman 85); Gudjohnsen (Jarošík 90); Drogba. **Yellow**
cards: Cole 52
Arsenal: Lehmann; Toure; Senderos; Lauren; Cole; Vieira; Pires; Gilberto
Silva; Fabregas (Aliadiere 81); Reyes; Bergkamp (Van Persie 78). **Yellow**
cards: Vieira 74; Reyes 90; Pires 90

23 April 2005   Chelsea 3 Fulham 1

Premiership Attendance: 42,081; Stamford Bridge; Referee: Alan Wiley
Chelsea: Cech; Johnson; Carvalho; Huth (Jarošík 46); Terry; Cole (Robben
46); Lampard; Makelele; Duff; Drogba (Tiago 74); Gudjohnsen. **Scorers:**
Cole 17; Lampard 64; Gudjohnsen 87. **Yellow cards:** Terry 44
Fulham: Van Der Sar; Volz; Goma; Knight; Clark; Pembridge (Malbranque
84); Rosenior; Boa Morte; John; McBride; Radzinski. **Scorer:** John 41. **Yellow**
cards: John 53

27 April 2005   Chelsea 0 Liverpool 0

Champions League Semi-Final 1st Leg Attendance: 40,497; Stamford Bridge;
Referee: Alain Sars
Chelsea: Cech; Johnson; Carvalho; Terry; Gallas; Tiago (Robben 59); Cole
(Kezman 78); Lampard; Makelele; Drogba; Gudjohnsen. **Yellow cards:** Cole
59; Kezman 79
Liverpool: Dudek; Finnan; Riise; Traore; Hyypia; Carragher; Alonso; Biscan
(Kewell 86); Gerrard; Baro? (Cisse 66); Garcia (?micer 90). **Yellow cards:**
Biscan 57; Alonso 87

30 April 2005   Bolton Wanderers 0 Chelsea 2

Premiership Attendance: 27,653; Reebok Stadium; Referee: Steve Dunn
Bolton Wanderers: Jaaskelainen; Ben Haim; N'Gotty; Speed; Hierro;
Candela (Jaidi 77); Okocha (Nolan 63); Giannakopoulos (Pedersen 63);
Gardner; Diouf; Davies. **Yellow cards:** Candela 51; Diouf 58; Jaaskelainen 60;
Nolan 89
Chelsea: Cech; Carvalho; Terry; Gallas; Tiago; Makelele (Smertin 90);

Lampard; Jarošík; Geremi; Gudjohnsen (Cole 85); Drogba (Huth 65).
Scorers: Lampard 60, 76. **Yellow cards:** Makelele 5

03 May 2005　Liverpool 1　Chelsea 0
Champions League Semi-Final 2nd Leg, Attendance: 42,529; Anfield; Referee: Lubos Michel
Liverpool: Dudek; Finnan; Traore; Riise; Hyypia; Carragher; Hamann (Kewell 73); Gerrard; Biscan; Garcia (Nuñez 84); Baro? (Cisse 59). **Scorer:** Garcia 5. **Yellow cards:** Baro? 8
Chelsea: Cech; Carvalho; Terry; Gallas; Tiago (Kezman 70); Makelele; Lampard; Geremi (Huth 76); Cole (Robben 70); Gudjohnsen; Drogba

07 May 2005　Chelsea 1　Charlton Athletic 0
Premiership Attendance: 42,065; Stamford Bridge; Referee: Mike Riley
Chelsea: Cudicini (Pidgeley 82); Johnson (Jarošík 67); Carvalho; Gallas; Terry; Cole; Geremi; Lampard; Makelele; Tiago (Forssell 67); Gudjohnsen. **Scorer:** Makelele 90
Charlton Athletic: Andersen; Young; Fortune; El Karkouri; Konchesky; Kishishev; Murphy; Hughes; Holland; Lisbie; Johansson

10 May 2005　Manchester United 1　Chelsea 3
Premiership Attendance: 67,832; Old Trafford; Referee: Graham Poll
Manchester United: Carroll; Silvestre; Neville; Brown; Ferdinand; Scholes; Keane; Fletcher (Saha 72); Ronaldo; Van Nistelrooy; Rooney. **Scorer:** Van Nistelrooy 7. **Yellow cards:** Keane 31; Van Nistelrooy 63
Chelsea: Cudicini; Johnson (Jarošík 72); Carvalho; Huth; Gallas; Tiago; Makelele; Lampard; Geremi; Cole (Grant 90); Gudjohnsen (Morais 86). **Scorers:** Tiago 17; Gudjohnsen 61; Cole 82. **Yellow cards:** Makelele 51; Lampard 64; Gallas 73

15 May 2005　Newcastle United 1　Chelsea 1
Premiership Attendance: 52,326; St James' Park; Referee: Howard Webb
Newcastle United: Given; Carr (Taylor 46); Bramble; Boumsong; Babayaro; N'Zogbia; Milner; Jenas; Ambrose; Shearer; Kluivert (Chopra 76). **Scorer:** Geremi og 33. **Yellow cards:** Babayaro 34; N'Zogbia 37; Kluivert 54; Jenas 60

Chelsea: Cudicini; Johnson; Carvalho; Huth; Tiago; Cole (Morais 89); Geremi; Jarošík (Watt 90); Lampard; Makelele; Gudjohnsen (Oliveira 84). **Scorer:** Lampard pen 35. **Yellow cards:** Cole 41; Tiago 59; Carvalho 59; Geremi 78

SEASON HIGHLIGHTS

---

2 June 2004
The 'Special One' arrives. Jose Mourinho is appointed manager on a three-year contract. The 41-year-old joins after winning the Champions League with Porto and says: 'We [Chelsea] have top players and, sorry if I'm arrogant, but we now have a top manager.'

15 August 2004
Chelsea enjoy the perfect start to Jose Mourinho's reign. Eidur Gudjohnsen's goal on 14 minutes secures a 1–0 victory against Manchester United at Stamford Bridge in the Barclays Premiership opener.

3 October 2004
Chelsea take all three points against Liverpool at Stamford Bridge to keep the pressure on leaders Arsenal. A vital strike by substitute Joe Cole after 63 minutes sees the Blues earn a narrow victory although they had plenty more chances to add to their advantage.

2 November 2004
With two matches to spare, Chelsea reach the knockout stages of the Champions League with a 1–0 success at CSKA Moscow. Arjen Robben's first goal for the club means they remain unbeaten and top Group H.

6 November 2004
Arjen Robben steals the show again as his second matchwinner of the week takes Chelsea to the top of the Premiership. Everton's stubborn resistance is finally broken after 72 minutes in West London as the flying Dutchman breaks the deadlock.

13 November 2004

Chelsea romp to a 4–1 win at local rivals Fulham to confirm their place at the top. Cottagers boss Chris Coleman believes they are there to stay. 'We've just lost to the Champions,' he declares.

27 February 2005

Chelsea clinch their first trophy in five years and the tenth major success in their history as the beat Liverpool 3–2 in the Carling Cup Final at Cardiff's Millennium Stadium. They overcome the setback of conceding a first-minute goal to take the tie into extra time. Goals from Didier Drogba and Mateja Kezman in the added thirty minutes secure the first silverware of the Mourinho era.

5 March 2005

A 3–1 win at Norwich City restores an eight-point lead at the head of the Premiership table. Petr Cech concedes his first league goal in 1,024 minutes – a new Premiership record. The Czech keeper takes the record from Manchester United legend Peter Schmeichel who concedes that the Premiership title is also on its way to Chelsea.

8 March 2005

On a magical night at the Bridge, Chelsea progress to the Quarter-Finals of the Champions League with a brilliant 4–2 defeat of Barcelona. Trailing 2–1 from the first leg, the Blues blitz Barca with three goals in the first half-hour from Frank Lampard, Damien Duff and Eidur Gudjohnsen. Captain John Terry caps a night of high drama with the fourth as Chelsea go on to a last-eight success against Bayern Munich before the Champions League adventure ends in the all-England semi against Liverpool.

20 April 2005

Arsenal postpone Chelsea's title celebrations for a few more days as they refuse to surrender their trophy in a goalless draw at Stamford Bridge. An eleven-point lead is maintained with just five games to go though, and Gunners manager Arsene Wenger adds his praise to the champions-elect: 'Chelsea will be worthy champions because they have been remarkably consistent. That's the most difficult thing to do in top sport.'

30 April 2005

Two goals from the inspirational Frank Lampard in a 2–0 win at Bolton means Chelsea are confirmed as Champions of England for the first time since 1955. An ecstatic Jose Mourinho captures the moment: 'The players deserve this more than anybody but I am very happy for the fans, especially those that have not seen a title win. The way we were champions was not easy. It shows the mentality, ambition and desire.'

7 May 2005

The Premiership trophy finally arrives at Stamford Bridge. The most successful season in the club's 100-year history ends in joyous scenes as Claude Makelele's last-minute goal earns a 1–0 win against Charlton Athletic. Former skipper Roy Bentley and many of his 1955 team-mates join the 2005 champions on the pitch as John Terry proudly accepts the treasured silverware.

RECORDS SET BY CHELSEA IN 2004/05

Most wins in a Premiership season – 29

Most points in a Premiership season – 95

Fewest points dropped in a Premiership season – 19

Fewest goals conceded in a Premiership season – 15

Fewest goals conceded in England's top division since the War – 15

Equal the all-time record for fewest goals conceded in
England's top division – 15

Most clean sheets in a Premiership season – 25

Most consecutive minutes without a team conceding a goal in the Premiership – 1,024

Most consecutive minutes without a goalkeeper conceding a goal in the Premiership – 1,024 by Petr Cech

Club record for longest sequence of unbeaten league games – 29

Club record for longest sequence of unbeaten away league games – 14

CHELSEA HONOURS 2004/05

Team
Premiership champions
Carling Cup winners

Players
Frank Lampard – England Player of the Year 2004
Frank Lampard – Footballer Writers' Association Footballer of the Year 2004/05
Frank Lampard – Barclays Player of the Year 2004/05
Frank Lampard – PFA Fans' Player of the Year 2004/05
Frank Lampard – Barclays Player of the Month April 2005

John Terry – PFA Players' Player of the Year 2004/05
John Terry – Footballer Writers' Association Footballer of the Year runner-up 2004/05
John Terry – Barclays Player of the Month January 2005

Arjen Robben – Barclays Player of the Month November 2004

Joe Cole – Barclays Player of the Month March 2005

Jose Mourinho – Barclays Manager of the Year 2004/05
Jose Mourinho – Barclays Manager of the Month November 2004
Jose Mourinho – Barclays Manager of the Month January 2005

THE PLAYERS 2004/05

Player	Nationality	Born	Signed	Fee
Celestine Babayaro	NGR	29/08/1978	20/06/1997	£2,250,000
Wayne Bridge	ENG	05/08/1980	21/07/2003	£7,000,000
Ricardo Carvalho	POR	18/05/1978	27/07/2004	£19,850,000
Petr Cech	CZE	20/05/1982	01/07/2004	Undisclosed
Joe Cole	ENG	08/11/1981	06/08/2003	£6,600,000
Carlo Cudicini	ITA	06/09/1973	03/07/2000*	£160,000
Didier Drogba	CIV	11/03/1978	20/07/2004	£24,500,000
Damien Duff	IRL	02/03/1979	21/07/2003	£17,000,000
Paulo Ferreira	POR	18/01/1979	05/06/2004	£13,000,000
Mikael Forssell	FIN	15/03/1981	18/12/1998	Free
William Gallas	FRA	17/08/1977	04/07/2001	£6,200,000
Geremi	CMR	20/12/1978	16/07/2003	£7,000,000
Anthony Grant	ENG	04/06/1987	01/07/2003	Trainee
Eidur Gudjohnsen	ISL	15/09/1978	12/07/2000	£4,000,000
Robert Huth	GER	18/08/1984	23/08/2001	From Trainee
Jirí Jarošík	CZE	27/10/1977	06/01/2005	£2,500,000
Glen Johnson	ENG	23/08/1984	15/07/2003	£6,000,000
Mateja Kezman	YUG	12/04/1979	12/07/2004	£5,000,000
Frank Lampard	ENG	20/06/1978	03/07/2001	£11,000,000
Claude Makelele	FRA	18/02/1973	31/08/2003	£16,000,000
Nuno Morais	POR	29/01/1984	28/08/2004	Undisclosed
Adrian Mutu	ROM	08/01/1979	14/08/2003	£15,800,000
Filipe de Oliveira	POR	15/07/1984	21/09/2001	£140,000
Scott Parker	ENG	13/10/1980	30/01/2004	£10,000,000
Lenny Pidgeley	ENG	07/02/1984	01/07/2001	From Trainee
Arjen Robben	NED	23/01/1984	01/07/2004	£12,000,000
Alexei Smertin	RUS	01/05/1975	25/08/2003	£3,450,000
John Terry	ENG	07/12/1980	18/03/1998	From Trainee
Cardoso Mendes Tiago	POR	02/05/1981	20/07/2004	£10,000,000
Steven Watt	SCO	01/05/1985	01/07/2002	Trainee

Notes
*On loan from 06/08/1999
Only players to have made a first-team appearance in 2004/05 included

GOALS BY COMPETITION

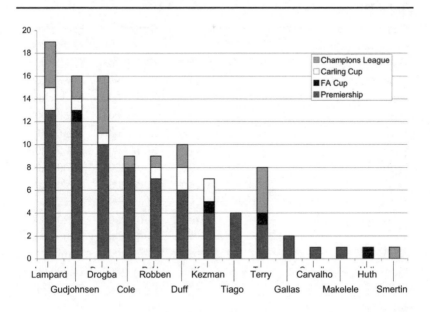

	Premiership	FA Cup	Carling Cup	Champions League
Lampard	13		2	4
Gudjohnsen	12	1	1	2
Drogba	10		1	5
Cole	8			1
Robben	7		1	1
Duff	6		2	2
Kezman	4	1	2	
Tiago	4			
Terry	3	1		4
Gallas	2			
Carvalho	1			
Makelele	1			
Huth		1		
Smertin				1

PLAYER APPEARANCES, GOALS AND MINUTES ON PITCH

Player	Premiership				FA Cup			
	App	Sub	Gls	Mins	App	Sub	Gls	Mins
Babayaro	3	1	0	282	0	0	0	0
Bridge	12	3	0	1149	2	0	0	180
Carvalho	22	3	1	1970	1	0	0	90
Cech	35	0	0	3150	0	0	0	0
Cole	19	9	8	1630	3	0	0	225
Cudicini	3	0	0	261	3	0	0	269
Drogba	18	8	10	1626	1	1	0	73
Duff	28	2	6	2400	1	1	0	90
Ferreira	29	0	0	2610	0	1	0	22
Forssell	0	1	0	24	0	0	0	0
Gallas	28	0	2	2445	1	0	0	90
Geremi	6	7	0	590	2	0	0	113
Grant	0	1	0	1	0	0	0	0
Gudjohnsen	30	7	12	2495	2	1	1	219
Huth	6	4	0	541	1	0	1	90
Jarošík	3	11	0	444	2	1	0	203
Johnson	13	3	0	1158	3	0	0	270
Johnson	6	18	4	753	3	0	1	229
Lampard	38	0	13	3412	0	2	0	76
Makelele	36	0	1	3240	0	0	0	0
Morais	0	2	0	7	1	0	0	90
Mutu	0	2	0	51	0	0	0	0
de Oliveira	0	1	0	7	0	0	0	0
Parker	1	3	0	128	0	0	0	0
Pidgeley	0	1	0	9	0	0	0	0
Robben	14	4	7	1256	0	2	0	55
Smertin	11	5	0	779	3	0	0	270
Terry	36	0	3	3240	1	0	1	90
Tiago	21	13	4	1970	2	0	0	135
Watt	0	1	0	1	1	0	0	90

Player	Carling Cup				Champions League			
	App	Sub	Gls	Mins	App	Sub	Gls	Mins
Babayaro	1	0	0	90	0	0	0	0
Bridge	4	0	0	360	4	0	0	360
Carvalho	3	0	0	270	10	0	0	900
Cech	2	0	0	180	11	0	0	990
Cole	4	2	0	312	8	1	1	650
Cudicini	4	0	0	360	1	0	0	90
Drogba	3	1	1	259	8	1	5	688
Duff	5	1	2	430	8	2	2	663
Ferreira	5	0	0	450	6	1	0	537
Forssell	0	0	0	0	0	1	0	2
Gallas	5	0	0	433	12	0	0	1043
Geremi	1	0	0	90	1	2	0	99
Grant	0	0	0	0	0	0	0	0
Gudjohnsen	1	5	1	150	9	2	2	723
Huth	0	0	0	0	1	3	0	137
Jarošík	1	2	0	65	0	0	0	0
Johnson	2	1	0	190	4	2	0	395
Johnson	2	2	2	222	3	6	0	374
Lampard	3	3	2	333	12	0	4	1052
Makelele	4	0	0	360	10	0	0	900
Morais	0	0	0	0	0	1	0	1
Mutu	0	0	0	0	0	0	0	0
de Oliveira	0	0	0	0	0	0	0	0
Parker	3	0	0	252	3	1	0	251
Pidgeley	0	0	0	0	0	0	0	0
Robben	3	1	1	260	2	3	1	225
Smertin	1	0	0	90	4	1	1	328
Terry	5	0	0	450	11	0	4	990
Tiago	4	0	0	335	4	7	0	449
Watt	0	0	0	0	0	0	0	0

PREMIERSHIP LEAGUE TABLES THROUGHOUT SEASON

3 October 2004

Team	Games	Wins	Losses	Draws	Goals For	Goals Against	Points
Arsenal	8	7	0	1	26	7	22
Chelsea	8	6	0	2	8	1	20
Everton	8	5	2	1	9	7	16
Manchester United	8	3	1	4	9	7	13
Tottenham Hotspur	8	3	1	4	5	3	13

Chelsea are in hot pursuit of Arsenal who have made a flying start.

6 November 2004

Team	Games	Wins	Losses	Draws	Goals For	Goals Against	Points
Chelsea	12	9	1	2	17	3	29
Arsenal	12	8	1	3	32	13	27
Everton	12	7	3	2	14	11	23
Bolton Wanderers	11	6	2	3	18	13	21
Middlesbrough	11	5	3	3	19	14	18

Chelsea go top.

25 December 2004

Team	Games	Wins	Losses	Draws	Goals For	Goals Against	Points
Chelsea	18	13	1	4	37	8	43
Arsenal	18	11	2	5	45	22	38
Everton	18	11	3	4	21	14	37
Manchester United	18	9	2	7	28	13	34
Middlesbrough	18	9	4	5	32	22	32

At Christmas Chelsea are 5 points clear.

30 April 2005

Team	Games	Wins	Losses	Draws	Goals For	Goals Against	Points
Chelsea	35	27	1	7	67	13	88
Arsenal	34	22	4	8	74	33	74
Manchester United	34	20	4	10	50	21	70
Everton	35	17	11	7	41	36	58
Liverpool	36	16	13	7	49	37	55

Chelsea clinch the Premiership title, with an unassailable 14-point lead over nearest rivals Arsenal.

Final Table 2004/05

Team	Games	Wins	Losses	Draws	Goals For	Goals Against	Points
Chelsea	38	29	1	8	72	15	95
Arsenal	38	25	5	8	87	36	83
Manchester United	38	22	5	11	58	26	77
Everton	38	18	13	7	45	46	61
Liverpool	38	17	14	7	52	41	58
Bolton Wanderers	38	16	12	10	49	44	58
Middlesbrough	38	14	11	13	53	46	55
Manchester City	38	13	12	13	47	39	52
Tottenham Hotspur	38	14	14	10	47	41	52
Aston Villa	38	12	15	11	45	52	47
Charlton Athletic	38	12	16	10	42	58	46
Birmingham City	38	11	15	12	40	46	45
Fulham	38	12	18	8	52	60	44
Newcastle United	38	10	14	14	47	57	44
Blackburn Rovers	38	9	14	15	32	43	42
Portsmouth	38	10	19	9	43	59	39
West Bromwich Albion	38	6	16	16	36	61	34
Crystal Palace	38	7	19	12	41	62	33
Norwich City	38	7	19	12	42	77	33
Southampton	38	6	18	14	45	66	32

AND FIFTY YEARS AGO...

1954/55 Final League Table

Team	Games	Wins	Losses	Draws	Goals For	Goals against	Points
Chelsea	42	20	10	12	81	57	52
Wolverhampton Wanderers	42	19	13	10	89	70	48
Portsmouth	42	18	12	12	74	62	48
Sunderland	42	15	9	18	64	54	48
Manchester United	42	20	15	7	84	74	47
Aston Villa	42	20	15	7	72	73	47
Manchester City	42	18	14	10	76	69	46
Newcastle United	42	17	16	9	89	77	43
Arsenal	42	17	16	9	69	63	43
Burnley	42	17	16	9	51	48	43
Everton	42	16	16	10	62	68	42
Sheffield United	42	17	18	7	70	86	41
Huddersfield Town	42	14	15	13	63	68	41
Preston North End	42	16	18	8	83	64	40
West Bromwich Albion	42	16	18	8	76	96	40
Charlton Athletic	42	15	17	10	76	75	40
Tottenham Hotspur	42	16	18	8	72	73	40
Bolton Wanderers	42	13	16	13	62	69	39
Blackpool	42	14	18	10	60	64	38
Cardiff City	42	13	18	11	62	76	37
Leicester City	42	12	19	11	74	86	35
Sheffield Wednesday	42	8	24	10	63	100	26

Players of 1954/55

	Date of Birth	Place of Birth	Appearances	Goals
Ken Armstrong	03/06/1924	Bradford	39	1
Roy Bentley	17/05/1924	Bristol	41	21
Frank Blunstone	17/10/1934	Crewe	23	3
Peter Brabrook	08/11/1937	Greenwich	3	
Alan Dicks	29/08/1934	Kennington	1	
Robert Edwards	22/05/1931	Guildford	1	
Ron Greenwood	11/11/1921	Burnley	21	
John Harris	30/06/1917	Glasgow	31	
James Lewis	26/06/1927	Hackney	17	6
John McNichol	20/08/1925	Kilmarnock	40	14
Seamus O'Connell	01/01/1930	Carlisle	10	7
Eric Parsons	09/11/1923	Worthing	42	11
William Robertson	13/11/1928	Glasgow	26	
Derek Saunders	06/01/1928	Ware	42	1
Peter Sillett	01/02/1933	Southampton	21	6
Robert Smith	22/02/1923	Langdale	4	
Leslie Stubbs	18/02/1929	Great Wakering	27	5
Charles Thomson	02/03/1930	Perth	16	
Stanley Wicks	11/07/1928	Reading	21	1
Stan Willemse	23/08/1924	Brighton	36	1

Notes

Most Expensive Player: Eric Parsons £23,000

Total Cost of Squad: £97,000

PREMIERSHIP TOP SCORERS 2004/05

Henry, Thierry	Arsenal	25 goals
Johnson, Andy	Crystal Palace	21
Pires, Robert	Arsenal	14
Hasselbaink, Jimmy Floyd	Middlesbrough	13
Lampard, Frank	**Chelsea**	**13**
Defoe, Jermaine	Tottenham Hotspur	13
Cole, Andrew	Fulham	12
Crouch, Peter	Southampton	12
Yakubu, Ayegbeni	Portsmouth	12
Gudjohnsen, Eidur	**Chelsea**	**12**
Fowler, Robbie	Manchester City	11
Keane, Robbie	Tottenham Hotspur	11
Cahill, Tim	Everton	11
Rooney, Wayne	Manchester United	11
Earnshaw, Robert	West Bromwich Albion	11
Phillips, Kevin	Southampton	10
Drogba, Didier	**Chelsea**	**10**
Heskey, Emile	Birmingham City	10
Wright-Phillips, Shaun	Manchester City	10
Ljungberg, Freddie	Arsenal	10

Average Goals Against Per Game

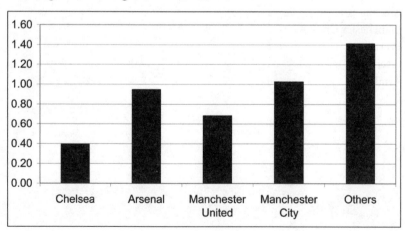

CHELSEA PREMIERSHIP SCORERS – SCORING RATE

	Total Minutes	Goals	Scoring Rate
Lampard	3,412	13	1 goal every 262 mins (2.9 matches)
Gudjohnsen	2,495	12	208 (2.3)
Drogba	1,626	10	163 (1.8)
Cole	1,630	8	204 (2.3)
Robben	1,256	7	179 (1.9)
Duff	2,400	6	400 (4.4)
Kezman	753	4	188 (2.1)
Tiago	1,970	4	493 (5.5)
Terry	3,240	3	1,080 (12)
Gallas	2,445	2	1,223 (13.6)
Carvalho	1,970	1	1,970 (21.9)
Makelele	3,240	1	3,240 (36)

Chelsea's Premiership record against the top teams

Team	Played	Won	Draw	Lost	Goals For	Goals Against
Arsenal	2	0	2	0	2	2
Manchester United	2	2	0	0	4	1
Everton	2	2	0	0	2	0
Liverpool	2	2	0	0	2	0
Total	**8**	**6**	**2**	**0**	**10**	**3**

PREMIERSHIP GOALKEEPER STATS 2004/05

Player	Team	Apps	Clean Sheets	%
Cech, Petr	**Chelsea**	35	24	**68.57%**
Carroll, Roy	Manchester United	26	17	65.38%
Friedel, Brad	Blackburn Rovers	38	15	39.47%
Martyn, Nigel	Everton	32	13	40.62%
Kiely, Dean	Charlton Athletic	36	12	33.33%
James, David	Manchester City	38	12	31.58%
Robinson, Paul	Tottenham Hotspur	36	12	33.33%
Sørensen, Thomas	Aston Villa	36	11	30.56%
Lehmann, Jens	Arsenal	28	11	39.29%
Kiràly, Gabor	Crystal Palace	32	10	31.25%
Jaaskelainen, Jussi	Bolton Wanderers	36	9	25.00%
Schwarzer, Mark	Middlesbrough	31	9	29.03%
Taylor, Maik	Birmingham City	37	9	24.32%
Van Der Sar, Edwin	Fulham	33	8	24.24%
Given, Shay	Newcastle United	36	7	19.44%
Green, Rob	Norwich City	38	7	18.42%
Hoult, Russell	West Bromwich Albion	36	6	16.67%
Dudek, Jerzy	Liverpool	24	5	20.83%
Niemi, Antti	Southampton	28	5	17.86%
Almunia, Manuel	Arsenal	10	5	50.00%
Howard, Tim	Manchester United	12	4	33.33%
Hislop, Shaka	Portsmouth	17	3	17.65%
Smith, Paul	Southampton	5	2	40.00%
Ashdown, Jamie	Portsmouth	16	2	12.50%
Jones, Brad	Middlesbrough	5	2	40.00%
Cudicini, Carlo	**Chelsea**	3	2	**66.67%**
Crossley, Mark	Fulham	5	1	20.00%
Kuszczak, Tomasz	West Bromwich Albion	2	1	50.00%
Cerny, Radek	Tottenham Hotspur	2	1	50.00%
Keller, Kasey	Southampton	4	1	25.00%
Kirkland, Chris	Liverpool	10	1	10.00%
Carson, Scott	Liverpool	4	1	25.00%

Suspensions

Start Date	Suspension	Match	Dates
Robert Huth	15/08/2004	One Match Ban	15/08/2004
Adrian Mutu	25/10/2004	Seven Month Ban	Multiple
Frank Lampard	08/01/2005	One Match Ban	08/01/2005
Arjen Robben	11/01/2005	One Match Ban	12/01/2005
John Terry	19/02/2005	One Match Ban	20/02/2005
Carlo Cudicini	21/02/2005	One Match Ban	27/02/2005
Didier Drogba	24/02/2005	One Match Ban	08/03/2005
Mateja Kezman	09/03/2005	One Match Ban	06/04/2005
Jose Mourinho	31/03/2005	Two Match Touchline Ban	06/04/2005 & 12/04/2005

Chelsea Players Nationalities

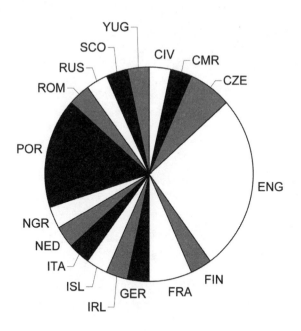

THE BACKROOM STAFF

		Date appointed
Manager	José Mourinho	2 June 2004
Assistant Manager	Steve Clarke	3 July 2004
Assistant Manager	Baltemar Brito	3 July 2004
Reserve Team Coach	Mick McGiven	1997
Youth Team Coach	Brendan Rogers	10 September 2004
Goalkeeping Coach	Silvino Louro	3 July 2004
Fitness Coach	Rui Faria	3 July 2004
Assistant Fitness & Conditioning Coach	Ade Mafe	1998
Physio	Mike Banks	1995
Assistant Scout	Andre Villas Boas	3 July 2004
Chairman	Bruce Buck	3 March 2004
Director	Eugene Tenenbaum	1 July 2003
Chief Executive	Peter Kenyon	1 February 2004
Director of Communications	Simon Greenberg	12 July 2004
Company Secretary	Alan Shaw	1998
Commercial Manager	Carole Phair	1994